J. Mordaunt Crook is a Lecturer in History
at Bedford College, University of London,
and an Executive Committee member of the
Victorian Society, the Georgian Group and
the Society of Architectural Historians of
Great Britain. He is editor of *Architectural
History*, co-author of *The History of the King's
Works*, 1782–1851 (H.M.S.O., 1972), and
author of an expanded version of Eastlake's
Gothic Revival (Leicester, 1970) and *The
British Museum* (Penguin, 1972) as well as
numerous essays, articles and reviews. He is
now working on a Biographical Dictionary
of Victorian Architects and a book about
William Burges.

THE GREEK REVIVAL

THE
GREEK REVIVAL

Neo-Classical Attitudes in
British Architecture
1760–1870

✳

J. MORDAUNT CROOK

JOHN MURRAY

Printed in Great Britain by
W & J Mackay Limited, Chatham
0 7195 2724 4

TO CECIL

Contents

---———————————————— ✳ ————————————————---

Acknowledgements

After a few years' gestation, and several changes of plan, this book was eventually written during the Spring and Summer of 1971. That it was written at all was principally due to the generosity of the Warburg Institute, London, which awarded me a Special Research Fellowship at a crucial moment. I owe the Warburg, and particularly its Director, Sir Ernst Gombrich, a special debt of gratitude. A number of other people gave generously of their time and knowledge. Nicholas Cooper, David Walker, Maurice Craig, Alastair Rowan, Desmond Fitzgerald, Patrick Rossmore and Kittie Cruft all helped in pursuit of photographs. Sandra Millikin (née Blutman) helped initially with some of the preliminary research. And latterly Frances Fergusson was an invaluable source of information. Sir John Summerson, Howard Colvin and John Harris cast learned and critical eyes over the typescript: I am most grateful for their patience and advice. My debt to Cecil Kerr merits much more than a mere dedication. Finally it was my good fortune to find a publisher who was not only historically appropriate but considerate beyond measure.

※

Introduction

The Greek Revival was a slow business. Starting in the 1750s, it reached its zenith in England in the 1820s, and lingered in Scotland until the end of the Victorian period. Its appreciation by architectural historians has been equally sluggish. Sir Albert Richardson's *Monumental Classic Architecture in Great Britain and Ireland during the 18th and 19th centuries* (1914) has been for a long time the only overall survey of Britain's later classical tradition. And A. T. Bolton's lavish folios on Robert and James Adam (1922) remained until recently the only full-scale study of any of the major architects involved.

During the last few years, however, interest in this neglected phase of architectural history has increased enormously. It all began in 1953–54 with the publication of two seminal works: Sir John Summerson's *Architecture in Britain, 1530–1837* and Mr. H. M. Colvin's *Biographical Dictionary of English Architects, 1660–1840*. Between them these books laid the foundations for a reassessment of British Neo-Classical architecture. Then came the late Emil Kaufmann's *Architecture in the Age of Reason* (1955): the culmination of a series of provocative and idiosyncratic attempts to analyse the theoretical premises of Neo-Classicism—an exercise magisterially continued in Professor Henry-Russell Hitchcock's *Architecture: 19th and 20th centuries* (1958). Those were all major works. Smaller in scale, but scarcely less significant in the 1950s and 1960s, were scholarly articles by Sir Nikolaus Pevsner, Dr. S. Lang, Dr. Robin Middleton and Dr. Helen Rosenau. Since the early 1950s different aspects of Regency archaeology and connoisseurship have been closely examined in T. Spencer's *Fair Greece, Sad Relic* (1954), and W. St. Clair's *Lord Elgin and the Marbles* (1967); the classical heritage of Glasgow and Edinburgh has been splendidly surveyed in A. Gomme and D. Walker's *The Architecture of Glasgow* (1968) and A. J. Youngson's *The Making of Classical Edinburgh*

(1966); and many of the late Christopher Hussey's *Country Life* articles on Neo-Classical houses have been incorporated in three superb volumes, *English Country Houses: Early, Mid and Late Georgian* (1954–58). Miss Dorothy Stroud has produced monographs on Sir John Soane (1961), Henry Holland (1966) and George Dance (1971). Mr. John Harris's *Sir William Chambers* (1970) has taken its place as the definitive study of the arch opponent of the Greek Revival. Dr. Damie Stillman has meticulously analysed the Adam style (1969). Dr. Wolfgang Hermann has established beyond all doubt the extent of Laugier's influence on Neo-Classical theory (1962). And the relationship between architecture, sculpture and painting in the age of Neo-Classicism has at last begun to be explained: allusively and evocatively by Mario Praz (*On Neo-Classicism*, 1969 ed.); succinctly by Dr. Henry Hawley (*Neo-Classicism, Style and Motif*, 1964); copiously by Dr. David Irwin (*English Neo-Classical Art*, 1966); and with great subtlety and finesse by Professor Robert Rosenblum (*Transformations in late 18th-century Art*, 1967). Mr. Hugh Honour's *Neo-Classicism* (1968) was the first popular introduction to the whole subject, concise, coherent and compulsively readable. Dr. David Watkin's *Thomas Hope* (1968) was the first detailed study of an individual Greek Revivalist. Mr. Wolfgang Leppmann's *Winckelmann* (1971) provided the first full-length account in English of the greatest of Neo-Classical heroes. And Dr. Dora Wiebenson's *Sources of Greek Revival Architecture* (1969) supplied the first documented analysis of the bibliographical revolution associated with the names of Stuart and Revett.

So, in less than twenty years, our understanding of Neo-Classicism has been transformed. The time seemed ripe, therefore—in the year of the Council of Europe's quinquennial exhibition, *The Age of Neo-Classicism*—to bring the threads together, to attempt a fresh survey of the whole phenomenon of Greek Revivalism in British architecture.

'Beginning around 1760', warns Professor Rosenblum, 'Western art becomes so hydra-headed that the historian who attacks it from a single approach is sure to be defeated'. Despite that *caveat*, I have in fact singled out one theme in the hope that it will illuminate the whole picture. That theme is the Greek Revival in British architecture. It is not a theme which can be easily isolated. Greek Revivalism was but one aspect of Neo-Classicism, and Neo-Classicism—I believe—cannot be entirely separated from Romanticism. But the Greek Revival was in many ways the main-spring of the Neo-Classical machine. And that machine was driven fast and furiously by the pent up forces of Romanticism.

Historians of the later eighteenth and early nineteenth centuries are in fact plagued by semantic confusion: how many can confidently use labels like 'Rococo', 'Romanticism', 'Neo-Classicism' and 'Romantic Classicism'? Piranesi has actually been classified under all four categories —and under 'Baroque' too. Clearly it is time to sharpen up our defini-tions, or abandon them altogether. 'Romantic Classicism' means no more than Neo-Classicism in the age of Romanticism. And in this book it appears only to be dismissed as superfluous. 'Rococo', however, is a valid category, sanctioned by near-contemporary use, and properly used to describe the romantic spirit of the mid-eighteenth century writhing within the strait-jacket of classic convention. That leaves two: 'Romanti-cism' and 'Neo-Classicism'. The theme of this book constitutes a denial of their existence as independent categories. Neo-Classicism is interpreted as stemming, at least in part, from a larger Romantic impulse. Indeed both classic and romantic attitudes are construed as permanent psychological states, interrelated, complementary, locked in creative conflict. During the late eighteenth and early nineteenth centuries this classic-romantic tension was creatively resolved in pursuit of a single goal: that romantic vision of a classic Arcadia which is summed up in the architecture of the Greek Revival.

Greek Revival architecture in Britain was the product of two factors: archaeology and theory. The subject falls naturally therefore into three sections. The first part of this book deals with the rediscovery of Greece in the seventeenth, eighteenth and early nineteenth centuries. The second part is concerned with architectural theory. And the third is a photo-graphic survey of the buildings themselves. If the first part seems in-coherent and episodic, then so were the activities of many of the early archaeologists. If the second section seems a little abstruse, that is perhaps because Neo-Classical thinking in the age of Romanticism had a weakness for cosmic abstractions. And if the third part of the book appears fragmen-tary, fragmentation is at least a hazard natural to any visual survey of more than a hundred years of architectural history—from 'Athenian' Stuart to 'Greek' Thomson. Those who wish to probe more deeply should turn to the bibliography. This is a work of explanation rather than documentation.

PART ONE

The Rediscovery of Greece

Where'er we tread 'tis haunted, holy ground;
No earth of thine is lost in vulgar mould,
But one vast realm of Wonder spreads around,
And all the Muse's tales seem truly told,
Till the sense aches with gazing to behold
The scenes our earliest dreams have dwelt upon

CHILDE HAROLD

For centuries few Englishmen set foot on the Acropolis. Wily Byzantines and cruel Turks guarded the holy ground of Greece and scarcely encouraged inquisitive visitors from Western Europe. Religion and trade, however, kept the channels of communication open. In the twelfth century, so Matthew Paris tells us, Master John of Basingstoke, Archdeacon of Leicester in the reign of Henry III, studied in Athens with the priests of the Orthodox Church. And over the years numerous European settlers and occasional groups of Levantine traders must have ventured beyond the Aegean. On 7 April 1436 the Italian traveller Cyriaco d'Ancona inscribed in his journal: *Athenas veni.*

After its foundation in 1586 the English Levant Company certainly made it easier for traders to penetrate the Greek archipelago. But such visits can only have been rare. The fall of Constantinople in 1453 and the Turkish conquest of the Greek mainland in 1460 destroyed Greece as a political entity and cut her off from the rest of Christendom. Western Europe trembled before the Ottoman—'those hellish Turks', lamented William Malim in 1573, 'horseleeches of Christian Blood'. Greece itself and the sites of Greek civilization in Thrace, Macedonia, Asia Minor and

I

the Archipelago, entered a kind of cultural limbo. Occasional antique marbles found their way back to Venice, like those collected by Poggio Bracciolini. But cultural contacts were minimal. Intrepid travellers brought back tales of woe and desolation. 'O noble Greece', wrote the future Pius II, 'behold now your end, now you are at last really dead. Alas, how many cities which once enjoyed fame and prosperity are now destroyed! Where is now Thebes, where Athens, where Mycenae, where Larissa, where Sparta, where Corinth, where those other memorable cities of old! If you seek for their walls you will not even find ruins'.

A young Cambridge scholar named Fynes Moryson is known to have visited Greece in the 1590s, the first of a long series of wandering Hellenists from that university. But it is not until the seventeenth century that historians have the benefit of reliable accounts—in English and French—relating to the penetration of the Greek mainland. Previous knowledge of the architectural monuments of Greece had been sketchy in the extreme. In 1465 the Italian architect Sangallo produced a distorted, Renaissance version of the Parthenon, probably based on hazy drawings made by Cyriaco. Not until three centuries later was the world provided with an accurate representation of that great monument.

Three of the earliest explorations for which documentation survives were conducted by William Biddulph, George Sandys and William Lithgow. Biddulph, a chaplain at Constantinople, toured the Levant with four other Englishmen in 1605. 'Athens', he reported with some surprise, 'is still inhabited. . . . This City was the mother and nurse of all liberal Arts and Sciences: but now there is nothing but Atheism and Barbarism there: for it is governed by *Turks*, and inhabited by ignorant *Greeks*. Some of the ancient buildings are yet to be seen.' Sandys and Lithgow both set out, independently, in 1610. Sandys—the first American to visit Greece—published a description of his travels in the Levant and the near East. Lithgow left a brief impression of the Parthenon—'a Castle which formerly was the Temple of Minerva'—and a graphic account of his wanderings in rocky Arcadia: 'my belly was pinched, and wearied was my body. . . . Yet . . . the remembrance of those sweet seasoned Songs of Arcadian Shepherds which pregnant Poets have so well penned, did recreate my fatigued corpse with many sugared suppositions'. With

Tom Coryate he scoured the Troad in search of Troy and even published a picture of himself astride the ruins of 'old Ilium'.

By the 1620s there was already a new and powerful incentive: the lure of antique fragments. Charles Cavendish and Sir Henry Blount were among the first of a new generation of treasure-hunters. William Petty, John Markham and Sir Thomas Roe, the English Ambassador at Constantinople, acted as agents during the 1620s for two of the greatest collectors of the day, the Duke of Buckingham and the Earl of Arundel. Arundel in particular will be remembered, in Henry Peacham's immortal phrase, as the first who consciously set out 'to transplant old Greece into *England*'. In the gardens and galleries of Arundel House one visitor, Francis Bacon, found so many naked marbles that he cried out: 'The Resurrection!'. And John Selden published a formidable catalogue: *Marmora Arundelliana* (1628).

Not far away, in the palace of Whitehall, Charles I began to expand the royal collection in the same direction with 'old Greek marble-bases, columns and altars . . . brought from the ruins of Apollo's Temple at Delos, by that noble and absolutely complete Gentleman, Sir Kenelm Digby Knight'. Another collector was Philip Herbert, Earl of Pembroke and Montgomery. The 1620s and 1630s saw a real, if haphazard, awakening of interest in ancient Greece. English sailors roamed among the ruins of Delos. English travellers disembarked at Alexandria Troas at the mouth of the Dardanelles to scrawl their names on what they thought were the remains of ancient Troy. And John Milton, 'the first English Philhellene', vainly dreamt of visiting

> *Athens*, the eye of Greece, Mother of Arts
> And Eloquence.

But it was the second half of the seventeenth century which saw the first systematic attempts at discovery and topography. The Turkish defeat at St. Gothard (1664), Sobieski's relief of Vienna (1683), Morosini's capture of Athens (1685–7)—the Ottoman Empire had begun to crumble. In 1645 the Jesuits arrived in Athens. By 1658 the Capuchins had founded a monastery there, incorporating the remains of 'Demosthenes' Lanthorn'. When de Monceaux travelled the Peloponnese and visited Tiryns, Mycenae and Corinth he was able to explore Athens with a plan produced by the resident monks as a supplement to Meursius and Pausanias. So could the Earl of Winchilsea when he visited Athens in search of antique marbles during the later 1680s. In 1672 a Jesuit named Jacques Paul Babin wrote the first detailed description of Athens compiled from direct observation. That was the year before Laisné's expedition and two years before Nointel's.

The Marquis de Nointel, a French diplomat backed by Colbert, travelled the Levant with a team of talented assistants: Antoine Galland, the translator of *A Thousand and One Nights*; Antoine des Barres and Cornelio Magno of Parma; and two artists, Rombault Faidherbe and Jacques Carrey, a pupil of Le Brun, who produced the first detailed drawings of the Parthenon pediments. Greece was beginning to yield up its secrets. And in 1675 began a series of voyages which together constituted a major step forward in the rediscovery of Greece: the journeys of a Frenchman named Spon and three Englishmen named Wheler, Vernon and Eastcourt.

George Wheler was a young graduate of Lincoln College, Oxford, who dedicated his *Journey into Greece* (1682) to Charles II and was rewarded with a knighthood. He became a parson—in gratitude for his safe return; lived on to become a Canon of Durham; and ended by presenting a valuable collection of marbles to his old university. Dr. Jacob Spon was a learned Hellenist who had already edited Babin's guide (1674). He became Wheler's physician and amanuensis and published his own experiences in three useful volumes (1678). One of these included an engraving of the Parthenon before the Venetian bombardment of 1687. And this celebrated view, together with those prepared by the engineers Plantier and Verneda, long remained the nearest thing to an accurate representation of the Parthenon which Western Europe possessed.

Wheler and Spon survived their adventures. Their two companions, however, never returned. Sir Giles Eastcourt died near Vitrenizza, between Lepanto and Delphi, on the road to Mount Parnassus. Francis Vernon, astronomer, linguist, mathematician, diplomat and most intrepid of the quartet, survived capture by Tunisian corsairs and even enforced slavery—prior to belated graduation at Christ Church—before being murdered in a quarrel over a penknife on the way from Trebizond to Persia.

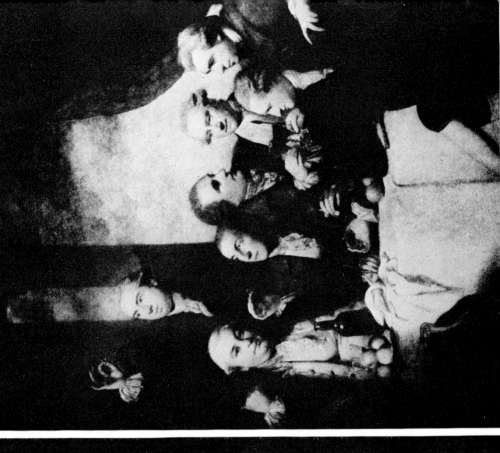

Sir Joshua Reynolds: Composite portrait of a meeting of the Dilettanti Society on the occasion of the induction of Sir William Hamilton (1777).

1(a). *l to r: foreground*, Sir W. W. Wynn (President), Mr Payne-Gallwey Sir W. Hamilton, Mr Smythe; *background*, Sir F. Taylor, Mr R. Thompson (Arch-Master), Mr Spencer-Stanhope.

1(b). *l to r: foreground*, Lord Mulgrave, Lord Seaforth, Duke of Leeds; *background*, Lord Dundas, Hon. C. Greville, Mr Crowle (Secretary), Sir J. Banks.

2. G. L. Taylor: A Distant View of the Acropolis (*c.* 1818).

3. Stuart, Revett, Dawkins and Wood admiring the Monument of Philopapus.

All four set out together from Venice and sailed down the Dalmatian coast to Corfu, Cephalonia and Zante before splitting up. Vernon and Eastcourt went straight on to Athens and the Morea. There Vernon composed the first descriptive account of Athens written by an Englishman, later published in epistolary form by the Royal Society. In the process he not only gazed upon the Parthenon but 'took all the dimensions with what exactness he could', considering the 'brutishly barbarous conduct' of the Turkish garrison. Meanwhile Wheler and Spon had sailed round the Peloponnese to Constantinople and travelled on into Asia Minor, visiting Smyrna and Ephesus. After calling at Crete they crossed the Peloponnese to Patras, sailed up the Gulf of Corinth to Amphissa, visited Delphi, Mount Parnassus, Mount Helicon, Thebes and Athens. There Wheler bribed his way on to the Acropolis with three okes of coffee and thought it a small price to pay for the privilege of seeing the Parthenon: 'absolutely, both for Matter and Art, the most beautiful piece of Antiquity remaining in the World. I wish I could communicate the pleasure I took in viewing it, by a Description that would in some proportion express the *Ideas* I had then of it; which I cannot hope to do'. He was almost equally impressed by the Theseion (Plate 94)—'a Master Piece of Architecture'; the Tower of the Winds (Plate 13)—'extremely well carved . . . with all the Comeliness of Nature'; and the Lysicrates Monument (Plate 54)—'a little round Edifice of white Marble very like a Lanthorn . . . and . . . very ancient'. He even supplied vignettes of all these antiquities, the first to be made available to antiquaries in the West. Visits to Marathon and Sunium, Salamis and Aegina, Megara, Corinth, Sicyon and Boeotia rounded off the tour, the most extensive yet undertaken by English travellers in that part of the world. Together Wheler, Spon, Vernon and Eastcourt had opened up Greece to Western inquiry. Appropriately all of them, except the unhappy Eastcourt, left their names inside the Theseion.

Naturally others followed. Bernard Randolph and Aaron Hill travelled the Morea in the 1670s. By the 1680s there were a sufficient number of Englishmen in Athens to warrant the appointment of a Consul, Lancelot Hobson. In 1699 a veritable troop of travellers began 'a journey round the ancient *Ionia*'. Their names were Whalley, Dunster, Coventry, Ashe, Turner, Clotterbrooke, Fry and Chishull. And the last at least left valuable accounts for publication. As yet, Greek antiquities were still regarded as curiosities. The most that Wheler could say was that Grecian marbles were nearly as fine as Roman ones: 'I dare prefer them before any place in the world, *Rome only excepted*'. The replacement of Rome by Athens at the head of the Neo-Classical hierarchy was a revolution reserved for the later eighteenth century.

The early eighteenth century saw something of a lull in Anglo-French exploration of Greece. After visits to Aphrodisias in 1705 and 1716 by William Sherwood and Dr. Samuel Lisle there is little to note until the 1730s. This brief hiatus in Grecian exploration may have been partly due to the Turkish reconquest of the Morea in 1717. Still, the English Ambassador at Constantinople, eccentric Edward Wortley Montagu, helped to negotiate the Treaty of Passarowitz (1718). And his wife, Lady Mary Wortley Montagu, in her *Letters from the Levant*, became the first Englishwoman to record her impressions of that part of the world. In fact she formed one of a new generation of English travellers—including the Earl of Sandwich (Plate 9), the future Earl of Bessborough, Richard Pococke and Richard Chandler—all of whom had their portraits painted in quasi-oriental dress, a conceit that was to outlive Lord Byron. But such conceits carry us forward into a new age, the age of the Society of Dilettanti.

✳ ✳ ✳

When Professor Kruse of Wittenburg published a work entitled *Hellas* in 1825, he divided it into five periods of which the fourth stretched from the fall of Constantinople to the foundation of the Society of Dilettanti. Such a comparison—between 1453 and 1732—was by no means absurd. Founded as a dining club for dissolute Grand Tourists, the Society had—well before the end of its first century—completely transformed the study of Greek antiquities. It did so by sponsoring and subsidizing the excavation, analysis and systematic publication of antique remains. By consciously extending the focus of the Grand Tour from Italy to Greece, the Dilettanti reinvigorated the waning energies of the classical tradition. By the 1740s Grand Tourism in Rome was already something of a ritual: the aesthetic ambitions of Shaftesbury's philosophy and Richardson's guide had dwindled into the petty world of *milordi* and *ciceroni*. Collecting mania kept it alive. Greece offered a fresh challenge to the adventurous and the acquisitive.

In many ways the history of the Dilettanti Society is the history of Neo-Classicism in England. First it was Roman. Then it was Greek. Then it was Graeco-Roman. And in all three phases its success was based on the labours of learned amateurs.

The Society's early members were mostly hedonists by instinct and scholars, if at all, only by accident. Horace Walpole complained that 'the nominal qualification' for membership 'is having been to Italy, and the real one being drunk: the two chiefs are Lord Middlesex and Sir Francis Dashwood, who were seldom sober the whole time they were in Italy'. Middlesex, later Duke of Dorset—in Shelburne's words, 'a proud, disgusted, solitary man'—had also travelled in France and was chiefly interested in opera. Dashwood (Plate 8), later Lord le Despencer, was a rather more complex person. He was a dedicated libertine, unfortunately married to 'a poor, forlorn Presbyterian prude', and stories of his sexual exploits were told and re-told with bated breath in London, Rome, Paris and St. Petersburg. Not surprisingly, his budget speech as Lord Bute's Chancellor of the Exchequer was greeted with hoots of laughter. After all he was, notoriously, self-styled Prior of Medmenham Abbey, patron saint of 'The Knights of St. Francis of Wycombe' and host at innumerable Hell-Fire orgies. But the very extent and ingenuity of Dashwood's licentious career bespeaks an artistic, if unbalanced, temperament. And as a patron of the arts he certainly had his merits. More than anyone, it was Dashwood who set the tone for the Society of Dilettanti: a mixture of ripe learning and ribald tomfoolery. And it was Dashwood's Hell-Fire crony Lord Sandwich (Plate 9)—Wilkes's 'Jemmy Twitcher', wit, gambler, politician, administrator, sailor and aesthete—who made sure that the best traditions of the Society were maintained. He had himself travelled in Italy, Sicily, the Greek Islands, Turkey and Egypt. He came back in 1739 laden with mummies, papyri, medals and marbles, and his logbook was posthumously published by his tutor in 1799. He measured the principal Athenian monuments and produced creditable ground-plans and a few brave elevations. He even drew cross-sections of the pyramids. Together Dashwood and Sandwich helped make classical archaeology something of a sport. They made it fashionable and they made it fun.

7

They were not short of companions. By 1736 the Dilettanti numbered forty-six, mostly young men of rank and fashion who could claim to have set foot on 'Classic Ground'. Before long membership had to be limited to fifty-four. Politically, they represented a variety of anti-Walpole factions. At least eight belonged to the Leicester House circle patronized by 'Poor Fred', George II's short-lived heir: Dashwood and Middlesex; Daniel Boone, a rich East India Merchant; Robert Darcy, Earl of Holdernesse, a diplomat who had served in Venice and the Low Countries and suffered from a 'passion for directing operas and masquerades'; and Sir Hugh Smithson (father of the founder of the Smithsonian Institution, Washington), John Howe, Bellingham Boyle and Viscount Middleton, all members of the Prince's private dining club known as 'The Gang' or 'The Harry the Fifth'. With these can be numbered the aesthetician and anecdotist, Joseph Spence, later Regius Professor of Modern History and Professor of Poetry at Oxford, and one time tutor and companion to Middlesex and the Earl of Lincoln during their travels in France and Italy. Lady Middlesex—'a vain girl, full of Greek and Latin, and music and painting'—ranks perhaps as an honorary member of this faction: she was Poor Fred's mistress. Other Dilettanti belonged to the circle of the future George III: Viscount Harcourt, for example, Horace Walpole's 'civil and sheepish' peer, who travelled France and Italy in the 1730s; David Mallet the poetaster; and handsome Sewallis Shirley, a famous rake with a complicated matrimonial career.

The fact that so many Dilettanti shared a common hostility to Sir Robert Walpole's régime made them equally hostile to the formalized Palladianism of the artistic establishment, and correspondingly sympathetic to the novel artistic heresies associated with the arrival of Rococo. High among the list of those heresies was a suspicion of Renaissance conventions and a Romantic, ill-defined enthusiasm for the antique.

Several of the early Dilettanti were important collectors. The Bessborough gems, the Ainslie coins, the Townley marbles, the Greville engravings, the Lansdowne marbles, the Sutherland paintings, the Weddell marbles, the Hamilton vases, the Worsley marbles, the Englefield vases, the Farnborough paintings, the Hope vases, the Hamilton manuscripts, the libraries of Heber, Bunbury, Windham, Storer and Cracherode— these were just a few of the rich and valuable collections built up by leading members. But the role of patron was interpreted fairly widely. Some, like Johnes of Hafod and Beaumont of Coleorton ('that giant of amateurs') were clearly men of taste and judgement. Others like Dr. Johnson's friend Bennet Langton and Horace Walpole's 'gallant Bristow' —perhaps even Samuel Rogers—were no more than minor stars in the literary firmament. Some were primarily politicians, men like Bedford, Barrington, Devonshire, Bubb Doddington and Charles James Fox. Others were national figures: military and naval heroes like Granby, Anson and Rodney; theatrical names like Garrick and Coleman; and leading painters like Reynolds, Lawrence and West.

Others were Dilettanti in only the popular sense of the term, professional eccentrics, littérateurs and lightweight aesthetes who contributed little to the Society's academic reputation: 'Old Q', the King of Piccadilly; Dick Edgcumbe, the Society's 'Bard'; Topham Beauclerk, wit and dandy; fashionable William Denney, a brief and unhappy Governor of Pennsylvania; George Augustus Selwyn, the wittiest man in London; the second Lord Palmerston—Mrs. Sheridan's 'good-natured, poetical, stuttering viscount'; Richard Fitzpatrick—Fox's charming and elegant companion in clubland. This was the breed of man satirized in *Ranelagh House* (1747): 'a coxcomb, just returned from his travels. He had set up as a Virtuoso, and brought home a headless Helen and a genuine "Otho", commissioned at Rome two years ago. He might be heard talking Italian in a loud voice and pronouncing the word "Gothic" fifty times an hour'.

Superficially the Dilettanti were devoted only to their own amusement. Their Sunday dinners were held in appropriately bibulous settings. The Bedford Head, The Fountain, The Star and Garter, The King's Arms, Almacks—these were their earliest headquarters. Schemes to build themselves a sober clubhouse either in Cavendish Square or else in Green Park, modelled on the Temple of Pola in Istria came to nothing. Their ceremonies combined the horseplay of Hell Fire junketings with the mysteries of Masonic ritual. The Secretary was dressed 'according to the dress of Machiavelli, the celebrated Florentine Secretary'. The President, enthroned upon a curule chair, wore a scarlet toga fastened with a brass buckle. When the original garment was stolen in 1790, Payne Knight designed a replacement on the lines of the Greek chlamys. The Arch-Master—accompanied at initiation ceremonies by an Imp with a red robe and two lighted tapers—was dressed in 'a long Crimson Taffeta Robe full pleated with a rich Hungarian cap and a long Spanish Toledo'. Actually, the sword was of Germanic origin, and the Baudrier or sword-belt—seen in Shee's portrait of J. B. S. Morritt—was a later gift of the Earl of Sandwich. As a concession, the Arch-Master was allowed to 'go to any Creditable Masquerade in the Robes of his Office'.

A group of early portraits by George Knapton—the Society's first painter, predecessor of Reynolds, Stuart, Lawrence, Eastlake, Leighton, Poynter and Sargent—certainly sets a libidinous tone. Bessborough appears as a Turkish dandy; Galway as a Cardinal warding off the Devil; Moira as a connoisseur stroking the legs of a bronze statuette of Aphrodite; and Dashwood, tonsured, as a Franciscan monk wearing a halo inscribed 'San Francesco di Wycombo', toasting the private parts of the Medici Venus with a silver chalice inscribed 'Matri Sanctorum' (Plate 8). On another occasion Dashwood was painted dressed as the Pope, 'raising his hand in an obscene form of benediction'. Clearly prurience and scholarship went hand in hand. As the Italians used to say: 'Inglèse italianato è un diavolo incarnato'.

At times the interest of certain members in the seamier side of antique art seems almost obsessional. Sir William Hamilton has become posthumously famous as the complaisant husband of Nelson's Emma. But as an early member of the Society his reputation was already more than a little *risqué*: his collection of antique vases was a happy hunting ground for connoisseurs of the erotic. It was a Frenchman, P. F. Hugues, who under the pen-name of d'Hancarville described Hamilton's first collection in a series of sumptuous volumes published in Naples in 1766–67—his second collection was published in monochrome by Tischbein in 1791–95. Michaelis dismissed d'Hancarville's later work on the *Origin, Spirit and Progress of Greek Art* (1785) as 'a fantastic farrago of mystico-symbolical revelation and groundless hypotheses'. And his lesser productions, notably *Veneres et Priapi*, are no more than elegant and facetious erotica. But at least his hand-tinted plates of Hamilton's vases (Plate 6) revealed in meticulous detail the more obviously phallic aspects of Greek and Etruscan art—a bowdlerized edition for popular consumption had to be printed in 1814.

Significantly enough, the Dilettanti chose Hamilton's election in 1777 as the occasion for a formal portrait of the Society. Sir Joshua Reynolds' composite painting (Plate 1) shows fourteen members relaxing after dinner: Hamilton with a vase and one of d'Hancarville's tomes; the President, Arch-Master and Secretary in ceremonial dress; and the rest of the group examining gems which are presumably obscene, or making ribald gestures in the background.

Several years later, in 1781, interest in phallicism was stimulated once more by a letter which Hamilton sent to Richard Payne Knight (Plate 7), the next generation's arch-pundit of the antique. In it he described a curious antique survival: the continued worship of Priapus in christianized form at the Feast of SS. Cosmas and Damian in the South Italian town of Isernia. Payne Knight published this and another letter together with a proto-Freudian commentary as *An Account of the Remains of the Worship of Priapus* (1786). With the help of d'Hancarville's 'infinite learning and ingenuity', he briskly traced the phallic principle right through ancient and oriental art—even the acanthus capital and honeysuckle frieze emerge as formalized symbols of generation. Although only privately printed, under the auspices of the Society, the book aroused a storm of protest. Mathias in his *Pursuits of Literature* denounced it as a 'record of the stews and bordellos of Grecian and Roman antiquity, exhibited for the recreation of antiquaries and the obscene revellings of Greek scholars in their private studies'. The Dilettanti decided that discretion was the better part of licence. And *Priapus* was withdrawn, to begin a new life as an inhabitant of the Victorian underworld.

Even at its foundation, however, the Society contained a hard core of members who were seriously interested in classical archaeology and topography. The bachelor brothers James and George Gray played a prominent part in the discoveries at Herculaneum and in the propagation of those discoveries in England. Sir William Hamilton deserves to be remembered as a scholar, antiquary and diplomat, for his Pompeian studies and Sicilian discoveries. For all its lubricity, his collection had a profound effect on a whole generation of designers, particularly Robert Adam and Josiah Wedgewood. And it was this side of the Society's activities—the promotion of archaeology and the control of taste—which developed significantly during the second half of the eighteenth century. The stream of French travellers did not of course run dry: Paul Lucas, who wandered across Asia Minor between 1705 and 1715, and the botanist Tournefort, for example; that formidable patron and scholar the Comte de Caylus; the Fourmonts, who excavated Sparta; J. P. d'Orville; and, later on, Dumont, Le Roy and Normand. But it was the Dilettanti who set the pace. In this respect nine names stand out: Lord Charlemont, patron and co-ordinator; the explorers James Dawkins and Robert Wood; James Stuart and Nicholas Revett, those 'great twin brethren' of the Greek Revival; the indefatigable topographers, Col. William Martin Leake and Sir William Gell; and, of course, the egregious Richard Payne Knight (Plate 7). Only one name is conspicuous by its absence: Lord Elgin's.

✳   ✳   ✳

The exploration of Greece by the Dilettanti Society began in an appropriately haphazard way with a series of expeditions which were privately organized and financed. In the 1730s Richard Pococke, later chaplain to Lord Chesterfield and Bishop of Ossory and Meath, travelled to Egypt and the near East, stopping briefly at Athens in 1740. Charles Perry was there about the same time. So was Alexander Drummond. All three published accounts of their travels. None was actually a member of the Society. But they were probably in touch with two men who soon became so: John Rawdon, Earl of Moira, who travelled Greece and the East in the later 1730s; and Robert Wood, who twice toured the Greek Islands, Egypt, Syria and Mesopotamia in 1742–43. Sandwich's voyage of 1737–39 was rather more important: he took with him two future Dilettanti, Bessborough and Mackye, plus a classical tutor, the Rev. J. Cooke, and a French painter named Liotard. They toured the Eastern Mediterranean, visited Athens, collected sculpture and inscriptions, and began to take measurements. The Dilettanti were starting to be systematic. And in 1749 this first hint of system assumed a slightly more definite shape.

In that year the Earl of Charlemont set out on an extensive tour. He visited Malta, Smyrna and the Dardanelles; Lesbos, Chios, Myconos, Delos, Paros, Alexandria, Rhodes, Cnidos and Cos; Halicarnassus, Corinth, Thebes and Euboea. With him went the future Lord Conyngham, a classics tutor named Edward Murphy, and Richard Dalton. Dalton

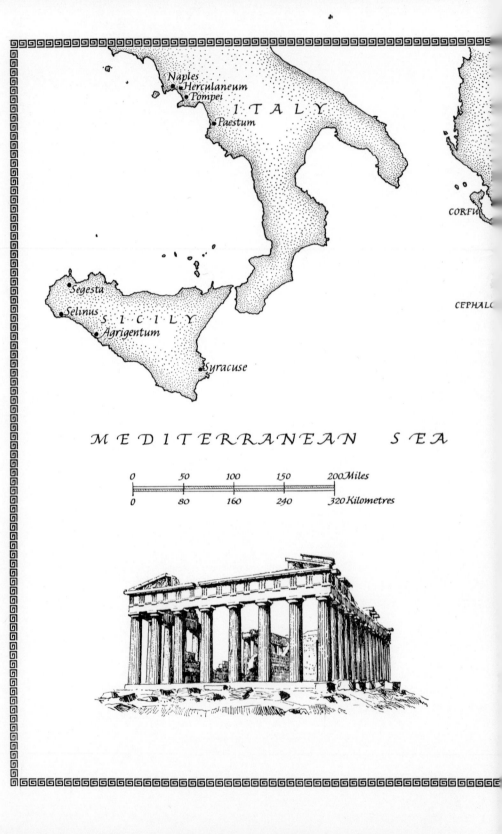

ITALY

Naples
Herculaneum
Pompei

Paestum

CORFU

SICILY

Segesta

Selinus
Agrigentum

Syracuse

CEPHALO

MEDITERRANEAN SEA

| 0 | 50 | 100 | 150 | 200 Miles |
| 0 | 80 | 160 | 240 | 320 Kilometres |

was a late-comer to the expedition. But he turned out to be its trump card.

Dalton became in fact the first British artist to make detailed drawings of Greek antiquities. His only predecessor—if we exclude Wheler's rough sketches—was a Scotsman named William Aikman who apparently made drawings in Greece in 1710. Dalton was an Irishman with an eye to the main chance. But he did produce the first hint of systematic coverage. He brought back crude impressions of most of the key monuments: the Theseion (Plate 94), the Parthenon (Plate 2), the Erechtheion (Plate 4), the Tower of the Winds (Plate 13), the Lysicrates Monument (Plate 54)— 'A Temple of Hercules . . . called the Lantorn of Demosthenes', the Monument of Philopapus (Plate 3) and even the fragmentary relics of the Mausoleum of Halicarnassus. These drawings formed the basis of several picture-books.

Dalton was quite rude about his predecessors. 'It would have given great Pleasure to the Lovers of Antiquity, if the worthy and indefatigable Dr. Pococke . . . had understood drawing or had such an Assistant with him'; and Dawkins and Wood had failed to record the sculpture at Bodrum (Halicarnassus) since 'Mons. Borra being only expert in the drawing of Architecture, could give no designs of Them'. But soon Dalton in turn failed to satisfy. *Cognoscenti* were already crying out for something better. By 1756 young Robert Adam could dismiss Dalton's efforts with scorn: 'He is well known at Rome, where those of true taste esteem him one of the most Ignorant of Mortals. He went with Lord Charlemont to Greece, Athens etc., and on his return publish'd a book of the Temples etc. he had seen there, which is so infamously stupid and ill done that it quite knock'd him in the head, and entitled him to the name Dulton which is generally given to him. But as he had commissions from my Lord to buy up prints and Drawings for him, he had got their names by Rott and so tips the Connoisseur with assurance and that presence of Mind that attends his Nation of Ireland'. Clearly Dalton belonged to the past rather than to the future of Greek archaeology. Even before he set foot in Greece, schemes had already been formulated for the measurement, delineation and publication of Greek antiquities on a much more ambitious scale.

It was in Naples, in the Spring of 1748, that Stuart and Revett first dreamt of the project which one day took shape as their *Antiquities of*

Athens. Travellers had visited Greece, and drawings had been made. But nothing approaching the completeness and precision of Antoine Desgodetz's *Edifices de Rome* (1682) had yet been attempted. In recording the monuments of Rome it was Desgodetz who established for the first time a methodology of architectural archaeology. Stuart and Revett set out to do the same for Greece.

The idea seems to have been at least partly due to two of their companions: the architect Matthew Brettingham Jnr. and the painter and art dealer Gavin Hamilton. Revett, the son of a Suffolk gentleman, had been in Rome since 1742, learning the techniques of draughtsmanship and acting as *cicerone* to visiting Englishmen. Stuart, the son of a Scots sailor, had travelled there on foot, paying his way by painting fans. And in Rome he had collected two major patrons: Lord Charlemont and the Earl of Malton, later Marquess of Rockingham; as well as two minor supporters who soon became colleagues in discovery: John Bouverie and James Dawkins. But the project would have remained a dream but for the Society of Dilettanti. It was Sir James Gray who first organized a subscription list, in Venice in the Spring of 1750. It was he who introduced Stuart and Revett to the Society and in 1751 proposed their names for membership. And it was another member, Consul Smith of Venice, who commended them to yet another member, Sir James Porter, English Ambassador at Constantinople. The Dilettanti Society made Stuart and Revett. And Stuart and Revett transformed the Dilettanti Society. For with their election in 1751—artists among *milordi*—the Society began to take on a rather more serious role. Toasts were still drunk—*Viva la Virtu*; *Grecian Taste and Roman Spirit*. Togas were still worn. But henceforward the Dilettanti were publishers as well as patrons.

The preparation and publication of the *Antiquities of Athens* was a slow and laborious process. And the work was hardly speeded up by the dilatory habits of the two chief participants. Between 1748 and 1751 they talked, they issued proposals, they organized subscriptions and they cut their archaeological teeth in Rome and Venice. In 1751 they set out for Athens, travelling via Zante, Chiarenza, Patras, Corinth, Cenchrea, Megara and Salamis. Between 1751 and 1754 they worked in Greece, excavating, measuring, reconstructing, undeterred by the presence of plague and the threat of assassination. Stuart produced the Picturesque views in gouache; Revett did most of the measuring. In 1753 they fled from Athens during the disturbances which followed the death of Osman, Chief of the Black Eunuchs. At one point Stuart became involved in a violent quarrel and knocked down the British Consul. On another occasion Revett was waylaid by a Maltese corsair *en route* from Athens to Salonica. Twice they were forced to retreat to Smyrna, visiting Delos and Chios on the way. It was certainly dangerous work.

From 1755 onwards they were back in England, toying with private architectural commissions and experiencing the delights and troubles of a new-found reputation. Hogarth's caricature—'The Five orders of PERRIWIGS, . . . measured Architectonically . . . from the Statues, Bustos and Basso-Relievos of Athens, Palmira, Baalbec and Rome'— appeared even before the great work saw the light of day. Not until 1762 was the first volume published. And even then the antique monuments which it did contain—the temple at Pola and the temple of Augustus, the temple on the Ilissus, the Lysicrates monument (Plate 54), the Tower of the Winds (Plate 13) and the Stoa, all at Athens—were all minor and mostly Hellenistic. One of the first subscribers—the poet Gray—waited so long that he lost his subscription receipt. But it was worth waiting for. As the *Annual Register* remarked, 'the labour employed in it must have been immense'. Still, this tardy rate of publication did mean that its impact on architectural design was at most gradual. Only in 1789 were the major monuments of the Acropolis published in volume two: Parthenon, Erechtheion (Plate 4), Propylaea, Thrasyllus monument (Plate 95), Theatre of Bacchus (Dionysus) and Temple of Jupiter Olympius (Zeus). And by that time the unworldly Revett had been bought out by 'Athenian' Stuart, and Stuart himself was dead. The second volume was in fact edited by William Newton. The third, fourth and fifth volumes—in 1794, 1814 and 1830—were all doubly posthumous and were all increasingly the work of other men: Willey Reveley (vol. iii); Joseph Woods (vol. iv); C. R. Cockerell, W. Kinniard, T. L. Donaldson, W. Jenkins and W. Railton (vol. v). But by the end of the project, Athens, Delos, Corinth, Salonica, Pola, Agrigentum and Bassae had all been dealt with.

All in all, from start to finish, the work took eighty-two years to complete. Part of the trouble lay in the principal authors' temperamental difficulties. Revett seems to have had a retiring, unambitious nature.

Stuart was the extrovert, lazy, good-natured and popular, dissipating his talents in a variety of competing interests. His first wife was a 'Grecian lady', perhaps his housekeeper. His second wife was a sixteen-year-old farmer's daughter—he chose her after her sister had refused him, and then had to send her to school to be educated. He ended his days playing skittles in the afternoon and drinking in public houses in the evening. To round off the picture, he chose as executor a 'person who . . . fell into loose and dissipated habits [and] . . . died of maddness in a London Workhouse'. Consequently, the bulk of Stuart's papers disappeared.

Despite its vicissitudes the *Antiquities of Athens* did maintain a basic consistency of purpose, or rather a multi-purpose consistency. The great project supplied several needs. Stuart and Revett summed up their aims in 1751 as follows:

> Many Authors have maintained these remains of [Greek] Antiquity, as Works of great magnificence, and most exquisite taste; but their Descriptions are so confused, and their Measures so inaccurate, that the most expert Architect could not from these Books form an idea distinct enough to make exact Drawings of any one building they describe. Their works seem rather calculated to raise our admiration than to satisfy our curiosity, or improve our taste.
>
> Rome, who borrowed her Arts and frequently her Artificers from Greece, has by means of Serlio, Palladio, Santo Bartoli, and other ingenious men, preserved the memory of the most excellent Sculptures, and magnificent Edifices which once adorned her; and though some of the originals are since destroyed, yet the memory, the exact form of these things, nay the Arts themselves were secured from perishing, since the industry of these men have dispersed examples of them through all the Polite Nations of Europe.
>
> But Athens, the mother of Elegance and Politeness, whose magnificence scarce yielded to that of Rome, and who for the beauties of a correct style must be allowed to surpass her, as much as an original excels a copy, has been almost entirely neglected, and unless exact drawings from them be speedily made, all her beautious Fabricks, her Temples, her Theatres, her Palaces will drop into oblivion, and Posterity will have to reproach us, that we have not left them a tolerable idea of what is so excellent, and so much deserves our attention. The reason of this neglect is obvious.
>
> Greece, since the Revival of the Arts [the Renaissance], has been in the possession of Barbarians. And Artificers capable of such a Work have been able to gratify their passion for fame or profit, without risking them-

selves among such professed enemies to the Arts, as the Turks still are, and whose ignorance and jealousy make an Undertaking of this sort still somewhat dangerous.

While those Gentlemen who have travelled there, though some of them have been abundantly furnished with Literature, yet have not any of them been sufficiently conversant with Painting, Sculpture, and Architecture, to make their Books of such general use, or even entertainment to the Public, as a man more acquainted with those Arts might do; for the best verbal Descriptions cannot be supposed to convey so adequate an idea of the magnificence and elegance of Buildings, the fine form, expression or proportion of Sculptures, the beauty or variety of a country, or the exact scene of any celebrated Action, as may be formed from Drawings made on the spot, measured with the greatest accuracy, and delineated with the utmost attention.

We doubt not but a Work so much wanted will meet with the Approbation of all those Gentlemen who are lovers of Antiquity, or have a taste for what is excellent in these Arts, as we are assured that those Artists who aim at perfection must be infinitely more pleased, and better instructed, the nearer they can draw their examples from the fountain-head.

In other words, the *Antiquities of Athens* was designed as both an archaeological record and an architectural treatise, a work of reference for scholars and a handbook for amateurs of the Grecian taste. In all these respects the volumes were a striking success. Initially at any rate, they were aimed at the patron, not the architect. Out of more than five hundred subscribers to volume one, only four were architects and three builders. Grecian *gusto* was expensive. Only gradually was the new learning assimilated into the common stock of architectural knowledge. Stephen Riou's *Grecian Orders* (1768), for example, acted as a filter: craftsmen and *milordi* subscribed, and even foreign pundits like Le Roy and Soufflot. Appropriately, Riou dedicated his work to Stuart, 'who three centuries after the revival of letters was the first to explore among the ruins of Athens and to publish to the world the genuine forms of Grecian architecture . . . thus rescuing [them] from that oblivion into which the ceaseless insults of barbarians would soon have plunged them'.

While the world of amateurs and scholars waited impatiently for Stuart and Revett, two speculative volumes, one French the other English, temporarily filled the gap. J.-D. Le Roy's *Ruines des Plus Beaux Monuments de la Grèce* (1758) was the result of a few months' hasty field-work during 1754. Here were perspective views, elevations and details of the major monuments of Athens, Corinth, Delos and Sunium. It was the work of a publicist rather than an archaeologist, even though its author had the backing of the French Academy in Rome and the support of the greatest of French antiquarian-connoisseurs, the Comte de Caylus. Stuart and Revett pointed out with relish that most of Le Roy's errors had 'been made before, tho' in fewer words, by Wheler and Spon'. And these errors and inconsistencies have supplied scholars with critical ammunition ever since. The other book was by an Englishman, Robert Sayer. His *Ruins of Athens and Other Valuable Antiquities in Greece* (1759) covered much the same ground and made much the same mistakes. Neither volume did more than whet the appetite of the Neo-Classical market. Much more significant were two complementary works on the late Roman ruins of Palmyra and Baalbek, produced by two men who were colleagues of Stuart and Revett rather than competitors: James Dawkins and Robert Wood.

Neither Baalbek nor Palmyra seems to have been noticed by Levantine traders before the later seventeenth century. After an abortive expedition in 1678, the vast desert city of Palmyra was eventually located by a group of English merchants in 1691. Baalbek's mighty ruins in the Bekaa valley remained hidden even longer. Not until 1697 did the English chaplain at Aleppo—Buckingham's 'chaste . . . accurate and . . . pious' Henry Maundell—visit the forgotten site on his way back from a pilgrimage to Jerusalem. Only in 1745 did Pococke's brief account of both sites appear: a pioneer effort, illustrated with plans, perspective views and Rococo vignettes. And it was not until 1750 that Dawkins and Wood set out with John Bouverie and G. B. Borra on their historic expedition from Naples.

Their ship carried a well-stocked library, 'chiefly of all the Greek historians and poets, some books of antiquities, and the best voyage writers'. They visited most of the islands in the Greek Archipelago and parts of the Greek mainland; then they went on to cover the Asiatic and European coasts of the Hellespont, Propontis and the Bosphorus, as far as the Black Sea, as well as a good deal of Asia Minor. In the Spring of

1751 they met up with Stuart and Revett in Athens, an encounter per-petuated in at least one of the plates of *Antiquities of Athens* (Plate 3). Wood and Bouverie were classical scholars, Borra and Dawkins were accomplished draughtsmen. And there were ample funds available: Dawkins—a wealthy Jacobite—hired a troop of Turkish cavalry to guard them from robbers. Despite Bouverie's death in Magnesia and several brushes with desert rebels, the trip went off without a hitch. *Palmyra* appeared in 1753: 'Palmyra is come forth', rejoiced Horace Walpole, 'and is a noble book'. *Balbec* followed in 1757. And Gavin Hamilton rose to the occasion with an heroic painting of the two explorers clad in Roman togas.

The drawings of both sites had been made in a matter of weeks, but their production was impeccable. Moreover, the text was designed to be both attractive and readable. Wood had been determined 'to read the Iliad and Odyssey in the countries where Achilles fought, where Ulysses travelled, and where Homer sung'. And both authors decided to 'intermix a few observations of our own, not so necessarily connected with the subject, . . . with a view to throw a little variety into a very dry enter-tainment'. The result was an undoubted success. 'The pomp of the build-ings', wrote Walpole, 'has not a nobler air than the simplicity of the narration'. Architectural decoration in Britain was profoundly affected. The excellence of Wood's volumes can best be judged by young Robert Adam's initial jealousy: 'Taste and Truth, or . . . even Accuracy are not [their] characteristics. . . . They are as hard as Iron and as false as Hell'. But in later years the Adam style owed more than a little to Palmyra. In fact Robert Adam and Charles Cameron flattered Wood by quickly publishing volumes of their own in a very similar manner: Adam's lavish *Spalatro* appeared in 1764, Cameron's *Baths of the Romans* in 1772. Paradoxically, it was such late Roman examples as these which helped to break up the dominance of Palladianism, and paved the way for the Greek Revival. 'Jamaica' Dawkins and 'Palmyra' Wood were not for-gotten.

But Robert Wood's contribution to Neo-Classical studies was not finished yet. Robert Adam, in mellower mood, once described him as one 'whose character is one of the most perfect among the Human Race. He is of universal learning possess'd of all Languages and having travelled over all the World to the best of purposes, has fund of Storys Serious and diverting which adapts him to all Capacitys as a Learned, or as a Jovial Companion. He is intimate with all the Great people of all Nations and esteemed by those of his own I mean of England. For his Birth is Irish, His Education is part Scotch and his improvements he made in Holland, in France and Italy'. Although Wood was a comparative latecomer to the Society of Dilettanti, he clearly played a significant part in its academic activities. Before leaving Homer aside and transferring his attentions from archaeology to politics, he took the lead in drawing up in 1764 a set of proposals for what was in many ways the most elaborate of the Society's projects: the first Expedition to Ionia.

This time the team was particularly strong. Responsibility for architectural measurement went to 'the indefatigable Revett'. Topographical drawing was the task of a talented young artist named William Pars. And responsibility for documentation and description went to an able Oxford epigraphist, Richard Chandler. Following the Society's detailed instructions, they sailed from England to Smyrna in the Summer of 1764, stopping off at the Dardanelles to explore the plains of Troy. From Smyrna they visited the temple of Apollo Didymaeus near Miletus, and the temples at Teos and Priene, besides several other sites in Asia Minor. Then plague drove them back to Athens, via Sunium and Aegina. From Athens they explored, among other sites, Eleusis, Delphi, Corinth, Mycenae and Olympia. Not until November 1766 did they arrive back at Bristol, sick but triumphant, laden with journals, drawings, marbles and inscriptions.

Years later, one dashing young Dilettante—J. B. S. Morritt—described Chandler as unnecessarily cautious: 'he strikes me as a college fellow turned fresh out of Magdalen to a difficult and somewhat fatiguing voyage, for which he was as unfit as could be; and though very good at an inscription, was sure to go in the beaten track, and be bugbeared by every story of danger and every Turk that pleased to take the trouble'. But it was Chandler's scholarly instincts which guaranteed the value of the three impressive works stemming from this expedition: *Ionian Antiquities* (1769), *Inscriptiones Antiquae* (1774) and *Travels in Asia Minor* (1775–76). The first volume of *Ionian Antiquities* contained the temples of Bacchus (Dionysus) at Teos, Minerva (Athena) Polias at Priene and

4. 'Athenian' Stuart sketching the Erechtheion.

5. Tailpiece from the Dilettanti Society's *Ionian Antiquities* (1769).

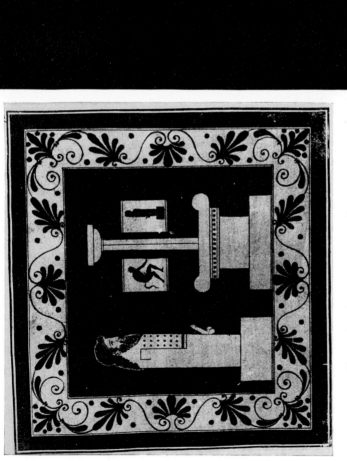

6. Priapus: an illustration from D'Hancarville's commentary on Hamilton's vases (1766–7).

7. Richard Payne Knight (1750–1824): a portrait by Sir Thomas Lawrence.

Apollo Didymaeus at Miletus. The second volume (1797)—partly the work of Joseph Windham—contained the temples at Aegina and Sunium, the temple of Jupiter Nemeus (Apollo) near Corinth, and the temple of Ceres (Demeter) at Eleusis. By any standards it was a formidable achievement. No wonder, in years to come, when Dr. Chandler was a retired country parson, he used to tell young visitors of his early travels, 'his bright eyes beaming with peculiar lustre'.

While Dilettanti were exploring Ionia, others were revealing to the world the Grecian sites in Southern Italy and Sicily. The Greek temples in Sicily were not too far outside the usual circuit of the Grand Tour. But they were not explored until d'Orville went there in 1724. No views were published before John Breval's *Remarks on Several Parts of Europe* (1738). And no detailed drawings appeared before G. M. Pancrazi's *Antiquities of Sicily* (1751). Robert Mylne was there during the 1750s. But his prospective publication materialized only in the writings of J. J. Winckelmann. Similarly, the Greek ruins at Paestum (Plate 12) were no more than seventy miles from Naples, clearly visible from boats sailing in the Gulf of Salerno. But it was not until the 1730s that they were 'discovered' by Comte Gazola and Bishop Berkeley. And it was not until the 1750s that their existence was acknowledged in the form of publication.

The reasons for this neglect were aesthetic rather than geographical. Before the 1750s few travellers thought the ruins worth looking at. Even as late as 1788, an average English traveller, Thomas Watkins, found his 'partiality for Vitruvius and Palladio' affronted by such 'rude and . . . unpleasing . . . Doric'. L. R. Iremonger and the future Earl of Guilford felt similarly uneasy in 1752–53. So did James Adam in 1761 and James Byres in 1766. But it was in fact the very primitiveness of these temples which eventually made them fashionable. When the German Baron Riedesel visited Sicily in 1767 he rejoiced in the patriarchal simplicity of the land, a world still peopled by shepherds from the idylls of Theocritus or the eclogues of Virgil.

The first important architect to interest himself in Paestum was the Frenchman J. G. Soufflot. In 1750 he was touring Italy with Madame de

Pompadour's brother, the Marquis de Marigny. While visiting some Roman remains near Naples they were told about Paestum by a local antiquary. The ruins had been described by D. G. Antonini in 1745 and drawings had been made three years later. But it was Soufflot who produced the first set of measured drawings, variations of which were published in slip-shod fashion by G.-M. Dumont (1764) and Filippo Morghen (1765). Soufflot's interest was still primarily historical. 'In spite of the materials and their proportions', he thought them interesting, if only to show 'the progress subsequently made by the Romans'.

Nevertheless, the French tried to adopt Paestum as a counter to the prestigious activities of Stuart and Revett elsewhere. Dumont produced an improved version of his book in 1769, and Piranesi's posthumous *Pesto* was published in 1778 with a French text. But it was in fact two English publications by John Berkenhout and Thomas Major in 1767–68 which first revealed in detail the architectural splendours of Paestum. As the *Annual Register* pointed out, those mighty temples had previously been as effectively hidden from architects and scholars as the buried cities of Herculaneum and Pompeii. Berkenhout and Major changed that.

Public taste, however, on either side of the Channel, had by no means accepted the crude detail and rugged proportions of primitive Doric. It was not until Payne Knight visited the Sicilian temples in 1777 and found them Picturesque that the tide of taste began to veer towards the primitive. The future Sir John Soane was there two years later—a visit not without effect on the development of British architecture. Then Payne Knight's description was taken up by Goethe, who translated it into German and made it the basis of his own reappraisal of the Paestum ruins.

When Goethe first caught sight of the rows of stumpy columns in the Spring of 1787 he found them strangely ugly:

> At first they excited nothing but stupefaction. I found myself in a world which was completely strange to me. . . . Our eyes and, through them, our whole sensibility have become so conditioned to a more slender style of architecture that these crowded masses of stumpy conical columns appear offensive and even terrifying. But I pulled myself together, remembered the history of art, thought of the age with which this architecture was in harmony, called up images in my mind of the austere style of sculpture— and in less than an hour I found myself reconciled to them and even thanking my guardian angel for having allowed me to see these well-preserved

remains with my own eyes. Reproductions give a false impression; architectural designs make them look more elegant and drawings in perspective more ponderous than they really are. It is only by walking through them and round them that one can attune one's life to theirs and experience the emotional effects which the architect intended. I spent the whole day doing this. . . .

Here indeed was a revolution in taste: nothing less than the collapse of Renaissance attitudes under the impact of antique fragments. From Paestum Goethe went on to Segesta, unfinished, rough-hewn—'it towers over a vast landscape'. Then on to Agrigentum: the Temple of Concord, its columns slightly more slender, 'like the image of a god as opposed to the image of a giant'; and the Temple of Jupiter (Zeus Olympius), 'scattered far and wide like the disjointed bones of a gigantic skeleton'. On his way back to Rome, the poet revisited Paestum: 'the last vision I shall take with me on my way north, and perhaps the greatest. . . . Sicily and Magna Graecia have given me hope of a new life'. Goethe's aesthetic conversion on the road to Paestum was of course symptomatic of a new awareness filtering through Europe. In the shape of Neo-Classicism, the classical tradition had been reborn.

Where Goethe went others followed. A new generation of Grand Tourists came from far and wide to gather 'Paestum's twice-blooming roses' and to share Forsyth's wonder at the rediscovery of a different world: 'I stood as on sacred ground. I stood amazed at the long obscurity of its mighty ruins'. With the author of *The Pleasures of Melancholy* (1815) travellers gazed bemused at such mighty symbols of mortality:

> They stand between the mountains and the sea,
> Awful memorials, but of whom we know not.

Frenchmen in particular made these antiquities in Southern Italy and Sicily their speciality. By 1819 Gourbillon, travelling in the footsteps of D'Orville, Brydone, Reidesel and Borch, could afford to treat the whole subject rather flippantly. 'Pedantic quotations', he claims, 'and measurements by lines and hair-breadths, have not entered into my plan. . . . Since we have been accustomed to publish travels in Greece, Egypt, Italy and Sicily, this scholastic lumber has but too much passed from book to book. There is not a temple standing, not a temple lost, not a god, not a marble, not a stone, which has not been quoted, described, praised, baptized, debaptized and measured in every way . . . .' By the time he reached Syracuse, his appetite for antiquities had been amply sated:

> I have been five days at Syracuse, and there, by land or by sea, on foot or on horseback, on the modern or the ancient road, in a heavy car, or in a balloon in the air, for five tedious days from morn to night, I have mortified my poor body for the good of my mind. What is there to see which I have not seen . . .? What astonishment! what pleasure! what instruction! what disgust! How can I describe to the reader so many rarities, so many wonders! To reckon them alone, is enough to make a professed scholar lose patience. Thus, I have seen towers, walls, gates, baths, circuses, courts, forums, temples, altars, museums, gymnasia, theatres, and tombs!
>
> I have seen ports, seas, rivers, streams, lakes, springs, fountains, cisterns, pits, ponds, marshes, and wells! I have seen rocks, mountains, valleys, hills, plains, orchards, and heaths!
>
> I have seen bodies, heads, thighs, feet, hands and arms, of which some belong to nobody, and others are the property of all the world.
>
> I have seen beautiful palaces without walls, without roofs, without doors, without windows; woods without verdure and without trees; and cellars without casks and without wine!
>
> I have seen speaking grottos and silent theatres, deserts open to the sun, and gardens a hundred feet under the earth!
>
> All this in five days!

The volumes sponsored by the Dilettanti—and the explorations encouraged in French court circles—recovered the remains of ancient Greece. But they hardly recaptured its spirit. That was the task of a person very different to the English *milordi* and French *savants*: a German scholar who never visited Greece, named Johann Joachim Winckelmann.

Winckelmann was the classic autodidact, a self-made polymath, a cobbler's son turned pedagogue. His learning had been fashioned by intense and solitary study. His youth was spent in provincial Prussia, in Halle, Jena and Seehausen, cut off from centres of classical scholarship. His biographer pictures him as an indigent schoolmaster in Seehausen, 'like a slave [who] only half belonged to himself in the day. His real life began at night, when he invited the ancients to be his guests. There he sat, . . . pale and lean . . ., in his narrow, bare, ice-cold monk's cell behind the cemetery, with his . . . dark, sparkling eyes over the aquiline nose peering out from the depths of his cloak into a parchment copy of Plutarch or Sophocles, dreaming, in the midst of impenetrable, snow-covered fields, of the Mediterranean and its people, while the northeast [wind] made the small, round panes rattle in their rotting frames and the moon set in the west behind the massive and gloomy steeples of St. Peter and St. Paul'.

Patronized by Augustus the Strong, Elector of Saxony and King of Poland, Winckelmann won favour at the court of Dresden, took orders in the Roman church and found means of visiting the Eternal City. In Dr. Johnson's phrase, 'a man who has not been in Italy is always conscious of an inferiority'. Winckelmann's inferiority was short-lived. In Rome 'this Saul among the classicists' was quickly transformed into 'the St. Paul of art historians'. He had served a long and arduous apprenticeship. 'Enjoy the best years of your life', he once told a young admirer; 'mine were wasted in sorrow, want and labour'. By the end of his career he was an international figure, boasting the title 'Papal Antiquary'.

Even before leaving Germany, Winckelmann had published *Reflections on the Imitation of Greek Works in Painting and Sculpture* (1755). 'Noble simplicity and quiet grandeur'—a refinement of Montaigne's *le grand et le simple*—had made their appearance as yardsticks of aesthetic excellence. And he had already enunciated the battle-cry of Neo-Classicism: 'The only way for us to become great . . . lies in the imitation of the Greeks'. Even in this first essay—the author modestly called it 'a brief brochure on the arts'—Winckelmann's powers and limitations were revealed. His judgements of sculpture opened the eyes of a whole generation, and indeed those judgements have remained among the very sinews of aesthetic thinking ever since. In this, his first work, however, his comments on painting were jejune, and his assessment of Greek architecture non-existent. The essay's opening words threw down the critical gauntlet: 'Good taste . . . was born under the sky of Greece'. But Winckelmann's awareness of that taste was limited by the circumstances of his upbringing. He made a name as a classicist before visiting Rome. And, despite several opportunities, he never set foot in Greece. Throughout his life he seems to have been comparatively insensitive to landscape and buildings. It was sculpture which moved him, particularly the idealization of the human form.

Perhaps for these reasons Winckelmann's influence in Britain was mostly indirect. His *Reflections* were twice translated into English, ten years after publication, once by no less a figure than Fuseli. But Englishmen, so runs the cliché, have never understood sculpture. It took an American to edit and translate his *History of Ancient Art* (1764) nearly one hundred years after its publication. His collected works have long been available in Italian. But his *Observations on the Architecture of the Ancients* (1762), although it appeared in French in 1783, has yet to appear in full in English. Among English Greek Revivalists only C. R. Cockerell seems to have taken that particular work seriously. Even Fuseli described him as one who 'reasoned himself into frigid reveries and Platonic dreams of beauty'. Perhaps he was right in taunting his English contemporaries with Philistinism. But then the lack of Anglo-German rapport was mutual. Although he called Robert Mylne 'a friend of mine' and admitted that Dawkins' death was 'a real loss to art and science', Winckelmann affected to despise the archaeological precision of Stuart and Revett and vehemently attacked their first volume: 'monstrum horrendum ingens, cui lumen ademptum'.

Perhaps it was simply a matter of jealousy. As Michaelis put it: Winckelmann 'was not permitted to see the promised land of Greek art as revealed by English energy'. Even so, his influence in Britain, belated and indirect, was enormous. Byron, Keats, Shelley and Landor, in different ways and in different degrees, breathed the heady atmosphere which Winckelmann had helped to create. Romantic Hellenism was born amid the frosty wastes of Seehausen and the provincial galleries of Dresden. Slowly, Winckelmann seems to have penetrated the consciousness of every Englishman with any pretensions to classical taste. As late as 1812, in ponderous couplets, Charles Kelsall's *Letter from Athens* lamented the 'tragical' murder of his hero—a squalid affair in a wayside inn:

> Could then no hand the felon's blade restrain?
> —Lo in cold blood Germania's boast is slain!—
> O Winckelmann! when thy vital sp'rit fled,
> The Graces wept, and Painting bow'd her head;
> Thee, whom the arts and choicest love adorn'd,

'Mid Rome's proud ruins Architecture mourn'd—
The Julian Alps return'd the Muses' shrieks,
Redden'd with scalding tears pale Sculpture's cheeks.

Few of his contemporaries read the whole Winckelmann *corpus*. But then how many people today have actually read Marx and Freud?

From a strictly academic point of view, Winckelmann's initial process of thought was precariously inductive: working largely from Hellenistic originals or Graeco-Roman copies, he adumbrated formidably generalized aesthetic categories. But towards the end of his life, in Rome, Herculaneum, Paestum and Florence, he developed a truer archaeological sense. His second book, the *Catalogue of the Engraved Gems of the late Baron Stosch* (1760), is impressively well documented. His accounts of the excavations at Pompeii and Herculaneum (1762 and 1764) helped not only to reveal but to explain those wondrous treasure houses. His *Observations on the Architecture of the Ancients*, the product of a brief visit to Paestum four years before, evoked the spirit of those mighty temples almost as powerfully as any engraving. And his encyclopaedic *History of Ancient Art* was no less than an attempt to describe and analyse the artistic achievements of the ancient world.

In this, his final work, Winckelmann set out to trace, 'wherever feasible on the strength of the surviving ancient works themselves, the origin, growth, changes, and decadence of art, as well as the styles of the various nations, periods and artists'. Unlike the works of Montfaucon or de Caylus, this was more than a mere compendium. Inevitably, however, such a cyclical theory failed to supply that 'systematic doctrine' for which he sought. Despite his formidable range of observation—climatology, mathematics, sociology, chemistry, numismatics, philosophy—he was working from insufficient evidence. 'Who in the world', asked Herder, 'unless he be a prophet, a god, or a devil, could write a *complete* History of Art?'. Or as Winckelmann himself put it, 'it is no disgrace, when hunting in a forest full of game, to miss a few shots'. If his greatest work was a failure, it was an heroic failure. In writing it he became in effect the founder of two new disciplines—art history and archaeology—as well as the prophet of Neo-Classicism. And his disciples carried on the work. J. H. von Riedesel's *Journey through Sicily and Magna Graecia* (1771) became the bible of Sicilian tourists from Goethe onwards. Lessing broke off his writing of the *Laocöon* with the words: 'Mr. Winckelmann's *History of Ancient Art* has just come off the press. I dare not take another step until I have read it'.

It was not so much what Winckelmann said that mattered. It was the unforgettable way that he said it. 'He tells me his feelings', said Gibbon of the ideal critic, 'and he tells them with so much energy that he communicates them.' That dictum might stand as Winckelmann's epitaph. His neo-Platonic idealism—Bellori plus Shaftesbury and Montesquieu—was less novel than language. His statements burned with pent up passion. His sentences were chiselled with rare economy and grace. At times his utterances assumed an almost messianic tone. The idea of Greece, if not its actuality, dominated his very existence. He even explained to Casanova that his homosexual instincts—'pederasty tempered by pedagogy'—arose out of admiration for the ambivalent exploits of his ancient heroes. Madame de Staël remarked that he 'made himself a pagan' in order to understand the aesthetics of paganism. Even before his death in Trieste he had come to be regarded as 'The Father of Archaeology'. And ever since his voice has been the voice of Neo-Classicism. Even in England, the Greek Revival was largely a movement of his own making.

Winckelmann spoke for the world of learning. But in diluted form his utterances percolated throughout the world of fashion. Greekomania in smart society was summed up in one trivial but significant phenomenon: the international acclaim accorded to Lady Hamilton's Attitudes. Emma Hamilton had apparently been trained in the chorus at Dr. Graham's Temple of the Muses. As consort of a celebrated antiquary she put her expertise to good use in a series of *tableaux vivants* modelled on Pompeian frescoes and Graeco-Roman statues. Her charades brought antiquity into the drawing room—though Goethe caustically remarked that she spoilt the effect as soon as she opened her mouth. 'Sir William Hamilton's pantomime mistress or wife', scoffed Horace Walpole, 'acts all the antique statues in an Indian shawl. I have not seen her yet, so am no judge, but people are mad about her wonderful expression, which I do not conceive, so few antique statues having any expression at all, nor being designed

to have it'. Younger men than Walpole, however, flocked to her Neapoli-
tan soirées and were overwhelmed by her Neo-Classical grace. Morritt's
eulogy will have to stand for the praises of a whole battalion of aesthetes.
He told his mother:

> We have not seen many new sights, but one of those we have seen is fairly
> worth all Naples and Rome put together . . . I mean Lady Hamilton's
> attitudes; and do not laugh or think me a fool, for I assure you it is beyond
> what you can have an idea of. . . . Her toilet is merely a white chemise
> gown, some shawls, and the finest hair in the world, flowing loose over
> her shoulders. These set off a tall, beautiful figure, and a face that varies
> for ever, and is always lovely. Thus accoutred, with the assistance of one
> or two Etruscan vases and an urn, she takes almost every attitude of the
> finest antique figures successively, and varying in a moment the folds of
> her shawl, the flow of her hair; and her wonderful countenance is at one
> instant a Sibyl, then a Fury, a Niobe, a Sophonisba drinking poison, a
> Bacchante drinking wine, dancing, and playing the tambourine, an Agrip-
> pina at the tomb of Germanicus, and every different attitude of almost
> every different passion . . . [all] entirely studied from the antique designs
> of vases and the figures of Herculaneum, or the first pictures of Guido
> etc. etc. Sometimes she does about two hundred, one after the other, and,
> according to the impulse of the moment, scarce ever does them twice the
> same. In short, suppose Raphael's figures, and the ancient statues, all
> flesh and blood, she would, if she pleased, rival them all. What is still
> better is that she acts with the greatest delicacy, and represents nothing
> but what the most modest woman may see with pleasure. . . . I never
> saw in my life *any* actress half her equal in elegance or variety. A painter
> who was of the morning party when she performed her attitudes cried
> with pleasure the whole time . . .

The last quarter of the eighteenth century was certainly an heroic
and romantic period in England's rediscovery of Greece. During the
1780s and 1790s sailing among the islands and wandering the Peloponnese became for the first time fashionable. 'The Athenian Reveley', who
travelled in 1785–86, was a scholar cast in Revett's mould. But James
Dallaway's thousand-mile tour of the Levant, sponsored by Lord Bute,
was published in 1797 with plates which were picturesquely vague rather

than precisely archaeological. Sir Richard Worsley's *Museum Worsleyanum* (1794) was as much a monument to his own taste as a contribution to scholarship. 'Buck' Whaley travelled to Jerusalem in 1788–89 merely to satisfy a bet with his colleagues in the Dublin Hell-Fire Club. And other travellers, such as Lady Craven, had no pretensions to learning whatever.

It was in 1786 that the beautiful Lady Craven, daughter of the Earl of Berkeley, left her husband for the Levant. Notoriously 'a democrate in love', she travelled the world with her paramours, 'breakfasted with the Empress of Russia, . . . dined with the Grand Signor, and supped with the Great Mogul'. She stayed in Constantinople as guest of the French Ambassador, Choiseul-Gouffier. She sailed to the Piraeus with Fauvel, doyen of French philhellenes. She carved her name upon the Theseion and felt the presence of Apollo's ghost within the confines of the Parthenon. She certainly fell in love with Grecian monuments, particularly that 'sweet little temple called the Lanthorn of Diogenes'. But her notoriety was such that, as she modestly admitted, she would probably have been 'Black Ball'd at Parnassus'. Later Margravine of Anspach, she returned to England and settled down to write French comedies. No wonder *The Lady's Magazine, or Entertaining Companion for the Fair Sex* delighted its readers with a 'Sketch of a Voyage to Athens' plagiarized from Wheler, Spon and Chandler. Not that travelling the Levant had become any easier. Dr. Sibthorp, the Oxford botanist, made three trips with John Hawkins as companion in 1786, 1787 and 1794, and died soon afterwards as a result of his exertions.

Saddest and most romantic of all was the fate of poor John Tweddell. Fresh from Cambridge and crossed in love, he set out for Greece in the Autumn of 1795, travelling via Russia, Northern Europe and the Near East. 'Athens especially is my great object', he wrote. 'I promise you that those who come after me shall have nothing to glean. Not only every temple, but, every stone, and every inscription, shall be copied with the most scrupulous fidelity'. He arrived there in the Spring of 1799 and began to work frenetically. Toiling in the sun all day, he soon completed fifty topographical scenes and two volumes of inscriptions. 'My collection of drawings of Athens', he boasted, 'is the most complete, without any doubt, of all those that have ever been carried out of the country'. By the summer he was dead. Wearied by travel, robbed by brigands, weakened by a vegetarian diet, he fell victim to a 'double tertian fever', dosed himself with James's powders and refused to be bled. Fauvel arranged for him to be buried exactly in the centre of the Theseion—he hoped to find a few traces of Theseus during the actual process of interment. Three salvoes of musketry bade him farewell, and the Archbishop of Athens walked in the funeral procession.

Such was the end of 'the exemplary and lamented Tweddell', a martyr to metempsychosis and excessive philhellenism. Even his papers were lost—Elgin was later unfairly accused of purloining them. But at least his tombstone was a fragment of the Parthenon, and he left his name on the pillars of Sunium. Nor did he lie alone. By his side in the Theseion—'that great mausoleum of British travellers'—were buried at least three more young Englishmen: Benjamin Gott, who died at Piraeus in 1817, far from his native Leeds; Thomas Melville Phillips, who died at Patras in 1819 after carving his name on a temple in Arcadia; and George Watson, victim of fever in 1810, whose gravestone still survives, thanks to its Latin inscription by Lord Byron.

But 'an antiquary', as Dr. Johnson put it, 'is a rugged being'—or at least successful ones are. And the Regency generation of British travellers certainly showed uncommon stamina. Of the various accounts which survive none catches the spirit of the time better than the letters and diaries left behind by Morritt of Rokeby. Heir to a great Yorkshire estate, a romantic Tory hot-foot from Cambridge, he set out with Dr. Stockdale as companion in the Spring of 1794. 'Quizzing the natives' in Belgium, France and Germany with all the arrogance of a *grand seigneur*— he preferred Frenchmen to Germans: 'folly in preference to stupidity'— Morritt began to show rather more interest as the going got rougher between Venice and Constantinople. The hills of Hungary and the wastes of Transylvania reminded him of 'what Mr. Gilpin would call *composition*'. With two more companions, Wilbrahim and Dallaway, he reached the coast of Asia Minor in September. 'We are now proceeding', he told his mother, 'by Brusa to Smyrna, and after visiting everything to be seen on the coast of Asia shall finish with the Troad; go in October and November by Cavallo and Mount Athos to Salonica; cross Macedonia and Thessaly through the Vale of Tempe etc., by land to Larissa, then by Thermopylae to Lividia, see Thebes, Boeotia, Phocis and Parnassus, and winter till February at Athens. In Spring see the Morea and cross to Sicily. N.B. With common precautions all this can be done, and the . . . robbers . . . may be very well avoided by common prudence. The Morea has hardly ever been visited except near Olympia. . . . Do you not envy me our winter's plan in Athens, where we mean to keep house, and send wine and English porter from Smyrna. I shall bring home drawings of every hill and grove in Greece . . .'.

'Dying with heat', in Smyrna; sleeping 'in a miserable mud cottage' near Miletus, 'with a legion of fleas and vermin'; threading the Greek islands in an open boat; dodging the plague—'we got away just in time'; eating hare, woodcock and wild duck, tasting honey from Hymettus; ogling the native girls—'I never saw a ball-room which compared with the quay at Scio'; despising the modern Greeks—'a people worn out'; reluctantly admiring the 'manly' Turks; living 'very primitively' in a cave on the island of Chalci 'in the true taste of the Golden Age'—Morritt's adventures were typical of a new generation of Grand Tourists. A cloudless sunset over the Bay of Smyrna made Gilpin seem irrelevant and a Claude Glass unnecessary. Memories of Loutherbourg's stage scenery at the Eidophusikon were soon obliterated by thunder and lightning amid the darkened ruins of Nicaea. 'I am more mad about Greece than ever', he wrote; 'except when on horseback I am reading or writing all day long. . . . Every hill I see here is interesting, and seems an old friend after what one has read'. Conditioned not only by the classics, but by the Picturesque as well, even Mount Olympus seemed familiar: 'something like Skiddaw . . . [but] about three times as high and covered with forests and rocks'. Besides, there was the Sublime to look for too. Hiding in 'a large cave by the seashore at the foot of Mount Mycale', he experienced a storm of tropical ferocity. With a 'sky . . . as black as ink. . . . The effect . . . was inconceivably grand . . . it burst over us in such a storm of thunder and lightning as I never in my life witnessed. The sea flew on one side of us, the thunder roared like a cannonade, almost deafening us with the sound among the tops of the mountains. The lightning was forked and continual, often followed immediately by the thunder . . . you will never imagine a sublimer scene. . . . Thunder in England is a perfect popgun to it. . . . It was worth being wet through to see'.

Of course the monuments themselves made a powerful impression. The Propylaea: 'chaste and simple architecture . . . nobleness of design'; the Parthenon sculptures: 'exquisite workmanship . . . brilliancy and exactness of execution . . . variety and imagination'; the columns of the Erechtheion (Plate 10): 'capitals extremely ornamented . . . the scroll around the whole seems worked in filigree, from the delicacy and lightness it is carved with. I never saw the Ionic order more beautiful, and begin really to think the ancient Grecians were inspired by some genius of elegance and taste that has since given over business, for we do not make any more of these kinds of miracles now'. 'On paper a pillar is a pillar, and there is no conveying to your mind the effect they produce upon mine . . . [But] my head is so full of these things that I can think of nothing else, for I have read of nothing else, heard of nothing else, and seen nothing else worth talking about. In short, my whole mind is entirely in Athens, and all my ideas are gone back some two thousand years'.

But it was the Arcadian setting of so many of the monuments which stirred Morritt's imagination most profoundly. 'The ruins of the [Ionic] temple at Priene', he reported 'are a great and splendid heap of architectural fragments, all on the ground; the blocks of marble are immense, and the worked stones very elegant. . . . After looking at the ruins, talking over Bias and old stories, we turned across the plain to the Maeander. The sun was now setting, the sky in a glow with its rays, and the islands and mountains round us glorious. Opposite us was the woody ridges and summits of Latmos, and more to the left a high, conical mountain whose outline was everywhere broken with crags and glittering in the parting lights of the sun. The moon over it grew brighter as the sun set, and when the evening came on—in memory, I suppose, of Endymion—did the honours of Mount Latmos gloriously'. The ruins of the Ionic Temple of Apollo at Branchidae were equally moving: 'A setting sun, when we saw it, shone full on the temple; beyond the sea was as smooth as a mirror, and the eye wandered over the neighbouring islands, or fancied distant ones. Samos, Icaria, Patmos, Leros, Calymna . . . you can hardly conceive a more delicious scene. The moon at night, and the sun at daybreak the day after, showed it off still more, in new lights and equal beauty'.

It was really a vision of Arcadia that Morritt was seeking. And he found it among the wild banditi of Maina. He rejoiced in their romantic simplicity, 'free in the midst of slavery'. 'Their virtues and vices', he wrote, 'are those of a half civilized nation'. Among them he stayed at a fairy-tale castle, 'waited on by beautiful girls, in the true mode of patriarchal times'. 'You know', he reminded his mother, 'how famous Arcadian pastorals always were. We found the country still as beautiful as possible throughout, and still, as usual, covered with sheep and shepherds, though not the opera kind of *pastorelli* which one admires at the Haymarket'. 'We were very often asked to marry and settle', he recalled wistfully, 'and think we should have made excellent Captains of a Mainote band'. Perhaps, instead, 'we will attend Ranelagh as Mainotes'.

Morritt was certainly among the most adventurous of his generation. But he had few pretensions to scholarship. His successors set quite a different standard. Their leader was Colonel William Martin Leake, the most impressive Levantine topographer of the nineteenth century.

In 1799 Leake went out to Constantinople to train Turkish gunners against the French. He took the chance to travel extensively through Greece, Egypt, and Syria. In 1802 he was in Athens and in September of that year he sailed with W. R. Hamilton in the very boat in which many of the Elgin Marbles were sunk off the shores of Cythera. During 1804–7 he made detailed drawings of the Greek mainland and archipelago. Later journeys to Turkey and Switzerland followed in 1808–10 and 1814. By the time he finally returned to England in 1815 he was clearly the most knowledgeable topographer of ancient Greece. And since then his *Topography of Athens* (1821), his *Tour in Asia Minor* (1824), his *Travels in the Morea* (1830; 1846) and *Travels in Northern Greece* (1835) have been indispensable reference books for classical scholars. A modest but indefatigable writer, he combined the integrity of a born scholar with the cool precision of a military engineer. Michaelis truly called him 'the founder of the scientific geography of Greece'.

Ahead of Leake in popular reputation, and not too far behind in achievement, was Sir William Gell. Byron immortalized him in a couplet:

Of Dardan tours let dilettanti tell,
I leave topography to classic Gell

—'classic' being an epithet which replaced 'coxcomb' in an earlier version
and was in turn replaced by 'rapid' when the poet discovered that Gell
had apparently 'topographized and typographized King Priam's domin-
ions in three days'. Rapid or not, the adjectives used by Michaelis—'dry
but indefatigable'—are rather more appropriate. Unlike Leake, he was a
clubbable companion with a natural appetite for publicity. Still, he was
more than 'the Augustus Hare of his day'.

In 1801, after coming down from Cambridge, Gell visited the Troad:
three years later came the *Topography of Troy*, a sumptuous folio with
hand-coloured plates. In 1803 he was in the Ionian Islands. In 1804 it was
the Greek mainland. In 1806 he toured Ithaca with Edward Dodwell.
Within a year he published an agreeable volume on its geography and
antiquities, and was duly elected a Dilettante. In 1810 he produced his
Argolis: the Itinerary of Greece, a combination of record, travelogue and
guide book. Next came his *Itinerary of the Morea* (1817) and *Journey in the
Morea* (1823), handbooks for travellers, factual and anecdotal respectively.
Later on he rounded off his career with *Pompeiana* (a joint work in two
stages with J. P. Gandy, 1817–19 and 1832), and settled in Naples as the
Dilettanti's Italian plenipotentiary. He lived in a house laughingly known
as the Villa Gellia. He even had the privilege of instructing Sir Walter
Scott in classical lore. When his two volume *Topography of Rome* appeared
in 1834 he must surely have wept that there was so little left of the ancient
world to topographize. Today he rests, improbably enough, in the same
tomb as Lady Craven, in the old British Cemetery at Naples.

In his own day Gell was probably best known for his *Pompeiana*. In
three attractive and reasonably priced volumes—prefaced by his own
profile—he summed up for an admiring audience the results of a century
of intermittent research amid the lava ashes of Pompeii and Herculaneum.
Both sites had been discovered piecemeal during the first two decades of
the eighteenth century. But excavation only began at Herculaneum in
1738 and at Pompeii in 1748. During the 1790s research was revitalized
by Napoleonic support. Work at Pompeii progressed more quickly under
the direction of Championnet and Arditi, and under the local patronage
of Queen Caroline. By the time Gell took up the subject Bayardi's massive

folios (1755 onwards) had already been supplemented with works by Mazois, Gau, Zahn and Ternite. But there was room for a popular illustrated survey. And Gell rapidly supplied it. His seductive drawings of Hellenistic decoration—composed with a *camera lucida*—were by no means architectural prototypes. But they did help to create the sort of Regency interior apotheosed in Thomas Hope's villa at Deepdene, Surrey. In fact Gell almost anticipated Bulwer Lytton in making Pompeii a popular cult.

But the work for which Gell should perhaps be best remembered began in 1812. In that year he was chosen to lead the Society of Dilettanti's second Ionian Expedition. With Francis Bedford and J. P. Gandy as architectural draughtsmen, with Keppel Craven as companion, and with William Wilkins as prospective editor, the team set out. Their itinerary had been mapped out by a fellow explorer, that 'travelled thane, Athenian Aberdeen'. And they went well prepared with bribes: 'Telescopes, Pistol barrels and Locks, some articles of cut Glass, and some Shawls of British Manufacture. . . . Bacshish under different names has a great deal of influence in every country yet known, but in the East it is indispensable'.

Of course by 1812 there were plenty of precedents for organized expeditions. But the steering committee knew the dangers only too well: 'For the ultimate Success of an Expedition like this, no human prudence or foresight can answer. Pestilence may render the access to many places too dangerous to be attempted; Insurrection . . . may completely shut up at once a great tract of country . . . .'. They need not have worried. Under Gell's firm and capable leadership, the trip was almost as big a success as Chandler's. The temple of Ceres (Demeter) at Eleusis, the temple of Juno (Hera) at Samos, the temple of Apollo Didymaeus near Miletus, the temple of Diana (Artemis) Leucophryne at Magnesia, the temple of Nemesis at Rhamnos—all these were excavated, examined and recorded. It had been 'the Intention of the Society of Dilettanti to engrave and offer them to the Public for the Improvement of National Taste'. But the heavy cost of the expedition made full and immediate publication impossible. In the end, Gell's discoveries appeared in two parts: *The Unedited Antiquities of Attica* (1817) and *Ionian Antiquities* vol. iii (1840). Not until 1881, well over a hundred years after Chandler's trip, was the

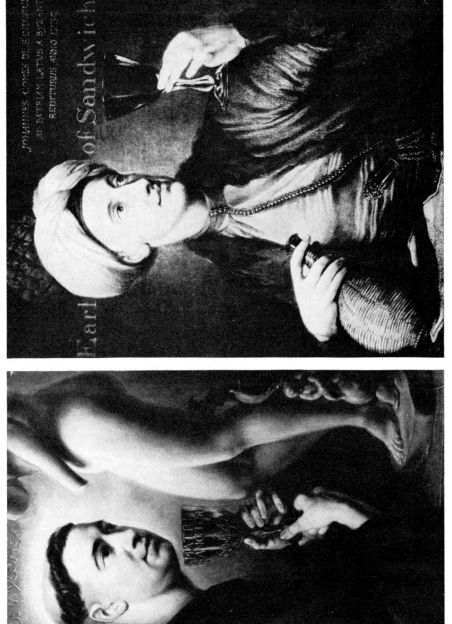

9. Lord Sandwich (1718–92) dressed à la Turk: a portrait by George Knapton.

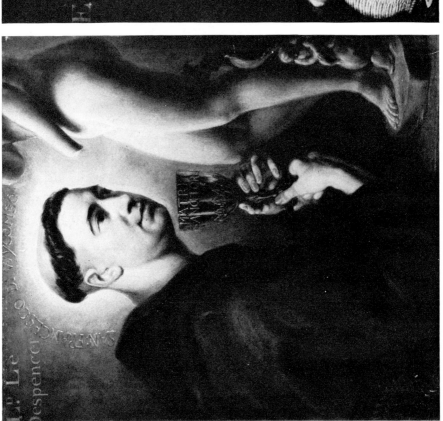

8. Sir Francis Dashwood (1708–81) as leader of the Hell Fire Club: a portrait by George Knapton.

Fig. 3.

Fig. 4.

Fig. 2.

Fig. 1.

Publish'd Oct.ʳ 27ᵗʰ 1787 According to Act of Parliament.

10. The Ionic order from the Erechtheion.

Ionian series completed, with a fourth and final volume edited by R. P. Pullan. Ironically, only a gift from John Ruskin—the bitterest opponent of all the Greek Revival stood for—enabled publication to be accomplished. The days of princely Dilettanti volumes were over. During the Victorian period initiative in classical patronage shifted from individuals to institutions. The early triumphs of the Dilettanti began to fade. And the classic battles between Elgin, Payne Knight and Byron had themselves become almost legendary.

*　　　*　　　*

The Elgin episode made the Greek Revival and nearly broke the Dilettanti Society. It was in 1799 that Lord Elgin set out as Ambassador to Constantinople, determined to bring back casts, drawings and specimens of Greek antiquities and thus accelerate 'the progress of taste in England'.

The idea seems to have sprung initially from Thomas Harrison, the architect of Elgin's Scottish seat at Broomhall, Fife. In 1802 Elgin wrote to Harrison as follows: 'I repeat it, you and you alone gave me the idea'. So Britain owes the Elgin Marbles, at least partly, to Thomas Harrison. That they were eventually secured for the British Museum was in no way due to the Society of Dilettanti. In fact the collection, transport and sale of the marbles was largely Elgin's own doing. True, he had able assistants: his secretaries, W. R. Hamilton and J. P. Morier; his chief painter, the painstaking Italian G. B. Lusieri; his assistant painter, Theodor Ivanovitch—'Lord Elgin's Calmuck'; his chaplain, the self-important Dr. Philip Hunt; and two architectural draughtsmen, a student named Ittar and a hunchback named Balestra. And his ambassadorial post gave him every opportunity of suborning the Turks and outmanoeuvring the French. But the removal of the Elgin Marbles—rightly or wrongly—was his own achievement.

'I should wish to have', Elgin told Lusieri, 'examples in the actual object, of each thing, and architectural ornament—of each cornice, each frieze, each capital—of the decorated ceilings, of the fluted columns—specimens of the different architectural orders and of the various forms of the orders—of metopes and the like, as much as possible. Finally everything in the way of sculpture, medals, and curious marbles that can be discovered by means of assiduous and indefatigable excavation. This excavation ought to be pushed on as much as possible, be its success what it may'. As the programme progressed, Elgin warmed to his work. 'The slightest object from the Acropolis', he wrote, 'is a jewel'. He even dreamed of chartering a Royal Navy ship to transport to England the entire caryatid porch of the Erechtheion (Plate 4)—'the whole Temple of the Cari-something', as Lady Elgin christened it, 'where the Statues of the Women are'.

Byron was not the first to disapprove. Dodwell and Clarke left moving accounts of Lusieri's depredations: 'down came the fine masses of Pentelican marble, scattering their white fragments with thundering noise among the ruins. The [Turkish] Disdar, seeing this, could no longer restrain his emotions; but actually took his pipe from his mouth, and letting fall a tear, said in a most emphatic tone of voice 'τέλος!'—'never again!'. Aberdeen saw and deplored 'the devastation which is indeed continual'. Robert Smirke, who might himself have been in Lusieri's shoes, claimed to be equally horrified: 'Each stone as it fell shook the ground with its ponderous weight with a deep hollow noise; it seemed like a convulsive groan of the injured spirit of the Temple'. But then Dodwell, Clarke, Smirke and Aberdeen, like every other traveller of the time, were all themselves guilty of antique petty larceny. Their trophies have, however, mostly vanished; Elgin's are at least safe in the British Museum. Much of the criticism which Elgin had to endure seems to have been prompted by envy rather than by justified self-righteousness. The same is equally true of attacks from his French rivals. Their intentions were identical. Choiseul-Gouffier, who became French Ambassador to the Ottoman Empire in 1783 sent instructions to his agent Fauvel as follows: 'piller dans Athènes et dans son territoire tout ce qu'il a de pillable'. Elgin—'un speculateur anglais'—was merely more successful.

Elgin's marbles began to arrive in London in 1803. With their arrival in stages controversy began in earnest and soon swelled to a mighty clamour. On one side were the artists. On the other the connoisseurs. The scene of the battle was a temporary museum opened in 1807 near the top of Piccadilly. Fashionable London flocked to this 'damp, dirty penthouse'—later the marbles were moved to the courtyard of Burlington House—to gaze upon these fragments of old Greece. John Flaxman, 'the

English Phidias', took one look and renounced the Medici Venus forever: compared with the Theseus, he told Hamilton, the Apollo Belvedere was a mere dancing master. His own master Canova, the greatest sculptor in Europe, refused point blank even to consider restoration: it would be sacrilege for any man to touch them with a chisel. 'The naked figures', he told Elgin, 'are real flesh, in its native beauty'. Benjamin West called them 'sublime' and wished he were forty years younger. Prize-fighters posed by them. Mrs. Siddons wept. Benjamin Robert Haydon was moved to ecstasy: 'That combination of nature and idea, which I had felt was so much wanting for high art, was here displayed to midday conviction. My heart beat! If I had seen nothing else I had beheld sufficient to keep me to nature for the rest of my life. . . . I felt as if a divine truth had blazed inwardly upon my mind and I knew that they would at last rouse the rest of Europe from its slumber in the darkness'. His companion, Henry Fuseli, the Swiss master of the Sublime, was overwhelmed: 'he strode about saying "De Greeks were godes! de Greeks were godes!" . . .'.

The artists were on Elgin's side. Chantrey, Lawrence, Westmacott, Rossi and Nollekens all supported him. It was the connoisseurs who cast doubt upon the value of the marbles. Trained in the appreciation of Ideal Forms, they rejected the naturalism of the Parthenon marbles; collectors of Roman and Graeco-Roman figures, they spurned the simplified architectural sculpture of the Greeks. They preferred the Apollo Belvedere to the Theseus, grace to grandeur. Their leader was Richard Payne Knight (Plate 7)—himself a collector of Graeco-Roman bronzes—strongly supported by Wilkins and Aberdeen. Before the marbles had even been unpacked, he called across to Lord Elgin at a dinner in 1806: 'You have lost your labour, my Lord Elgin. Your marbles are overrated; they are not Greek; they are Roman of the time of Hadrian'. That Hadrianic tag was an error dating back to Dr. Spon. Soon it hung like an albatross round Payne Knight's neck. Later he changed the ground of his attack, from chronology to quality. But the damage was done. Not until 1816— partly on the testimony of foreign experts like Visconti and Canova— did the government agree to purchase the marbles for the nation, largely to prevent them going abroad. Haydon noted in his diary: 'This year the Elgin Marbles were bought and produced an Aera in public feeling'. Next year he introduced the Theseus to John Keats.

39

Elgin emerged from the affair bankrupt and broken. In the *Quarterly Review* J. W. Croker made mincemeat of the egregious Payne Knight. But that was small consolation to Elgin. He received only £35,000—less than half his expenses. Eventually most of the Dilettanti came round to his side. Morritt never wavered in his support. In the public inquiry even Aberdeen changed sides. Payne Knight's erstwhile ally, William Wilkins, softened sufficiently to urge that Elgin be belatedly elected a Dilettante. Hamilton despatched the good news in 1831. With proper dignity, the offer was declined.

✳   ✳   ✳

Whatever Elgin's personal troubles—Byron made him immortal with a curse—the controversy over the marbles did much to establish Grecian as the style of the moment. In 1812 the Pilgrim awoke and found himself famous: copies of *Childe Harold* rested on Grecian sofas in half the drawing rooms of London. Few of the 'classic Thieves' in the Athenian Club could hope to escape *The Curse of Minerva*. Neither

> Dark Hamilton and sullen Aberdeen
>   . . . nor that lesser wight
> The victim sad of vase-collecting spleen
> House furnisher withal one Thomas [Hope] hight

—none of these was wholly innocent of marble mongering. But it was Elgin who drew the poet's fire. 'Quod non fecerunt Goti, hoc fecerunt Scoti' was inscribed near the missing Caryatid on the Erechtheion. And so, despite Payne Knight's defeat and despite the slur which Byron cast over the whole business of connoisseurship, the collective influence of the Dilettanti Society remained undiminished. Payne Knight's gibes and Byron's scorn merely heightened the fever of Greek Revivalism. At home every shop-girl tried to dress her hair *à la grecque*. Abroad every wandering midshipman tried to bring back a piece of the Parthenon. Away in Weimar Goethe collected Haydon's drawings of the Theseus. And Hazlitt predicted that the presence of the marbles in London might 'lift the Fine Arts out of the limbo of vanity and affectation . . . in which they have lain sprawling and fluttering, gasping for breath, wasting away, vapid and abortive'.

The Regency period was in many ways the heyday of the Dilettanti. With members like the Duke of Hamilton—'the proudest man in England'; the Duke of Sutherland—that 'leviathan of wealth'; and Charles Long M.P., later Lord Farnborough, 'the Tory aesthete of Bromley Hill . . . the Vitruvius of the . . . age'—the Society still maintained something approaching a dictatorship of taste. But it was about this time that the Society's virtual monopoly of English classical exploration was broken. Travelling in Greece became so frequent as to be almost commonplace. The Napoleonic blockade of the rest of Europe made the neutral Turkish empire doubly attractive to Grand Tourists. The Greek War of Independence (1821–30) supplied a great symbolic cause. And the poetry of Lord Byron turned philhellenism from an aristocratic cult into a bourgeois fashion.

Philhellenism even crossed the Atlantic, and there found in the democratic soil of the United States its happiest adoptive home. Jefferson had never reached Greece: he was only a Philhellene at second hand. American exploration of Greece belonged to a later generation. Perhaps the first of the new wave was Nicholas Biddle of Philadelphia. In 1806 he 'at last touched the holy soil of Greece', and after many adventures returned with one overriding conviction: 'the two great truths in the world are the Bible and Greek architecture'. The Doric columns of Philadelphia's Biddle Bank were but a portent of thousands more to come. America's emotional involvement with the Greek mystique was heightened by the Greek War of Independence. 'The Star-Spangled Banner', cried General Harrison of Cincinnati, 'must wave in the Aegean'. Such cultural reciprocity as there was, however, turned out to be mainly in the other direction. Grecian became the official style for governmental buildings all over the New World. And in 1857 one marble fragment from the ruins of the Parthenon was installed with appropriate ceremony among the granite stones of the Washington Monument. But that is another story. The rediscovery of Greece in the early nineteenth centuty was predominantly a British affair.

Thomas Hope was travelling in Greece in 1799–1800. In 1801 Wilkins, Gell, Dodwell and E. D. Clarke all visited Athens. So did Elgin's parents-in-law, the Nisbets. So did Elgin's maritime assistant Capt. Thomas Lacy. So did Dr. Carlyle, Professor of Arabic at Cambridge, and

Dr. Philip Hunt. Leake was there in 1802 with Col. John Squire and W. R. Hamilton. Sir William Drummond and 'Athenian' Aberdeen were visitors in 1803. So was the future Sir Robert Smirke, architect of the British Museum, with his travelling companion William Walker. In 1805 Gell was there with Sir Charles Monck of Belsay and Dr. Macmichael. Professor John Palmer of Cambridge followed in 1806. Byron called them the 'Levant lunatics'. By 1810 there was a veritable flood: John Cam Hobhouse, John Galt, Gally Knight, J. N. Fazakerley, Lord Sligo, Frederick North 5th Earl of Guilford, and of course Byron himself. 'Athens', he wrote, 'is at present infested with English people'. Lady Hester Stanhope even caught him bathing off the coast of Attica by the rocks of Cape Colonna. Lord Sligo later engineered a more formal introduction.

That was the year the 'loquacious' Dr. Clarke began to publish his *Travels*, making £7,000 in the process. In architecture, dress, furniture, sculpture, painting and poetry, Grecian was the style. Greekomania had gripped the British public. In 1814 *The Times* carried the following advertisement: 'To the Nobility, Gentry and Fashionable World—Ross's newly invented GRECIAN VOLUTE HEADDRESS, formed from the true marble models, brought into this country from the Acropolis of Athens by Lord Elgin, rivals any other hitherto invented. The elegance of taste and simplicity of nature which it displays, together with the facility of dressing, have caused its universal admiration and adoption'. Edward Dodwell returned from his travels in 1806 carrying upwards of a thousand drawings, later distilled into deliciously coloured *Views in Greece*. His reputation soared; he went out to Greece and Italy again in middle age, and died after being stricken by sunstroke among the Sabine Hills. Miss Sydney Owenson, later Lady Morgan, made quite a name for herself with four volumes of gushing romance entitled *Woman: or Ida of Athens* (1809). In the same year appeared Thomas Hope's *Costume of the Ancients*: Grecian decor was *de rigueur*. Five years later came his *Anastasius: or the memoir of a Greek*, and Byron wept twice: once because he had not written it, and once because Hope had.

Grecian *gusto* had radiated far beyond the charmed circle of the Dilettanti. As the *Quarterly Review* put it, *à propos* Leake's *Researches*: 'No man is now accounted a traveller, who has not bathed in the Eurotas and tasted the olives of Attica; . . . it is an introduction to the best company, and a passport to literary distinction, to be a member of the "Athenian Club", and to have scratched one's name upon a fragment of the Parthenon'. What the Athenian Club did in London, the Ottoman Club did in Constantinople. There the English *chargé d'affaires*, Spencer Smith—husband of Byron's 'fair Florence'—acted as pivot for quite a band of émigrés: Sibthorp, Hawkins, Liston, Dallaway, Wilbrahim, Morritt, Stockdale, Tweddell and Clarke all valued his hospitality. In 1811 Chateaubriand met up with numbers of Englishmen on the roads of the Peloponnese. At Mistra he even found an *English Inn* serving port and roast beef. After all, Nelson was a popular hero among the Greeks. And Byron was offered the field of Marathon for £900. By 1826 one traveller reported with disgust that there were literally thousands of names carved or painted on the columns of Sunium.

Athens (Plate 2), of course, was the goal of every traveller and the focus of enthusiasm. Its attractions were both classic and romantic: chaste monuments and exotic natives. 'Romans burn it', wrote the Rev. T. S. Hughes in 1820, 'Goths sack it, Venetians bombard it, Turks grind down monuments for mortar, and cold-blooded connoisseurs export them as articles of commerce: still Athens is the best school in the world for an architect'. Certainly the old walled town was cramped and squalid—Hobhouse 'walked round . . . at a brisk pace in forty-seven minutes'. And its treasures were in ruins. Morosini, Haseki and Elgin had all left their mark. The Parthenon sports a minaret. A Capuchin friar writes letters in Lysicrates' monument. A Turkish band plays each afternoon outside the Erechtheion. The Propylaea bristle with the muzzles of Turkish cannon. An English poet talks in the bazaar with 'French, Italians, Germans, Danes, Greeks, Turks, Americans . . .'. Wrestlers try their strength near the temple of Zeus Olympius. Before the Theseion at Eastertime dance 'Turks, Greeks, Albanians and Blacks'. And dancers of another sort twist and turn inside the Tower of the Winds.

Every Friday, according to Dodwell, the Dervishes gathered in the Tower. 'The spectator will find it as difficult to remain serious as it would be dangerous to appear otherwise. . . . The dance . . . is one of the most ridiculous ceremonies of Islamism. . . . They first sit upon the floor in a circle, and begin by singing the praises of God and Mohamed. The only instrumental accompaniment consist[s] of two small kettle drums. By degrees the song increases in animation, till on a sudden the company all start up, and sing and dance in a circle with vivid alacrity and obstreperous violence. After a certain time they make way for the two principal performers, who, holding each other by the sash, turn round with incredible rapidity. The Sheikh, or chief of the Derwisches, habited in the sacred *green*, with a large white turban, animates them by the powers of his voice and by the agitation of a large tambour. After the Derwisches have continued turning and screaming for a considerable time, they at length sink into the arms of the by-standers, and are for a few minutes apparently deprived of their senses, and filled with divine enthusiasm. . . . This curious ceremony has a strong resemblance to the festivals of the Corybantes. . . .'

✳   ✳   ✳

Many of the new generation of Regency Hellenists were Cambridge men. Gell, Dodwell, Clarke, Kelsall, Wilkins—all paid their respects to the memory of their fellow Cantabrian, John Tweddell. So did prize-winning Cambridge undergraduates:

> There in his early bloom, 'mid classic dust . . .
> [the Muses'] favourite sleeps; . . . far from Granta's bowers.

But Oxford's prize poets were similarly preoccupied. In 1806 'Ancient Art' was the competition theme and the winner, John Wilson, bade slumbering Genius

> . . . turn the eye, where, spurning time's controul,
> Art stamps on stone the triumphs of the soul.

In 1811 the subject was the Parthenon and Richard Burden produced the winning meditation on a building whose

> . . . beauty still appears
> Amid the wreck of thy forgotten years.

In 1815 it was the Theseion's turn. Samuel Richards directed his muse to the land where

> . . . rear'd in monarch state that fane appears
> Proud o'er the lapse of twice ten hundred years . . .
> Such the fair pile, where, shrin'd in holy cell,
> The slumb'ring ashes of the mighty dwell,
> Where Tweddell, youthful shade, to classic rest
> Sinks, like a wearied child, on Science' breast,
> And in the sacred scenes he lov'd to roam,
> Finds the last honours of a kindred home,
> While Muses, mourning whom they could not save,
> Still guard his fame; for Athens is his grave.

If anything, the Cambridge prizemen were rather less fashionably Hellenic. Macaulay's 'Pompeii' dates from 1819, Bright's 'Palmyra' from 1822, and Praed and Marshall's 'Athens' from 1824. But then the balance was soon amply redressed: Lord Byron was a Cambridge man.

Byron's role in the rediscovery of Greece was really a combination of inspiration and *haute vulgarisation*. His approach was fundamentally romantic, not archaeological, and scarcely even aesthetic. When Trelawney suggested a visit to Ithaca, Byron responded: 'Let's have a swim. I detest antiquarian twaddle'. He had little or no feeling for architecture. When Hobhouse remarked of the Parthenon, 'Well, this is surely very grand', the poet replied: 'Very like the Mansion House'. It was the associations which meant everything to him—'land of lost gods and godlike men'—and to most of his readers as well. 'Ask the traveller', he wrote in 1821, 'what strikes him as most poetical—the Parthenon, or the rock on which it stands? The COLUMNS of Cape Colonna, or the Cape itself? The rocks at the foot of it, or the recollection that Falconer's *ship* was bulged upon them? There are a thousand rocks and capes far more picturesque than those of the Acropolis and Cape Sunium in themselves. . . . But it is the "art", the columns, the temples, the wrecked vessel, which gives them their antique and their modern poetry, and not the spots themselves'. Confused, certainly. But at least he displayed a generalized feeling for the Picturesque. And when he slept and wrote inside the Choragic Monument of Lysicrates he could hardly avoid a sense of the *genius loci*. 'I am living', he wrote in 1811, 'in the Capuchin Convent, Hymettus before me, the Acropolis behind, the temple of Jove to my right, the Stadium in front, the town to the left; eh, Sir, there's a situation, there's your picturesque!'

As a traveller Byron was treading well-worn ground. As a poet he worked within an established Hellenic tradition. Long before *Childe Harold*, the poet's

> . . . wandering step
> Obedient to high thoughts, [had] visited
> The awful ruins of the days of old:
> Athens, and Tyre, and Balbec . . .

James Thomson in the 1730s, Thomas Warton and Thomas Gray in the 1750s, William Falconer and William Whitehead in the 1760s—all these had relished the flavour of Augustan melancholy and felt the urge to

> . . . trace with awe the dear remains
> Of mould'ring urns, and mutilated fanes . . .

William Haygarth's illustrated *Greece* (1814), in sonorous blank verse, took the form of a veritable Picturesque epic. In the 1820s George Canning's *Slavery of Greece* anticipated the spirit if not the diction of *The Isles of Greece*. And a Cornishman named Richard Polwhele even pre-empted Byron's Spenserian stanza as well as his philhellene sentiments.

But it was Byron who united the Augustan and the Romantic. He spoke the classical language of the eighteenth century with the accents of nineteenth-century liberalism. Of course his greatest contemporaries shared something of the same vision. Shelley's *Hellas* reveals the mind of a scholar and the soul of a poet, dreaming fond dreams of 'Temples and cities and immortal forms'. By a magical process of identification Keats, Greekless, was himself a Greek. Landor's epigrams rival the Delphic beauty of their antique originals. But only Byron's words managed to evoke—for the general run of Englishmen—the timeless spirit of old Greece. Besides, there was the manner of his death.

✳   ✳   ✳

More than any other category of men, however, it was the architects of the Greek Revival who supplied the link between imagination and discovery, the world of fashion and the world of scholarship. Such a man was William Wilkins.

A Cambridge don with a theatrical background, a classicist turned archaeologist and architect, Wilkins toured Greece, Asia Minor and Italy between 1801 and 1804. On his return to Cambridge he took the architectural world by storm. Championed by Thomas Hope, his Grecian design for Downing College defeated a Roman version submitted by no less a competitor than the Surveyor General, James Wyatt. Downing's Ionic columns established the Greek Revival as the dominant architectural fashion, and effectively launched Wilkins on a professional career which included the National Gallery and University College, London. As an archaeologist his talents were descriptive and analytical: he was almost the last of a generation not yet primarily concerned with excavation. His reputation as a scholar was established with *Antiquities of Magna Graecia* (1807), a lavish folio illustrated with fine drawings—plans, sections, elevations and Picturesque views—of the temples at Syracuse, Selinus, Agrigentum, Aegesta and Paestum. Subscribers included architects like Aikin, Byfield, Foster, Nash, Plaw, Porden and Saunders, as well as patrons and pundits like Aberdeen, Elgin, Gell, Hope, Lansdowne, Moira and Spencer. His *Atheniensia* (1816) contained several essays, lucidly argued, on the topography and antiquities of Athens. His *Civil Architecture of Vitruvius* (1812, 1817) combined a scholarly commentary on the Roman master—he was the first to interpret *scamilli impares* in terms of optical deviations—with a challenging essay on 'The Rise and Progress of Grecian Architecture' by no less an authority than 'Athenian' Aberdeen. Finally, his *Prolusiones Architectonicae* (1837), contained a number of valuable observations on the Erechtheion, illustrated by meticulously measured elevations and sections.

The travels of one architect in particular—the future Sir Robert Smirke, Wilkins' rival as leader of the English Greek Revival—happen to be especially well documented. Thanks to his penchant for writing voluminous letters in a miniscule hand, we can plot the progress of his journeys in some detail. His experiences were not particularly remarkable. In fact they were typical of his generation. But their very typicality merits examination—if only because his descriptions of Greek antiquities can be compared with his comments on the architectural products of the Renaissance.

Smirke made two expeditions between 1801 and 1805. The first was a disaster, the second something of a triumph. It was the war with France which made his first expedition abortive. Fortunately, the Peace of Amiens made Continental travel easier, and at last provided an *open sesame* to the artistic treasures of Paris. Among the herd of Englishmen who flocked abroad were numbered several Royal Academicians: the sedate West and the explosive Fuseli, the petulant Shee and the irritable Hoppner, the bohemian Turner and the thoughtful Opie. Kemble the actor was there; and Farington, 'the Dictator of the Academy'. Young Smirke, bruised by his journey from Boulogne, joined them in September 1802. Paris struck him as a city of contrasts, 'like a dream . . . grandeur and opulence, poverty and dirt'. With the Academicians he dined at Savary's, visited the Tivoli Gardens, and saw the ballet. He visited the site of the Bastille, the Museum of Arts—'what a striking place!', the Champs Elysées, the Palais Royale—'an extraordinary place', the Tuileries, the Ecole Militaire, the Palais de Bourbon and the Hospital of the Invalides. The Louvre façade he considered 'in a very grand style of architecture [with] a simplicity that one wonders should be the production of a Frenchman'. But he found no building that might be described as perfect. 'The present taste (I speak chiefly from external appearances for I have seen little of internal) appears either a strange mixture of Egyptian and the simple Grecian style or an extreme profusion of decoration'. Versailles, he admitted, 'is an immense building and when it was in high order must have been a most splendid sight'. Farington, however, spoke for most of the party when he complained that its style was 'bad and overloaded', adding that many French buildings still had a 'common and disgusting . . . very high, heavy, old fashioned French roof'.

Next month Farington's company returned to London. Smirke, with the young artist William Walker, began his journey to Italy: first from Lyons by water to Avignon; then from Nismes, where he was duly impressed by the Pont du Gard, the Roman Amphitheatre and the Maison Carrée, down the Rhone to Arles, where he studied the Amphitheatre, Baths and Palace of Constantine. 'The Frenchmen guess we are English', he wrote to his father, 'and we must consequently in their opinion be made of money. I never have a dinner, breakfast or bed . . . without first bargaining what I shall pay for it, and yet hardly ever go out of an inn without being imposed upon. . . . The French do bow and scrape to us as if we were Lords of the Universe; we are all 'des Gens, si braves, si honnêtes, si genereux, Oh, Mon Dieu!'. The two young travellers proceeded through wild country to Aix and Marseilles; then on to Toulon and so, by mule, to Antibes.

A troubled passage from Antibes to Genoa occupied almost a week, gales forcing the boat into Monaco. In Genoa, where Smirke spent a rainy Christmas, the architecture turned out to be disappointing: 'I saw many immense houses and much marble but little real magnificence. Where architectural embellishments have been employed they are chiefly in a miserable taste, but I was disgusted with the number that had nothing but columns and decorations painted upon them . . . [as for] the churches . . . it would be difficult to conceive how marbles of all colours, oil and frescoe paintings, an immense profusion of gilded decorations, and the necessary appendages of Catholic altars could be introduced and good taste preserved'. The streets in Pisa were wider, but the architecture was even less impressive—'rather too much of a mixture between Grecian and Gothic'—though the Leaning Tower was at least 'curious'. After a pressing visit to a banker in Leghorn, the journey South, through ice, frost and snow, was interrupted for one day at Florence and three at Siena, where the striped marble buildings seemed particularly distressing.

Almost two months were spent in Rome. 'With regard to the antiquities', Smirke decided, 'there has not been *so much* novelty as one might have expected. I have seen them so often in drawings, prints and paintings; have pored so often over the cathedrals and ornaments, that it seemed like visiting an old acquaintance, and I recognized and knew the names of many of them as if I were an old Cicerone'. He admired the Colosseum, the baths of the emperors, Trajan's Column, the Pantheon and the Triumphal Arches of Titus and Constantine. He was impressed by the figures on the Monte Cavallo, the galleries of the Vatican and Capitoline, the equestrian statue of Marcus Aurelius, and the frescoes of Michelangelo and Raphael.

But as a Neo-Classicist, Smirke was rather less impressed with the architecture of the Renaissance: 'with respect to the modern architecture, both in its churches and palaces, I must confess myself somewhat surprised that the excellent models of ancient art constantly before them have not been more successfully studied. In general I think the taste is rather of a heavy, disagreeable kind, but often a sort of magnificence in the whole effect which is rather imposing'. While admiring Bernini's colonnades, he decided that with regard to St. Peter's, 'immense and superb as it is, I think I never saw a building so much lost from injudicious proportions and design. Every object is on so extravagant a scale that notwithstanding there are so many people in it which might serve to show its real size, still it was to no purpose—they looked like pigmies. One is astonished at the time it requires to walk from one end to another when it appears comparatively so little. . . . A disagreeable effect is produced on the outside by the steps in front all starting from the building—it gives a weak and very unfirm appearance'. However Galilei's gorgeous chapel in St. John Lateran struck the young architect as 'one of the most elegant examples of modern architecture I ever saw, and an instance of the richest, gaudiest materials introduced with the least possible disgust. I leave it every day admiring it more than before.'

It was in Rome that Smirke and Walker finally decided to visit Greece. After stopping for a while at Naples, they set out by boat from Messina for the islands of Cephalonia and Zante, where their 'curiosity was satisfied by the sensation of a tolerable . . . earthquake'. Leaving Ithaca behind, they reached the mainland at Patras, with its mud houses, narrow streets and dirty bazaar. Accompanied by a guide, a porter, a janissary and an Italian servant, their horse-borne cavalcade pressed on into the hinterland, through wild country to Vestiza. Another boat took them to Corinth. And there the Doric columns of the Temple of Neptune (Poseidon), Smirke recorded, made this place 'the first in Greece where I saw any Antiquity . . . the proportion and shape pleased me very much and are not unlike those of the Paestum Temples'. However the Turkish landowner, frightened of his neighbours' anger, refused permission to measure, for 'by being raised so high as the entablature of the columns I might be enabled to overlook the areas in which their wives might chance to be walking'. On the way to Argos he passed the site now famous as Mycenae: 'Doric columns . . . in the plain famed anciently for the celebration of the Nemian Games; and a subterranean building lately dug out at Lord Elgin's expense and supposed by him to be the Tomb of Agamemnon'. The road to Sparta lay via Tripolizza. But at this point they were warned to go no further. The province of Maina—that 'haunt of Banditti'—was too dangerous for such a small party. The site of Sparta at that time displayed 'no ruin sufficiently perfect to enable even an antiquarian to ascertain its name, or to trace the various buildings mentioned by Pausanias'. Megalopolis, however, proved more rewarding: 'I could not help alighting and making two sketches of these beautiful ruins—I absolutely tore myself from them, for I do not remember feeling so much regret upon leaving any place'.

Smirke's route to Athens next included picturesque Calamata and ancient Messene. 'Of all the interesting spots I have seen', he wrote, Messene, 'next to Athens, is the most so, and I lose my patience when I remember how provokingly I have been disappointed of enjoying it. It is built among hills, or rather mountains, and is the corn ground of a few peasants of a village near it. Upon leaving Andrussa, six miles off, we were obliged to increase our guards with seven soldiers from the apprehension of robbers who were known to be among the hills, and it was this circumstance which prevented me stopping. . . . There were probably no remains of very large buildings, but the ground was for a great extent covered partially with fragments of columns, terraces, flights of steps and everything calculated to raise the imagination. . . . You may conceive how great was my desire to clear away the ground when ranges of columns broken off at the height of six or seven feet from their base appeared just rising above the tall ears of corn.' The site of Olympia, near the village of Andilaro, appeared, if anything, still more intriguing. 'It had a romantic appearance. Who could suppose we were near the spot where formerly was displayed a magnificence and luxury the descriptions of which will always raise astonishment? Who could imagine that in a small silent plain . . . had once been celebrated the Olympian Games? It is a change that makes one shudder. But, if . . . the Stadium, Temple of Jupiter etc. as described by [Fauvel] . . . are still there, the high standing corn prevented me from discovering them'. After Olympia, the two travellers revisited Megalopolis and Corinth before finally reaching the Piraeus, via Pidaura.

In making their tour of the Morea, Smirke and Walker covered in all between four and five hundred miles, with 'a small, thin, light mattress with a piece of greenbaize as a coverlid each . . . a couple of wretched maps . . . a Latin edition of Pausanias, and a Greek Dictionary'. Neither man showed any sign of illness, though they frequently averaged ten or twelve hours a day on horseback in intense heat. 'Our eating is very simple', Smirke told his father; 'we drink nothing but lemonade and the wine of the country which in general is very bad, as they are obliged to put a sort of pitch in it. . . . I am sure you would have stared to have seen us surrounded with our attendants having near us a whole sheep roasting for their provisions'. Yet 'we could never be anything else than *due Mylordi Inglesi*—neither could my 5 ft. rods, my 2 ft. ruler, measuring or sketching, at any time during our tour . . . convince the people to the contrary'. 'We are entitled certainly to some credit for any industry we may have used in these parts; conceive how much exertion is necessary for us unused to so hot a climate, when in making a sketch, the paper has been almost spoilt by sweat dropping from the face'.

The variegated scenery was continuously impressive: Sparta set in a fertile plain bounded by snow-capped mountains; Achaia and Arcadia, wild and mountainous. 'Nothing could exceed the grandeur of the mountain scenery as we sailed up the gulf of Corinth . . . but in the ride up the banks of the Alphaeus we saw really a fairy land. The river winds through a narrow valley bounded by the irregular hills covered with various sets of trees. In the valley we passed through groves and over lawns, all formed by nature, which in description even Shakespeare could scarcely do justice to'. 'The present appearance of Arcadia does not exactly correspond with our pastoral ideas of it; it is a cluster of round topped mountains, for the most part barren and where fit for cultivation producing only partially olives and vines; the shepherd has exchanged his pipe for a gun which he always carries slung over his shoulder, and the songs of content have long been forgotten'.

But it was of course the monuments in Athens which electrified the young architect. 'How can I', he told his father, 'by description give you any idea of the great pleasure I enjoyed in the sight of these ancient buildings of Athens! How strongly were exemplified in them the grandeur and effect of simplicity in architecture! The Temple of Theseus . . . cannot but arrest the attention of everyone from its appropriate and

11. C. R. Cockerell: The Temple of Apollo at Bassae (1811).

12. James Elmes: Paestum.

13. The Tower of the Winds.

dignified solemnity of appearance. The Temple of Minerva . . . strikes one in the same way with its grandeur and majesty. We were a month there. The impression made upon my mind . . . had not in that time in the least weakened by being frequently repeated and I could with pleasure spend a much larger time there, while those in Rome (with a few exceptions) not only soon grow in some degree uninteresting but have now entirely sunk into disregard and contempt in my mind. All that I could do in Athens was to make some views of them . . . hoping that they will serve as a memorandum to me of what I think should always be a model'.

Stuart's engravings, Smirke decided, must have been a trifle optimistic, particularly those of the Monument of Thrasyllus (Plate 95), the Lysicrates Monument (Plate 54) and the Tower of the Winds (Plate 13): 'how Stuart contrived to get his hundredths of an inch or even twelfths . . . I cannot imagine; those of the Acropolis and Temple of Theseus might certainly be measured with great accuracy, for in many places the edges of the marble are as perfect as if executed yesterday'. His own drawings on the Acropolis were not made without difficulties. The notorious Disdar—'the most impolite of petty officers', as Byron called him, 'the greatest patron of petty larceny that Athens ever saw except Lord E.'—had to be propitiated with gifts of coffee, sugar and silk. Smirke set his heart on making casts of the architectural ornament of the Erechtheion 'which appeared to have an unusual effect. Great richness was given without cutting up too much the surface of the object or interfering with the general effect, which is so universally the case with our modern enrichments. The order under the capitals of the pilasters (the Acanthus) (Plate 10) is a most striking instance of this'. However, 'no man had the least idea of what making a cast was'. Some of Elgin's surplus moulding earth was still available, but no one knew how to use it. So one morning Smirke and Walker selected a fragment of an ovolo enriched moulding, 'carried it to the side of one of the fortress walls and hurled it over. When it reached the ground, it dashed along for a considerable distance, stopping at length in the road which winds up to the entrance of the Acropolis. Fortunately no one was passing at the time; we wrapped our handkerchiefs over it and brought it safely home where I afterwards got the useless part cut off'.

After Athens Smirke visited Thebes and Delphi. As he goes we are reminded constantly that he was travelling in the early days of archaeology. 'One fragment of an inscription', he wrote, 'is all that remains of the ancient extensive city of Thebes, and the magnificent temples and buildings of Delphi have been as effectively swept away. Nothing of this city remains but the embankments made for the houses, being on the steep slopes of Parnassus'. As he was confessedly 'more interested in looking about for bits to which everyone is not directed by a sixpenny guide', he was, during his hurried travels, constantly confronted by the problem of badly preserved and inadequately excavated antiquities. Throughout his architectural career, he must, to a large extent, have relied on the measured drawings of his more leisurely predecessors and successors.

Smirke's Grecian tour ended ignominiously at Zante. 'Surrounded on all sides by accounts of hostile movements, shut out from every port in Italy . . . every town in Italy except perhaps Naples is occupied by French troops, hundreds of English travellers have been arrested by them . . . our resources of money have failed, and we are little better than beggars wandering from town to town seeking charity at each with promises of repayment on our return to Italy'. At this time letters to his father across battle-torn Europe could take almost a year to reach their destination. He was forced to spend the Autumn of 1803 at Messina, including several weeks in the Lazaretto: 'we have no communication with anyone, and everything going out of our hands is treated as if we were infectious beings.' Hostilities seemed to rule out that long-awaited trip to Pompeii, and the revisiting of Florence and Paris. A home-bound convoy from Malta, via Holland, seemed the only hope.

But Smirke still had another year of travelling ahead of him, this time without Walker. In December 1803 he sailed from Malta to Rome. Here he remained until April when he left for Naples. An injury to his knee—he fell while measuring a lofty monument—prevented him from making the journey on foot as he intended. It was from a mule that he inspected the cascades at Tivoli, the sweltering Baia coast, and the celebrated ruins of Paestum and Pompeii. One night he was reduced to sleeping on the floor of a cottage wine store. The long journey northwards was eventually begun in the company of two more young architects temporarily resident in Rome, Joseph Kay and Thomas Martyr, pupils of S. P. Cockerell. The trio travelled via Foligno, Perugia and the Papal States, Florence, Venice and Padua, to Vicenza. 'My stay at Vicenza', wrote Smirke, 'was architecturally of very little use to me'. He found it 'a handsome town on the whole, but Palladio, the boast of the country has sunk low in my estimation.'

After Vicenza, where Smirke learnt to speak German, the party proceeded to Verona, Trent and the Tyrol, Innsbruck and Salzburg. At Salzburg Smirke confessed that he found 'a greater degree of merit in its architectural character than I expected'. In October 1804 he sent his sister a description of the palace of Prince Leichtenstein and of the town of Vienna with its swirling waltzes and crowds of soldiers arrayed in military boots and medals. As for Viennese architecture, Smirke commented: 'although there were few specimens of good taste, yet judging from what I had seen before of German building, I did not expect it altogether so well. In their more modern works I found them closely imitating the French, but they succeed very indifferently'. His route then passed through Prague to Dresden. Of the latter town he brusquely noted: 'popularly the Athens of Germany—in fact there is nothing at all for me here'.

Harassed by the proximity of French troops, the three young architects eventually reached Berlin. 'The style with which the more recently erected houses are decorated is new', wrote Smirke, 'at least on the Continent, for it resembles more what has been lately introduced by Soane with sunk frets and grooves'. German architects fresh from tours of Italy and Sicily were bringing back the newly fashionable 'Paestum proportioned columns'. But this search for novelty produced unfortunate results: the imitations of the Propylaea, as of the Parthenon, were badly proportioned. 'Even the famous palaces of Sans Souci gave me scarcely a new idea'—but those, of course, were in 'the bad old fashioned Italian style'. For it was the influx of Grecian idioms, however misapplied, which made Smirke's tour of Germany more rewarding than his stay in Italy. In Dresden, Prague, Vienna, Potsdam and Berlin, he was delighted to discover 'some novel style and public spirit instead of the dull formal insipidity which mostly characterizes the old German school'.

After travelling through Schleswig Holstein, Smirke delayed at

Husum early in January 1805 before boarding a boat bound for England via Heligoland. He finally reached London later that month, after an absence of more than two and a quarter years. The process of preparation for a professional career had been completed. Smirke was now a Greek Revivalist. And when he conquered London in 1809 with his Grecian design for Covent Garden Theatre he had working in his office a still younger man who was soon to eclipse his master: Charles Robert Cockerell.

✻   ✻   ✻

It was in 1810, outside Athens, that C. R. Cockerell and John Foster of Liverpool first introduced themselves to Lord Byron. They drew alongside his boat, sang a song to attract his attention, and were invited up for a drink. Cockerell had set out from England—leaving Smirke, his 'good friend and master in Art', at Salisbury—in the guise of King's messenger, with despatches for the fleet at Cadiz, Malta and Constantinople. At Constantinople he made friends with Foster—'a most amusing youth'—and Sir William Ingilby, a Yorkshire baronet. Together they set out for Athens in high spirits, via Troy, Salonica, Myconos and Delos. When they reached—or thought they reached—the tomb of Patroclus, Cockerell went wild with excitement, stripped off his clothes and, naked as Achilles, ran three times round the site.

In Athens they joined forces with a group of slightly older men who had previously come together in Rome: two Danes, Peter Oluf Brönstedt and his brother-in-law Koes; a Livonian antiquary, Baron Otto Magnus von Stackelberg; a Nuremberg architect, Baron Haller von Hallerstein; and a Suabian painter, Jarob Linkh of Constatt. In 1811 Stackelberg, Koes and Bronstedt set off for Asia Minor. Haller, Linkh, Cockerell and Foster directed their attention to the Island of Aegina, and in particular to what was then known as the Temple of Jupiter Panhellinus. Excavation began at once.

'We got our provisions and labourers from the town', Cockerell reported; 'our fuel was the wild thyme, there were abundance of partridges to eat, and we bought kids of the shepherds; and when work was over for the day, there was a grand roasting of them over a blazing fire with an accompaniment of native music, singing and dancing. . . . On the second day one of the excavators working in the interior portico, struck on a piece of Parian marble which, as the building itself is of stone arrested his attention. It turned out to be the head of a helmeted warrior, perfect in every feature. It lay with the face turned upwards, and as the features came out by degrees you can imagine nothing like the state of rapture and excitement to which we were wrought. . . . Soon another head was turned up, then a leg and a foot, finally, to make a long story short, we found . . . no less than sixteen statues and thirteen heads, legs, arms, etc., all in the highest preservation not three feet below the surface of the ground'. Working fast with thirty men, they uncovered, in sixteen days, the majority of the glorious sculptures of the temple of Zeus. Bought from the islanders for £40, they were secretly moved to Athens by night and auctioned next year at Zante for £6000. The purchaser was Martin Wagner the sculptor, acting as agent for Crown Prince Louis of Bavaria. Britain's representative went to Malta by mistake. The French only offered cash on delivery. So the Aegina Marbles ended up in the Glyptothek at Munich instead of the British Museum or the Louvre. And there they were unfortunately restored by Thorwaldsen.

Cockerell's appetite for discoveries had been whetted—'our friends', he noted with relish, 'are dying with jealousy'. With the same three companions he next hurried off across the Peloponnese in pursuit of the Temple of Apollo Epicurius at Bassae (Plate 11). He found the ruins near the town of Phigaleia in July 1811. A Frenchman named Joachim Bocher had been there before him in 1765. Bocher, however, fell foul of brigands: they killed him for his brass buttons. Later on the intrepid Morritt visited the site. So did Smirke. But it fell to Cockerell, rummaging among the debris, to locate the Bassae Frieze. He glimpsed one of the marbles hidden in a fox-hole, told his friends, covered in his find, and set off quickly for other sites.

Cockerell's description of Bassae is as eloquent as his watercolour sketches (Plate 11). 'It is impossible', he writes, 'to give an idea of the romantic beauty of the situation of the temple. It stands on a high ridge looking over lofty barren mountains and an extensive country below them. The ground is rocky, thinly patched with vegetation, and spotted with splendid ilexes. The view gives one Ithome, the stronghold and last defence of the Messenians against Sparta, to the south-west; Arcadia with its many hills, to the east; and to the south the range of Taygetus, with still beyond them the sea'. Cockerell also penned the best description of the progress of the Bassae excavation. 'On the top of Mount Catylium, whence there is a grand prospect over nearly all Arcadia, they established themselves for three months, building round the temple huts with the boughs of trees, until they had almost formed a village (a city I should have said), which they denominated Francopolis. They had frequently fifty or eighty men at work in the temple, and a band of Arcadian music was constantly playing, to entertain this numerous assemblage; when evening put an end to work, dances and songs commenced, lambs were roasted whole on a long wooden spit, and the whole scene, in such a situation, at such an interesting time, when every day some new and beautiful work of the best age of sculpture the world has ever known was brought to light, is hardly to be imagined. Apollo must have wondered at the carousals which disturbed his long repose, and have thought that his glorious days of old were again returned'.

Glorious too were Cockerell's days among the wild Mainotes, 'the Greeks who had always been free from the days of Sparta, who had maintained their independence against Rome, Byzantium, the Franks, the Venetians, and Turks'. Romance and danger formed part of the atmosphere: 'Sometimes the shepherds on the precipices above us would call out, "What men are ye?" And we answered, "Good men". There was no step of the road that had not its annals of murder or robbery. . . . For three weeks I . . . slept with my clothes on, without a bed, and with only one blanket to wrap myself in'. At one point in Athens Cockerell and Foster met up with Frederick Douglas, author of *Ancient and Modern Greeks,* and Frederick North, later Lord Guilford, a vintage eccentric who dressed Greek and prayed Orthodox and is still remembered in Corfu as the founder of the Ionian Academy and first President of the Philomuse Society. Together all four planned an expedition to Egypt. But nothing came of the idea: North changed his mind, Douglas went home in a sulk, and Foster promptly fell in love. Cockerell had to be content with Ephesus, Priene and Didyma. Then on he went to Sicily, to the temple at Segesta, mighty and rough hewn, the three temples at Selinus, and the temple of Jupiter Olympius (Zeus) at Agrigentum, where he produced a visionary restoration of that temple of the giants.

Meanwhile, negotiations for possession of the Bassae treasures were taking place. Veli Pasha, governor of the Morea, was bought out for £400. Stackelberg replaced Cockerell as draughtsman—in fact it was Stackelberg who eventually published the discoveries in a formidable folio. Haller supervised the digging: up to one hundred and twenty men were employed. And in 1814, after being literally snatched from the Turkish troops, the Bassae frieze was bought by Britain for £15,000. By the time he returned to England in 1817, after further expeditions to Naples, Pompeii, Rome and North Italy, Cockerell had overawed the Greeks, bribed the Turks, outdistanced the French, outmanoeuvred the Germans and even impressed the Italians: with Canova, Thorwaldsen, Ingres and others he carried Hellenism into the heart of the Eternal City and dined regularly in the pronaos of the Cafe Greco.

Cockerell's years abroad were dramatic and dangerous. Brönsted was robbed by bandits. Stackelberg was captured by pirates. Haller sickened and died in the Vale of Tempe. And Cockerell himself narrowly escaped death by fever and an inevitable burial in the Theseion: 'if ever I get away from this country in health and safety', he once told his father, 'how I shall thank my stars!'. The lure of antiquity and the pressure of competition spurred him on. As the nineteenth century progressed, the rediscovery of Greece sometimes came near to degenerating into a mad scramble. But then, as one French critic put it: 'Antiquity is a garden which belongs by natural right to those who cultivate and harvest it'.

Cockerell's travels made him an international figure. And the fame of his discoveries was a standing incentive to any young British architect worth his salt. During the next decade he had many imitators, but none with quite the same combination of talent, bravery and luck. Thomas Allason was in Greece in 1814, divining the entasis of classic columns in the same year as Cockerell. R. H. Sharp, later a colleague of Wilkins, set out on a three year trip in 1816. Between 1817 and 1820 G. L. Taylor and Edward Cresy were there, with John Sanders and W. Purser, measuring and drawing with enthusiasm and precision.

Taylor and Cresy's tour coincided with that of the future Sir Charles

Barry. Barry began in 1817 with a conventional progress in France and Italy. Then he joined up with W. Kinnaird and the future Sir Charles Eastlake for a tour of Greece and Turkey. Next, in company with David Baillie, he penetrated Egypt and Syria. Finally he rounded off nearly four years of travel with visits to Cyprus, Rhodes, Malta, Sicily and Italy, where he met his future colleague J. L. Wolfe. Barry's travels are fortunately well documented. At the start he still belonged to the Regency generation, omnivorously pursuing the Picturesque and the antique. As his friend Eastlake put it: 'Our luggage [is] small—mine consists of materials for drawing and painting . . . and a mattress . . .; and we take Pausanias Anarcharsis, and maps. . . . I have no other object than the picturesque, and shall consider myself at liberty to put the mosque and the temple in the same picture, and to pay the same attention to the Turk's beard and turban as to the bas-relief he sits on'. But by the end of the tour Barry had laid in a store of archaeological information ranging from the Farnese Palace to the ruins at Agrigentum; from the temples at Luxor and Karnac to the Pantheon and the Baths of Diocletian. His addiction to Grecian purity was no longer exclusive. He would soon be qualified as a High Victorian eclectic.

Meanwhile, there was still plenty to find in Greece. H. W. Inwood began a memorable record of the Acropolis in 1819, the start of a brilliant career cut short in 1843 when he was drowned on a voyage to Spain. His *Erechtheion* (1827) is indeed a major key to our understanding of Greek Revival architecture. Its author modestly set out 'to increase more or less the general store of architectural knowledge'. But subscribers included all the leading Neo-Classical pundits: Aberdeen, Hope, Soane, Wilkins, Smirke and Cockerell. And the thirty-nine detailed engravings, including the Parthenon and the Tower of the Winds, constituted a valuable supplement to Stuart and Revett. W. Jenkins and Edward Jones followed in the early 1820s. Next came William Harris, who died of malaria at Palermo, but not before he had joined with Samuel Angell in discovering the sculptures of Selinus. William Railton visited Corfu and Greece in 1825–27. And at various dates during the 1820s and 1830s J. J. Scoles, Joseph Bonomi, Henry Parke, Frederick Catherwood and Francis Arundale began an extraordinary series of travels which took them beyond Italy, Sicily and Greece, to Asia Minor, Palestine, Arabia and the Nile Valley.

Already the scope of scholarly exploration was widening. Architectural fashion was moving on from Greek to Italianate. And archaeology ceased to be primarily concerned with the rediscovery of Greece. Arundale's Egyptomania induced him to take up residence in one of the tombs he excavated on the Nile: not surprisingly he contracted a fatal illness. Catherwood's wanderlust took him first to Jerusalem and then to the New World, to the Mayan cities of Central America. He ended as a railway engineer in California and went down in the steamer *Arctic*. Victorian archaeologists soon learned to look beyond the Mediterranean and the Aegean. The bravest English travellers were no longer buried in the Theseion. That was a privilege reserved for the Regency.

It would be wrong to think that travel in Greece was in any way a *sine qua non* of architectural practice during the Regency. Many of the most celebrated Greek Revivalists never got beyond Italy. Dance, Holland, Soane, Harrison and Nash were all vicarious Grecians, archaeologists at second hand. So were Goodwin, Hopper, Latrobe and Foulston as well as several leaders of the next, Graeco–Roman, generation: Burton, Elmes, Hardwick, Papworth, Wightwick and Basevi—to say nothing of all the Wyatts. But it was the archaeologists who supplied the mainspring, the impetus behind architectural fashion. And the dissemination of archaeological knowledge owed everything to the pioneer efforts of the Dilettanti.

With the Society of Dilettanti the rediscovery of Greece begins and ends. Before its foundation archaeology was still in its infancy. After the Society's Regency meridian the subject slowly took on institutional form. The French School at Athens was founded in 1846, the American in 1882, the British in 1885. The Society for the Promotion of Hellenic Studies was set up in London in 1879. Fellowes and Newton succeeded Stuart and Revett. Hittorf and Semper followed Dumont and Le Roy. And the era of Schliemann, Dörpfeld and Evans was very different to the age of 'rapid' Gell. In 1932, at the Society's bicentenary dinner, Lord Crewe spoke of the Dilettanti's 'marvellous combination of cultivation and dissipation . . . to their table the Muses invited Bacchus and other less respectable divinities with the happiest results'; members 'left behind them traditions which are not exactly those of piety and continence', but they 'devoted their soberer moments' to important and valuable work. Between 1734 and 1852 the Dilettanti spent some £30,000 in equipping expeditions to Greece and in publishing their discoveries. Classical archaeology owes a great debt to a Society which has numbered among its members statesmen and rogues, rakes and scholars, seven Prime Ministers and one murderer—an Irishman named 'Fighting Fitzgerald'.

In Britain—if not in Europe—the Dilettanti presided over a cultural revolution, a veritable second Renaissance. The first Renaissance sprang from the rediscovery of ancient Rome, the second stemmed from the rediscovery of ancient Greece. And that second Renaissance produced, among other things, the architecture of the Greek Revival.

PART TWO

The Greek Revival: Classic and Romantic

The history of art has suffered as much as any
history by trenchant and absolute divisions.
WALTER PATER

First of all, a few definitions. 'Greek Revival' is a term current in England in the 1860s, popularized in America in the later nineteenth century and used to describe the architecture of the final phase of Neo-Classicism. 'Neo-Classic' is a label first widely used in Europe in the 1880s to describe the flight from the Renaissance and the return to the antique during the late eighteenth and early nineteenth centuries. The architecture produced by this process can be recognized by its distribution of antique elements according to rationalist theories of design. 'Romantic Classicism' is a recent art-historical invention, an attempt to pin down more precisely the qualities of Neo-Classical architecture in the age of Romanticism. By elevating a descriptive phrase into an aesthetic category it confuses rather than clarifies the issues. But its very ambivalence concentrates attention on something which might otherwise be overlooked: the presence of Romantic elements in Neo-Classical design.

The attempt to separate Classic and Romantic is of course by no means new—and by no means easy: one is tempted to agree with the critic who dismissed both labels as 'thought-confounding words'. In 1814 a contributer to *The Quarterly Review*, probably Coleridge, noted that Madame de Staël had 'made the British public familiar' with the habit of distinguishing 'the productions of antiquity by the appellation of *classic*, those of modern times by that of *romantic*'. Six years later these distinctions had already taken up embattled positions, guarded by capital letters. 'I perceive', wrote Byron to Goethe, 'that in Germany as well as in Italy, there is a great struggle about what they call *Classical* and *Romantic*'. In 1832 Arnold's *Library of the Fine Arts* confidently defined the virtues and vices of 'Classicality' and 'Romanticism' as follows: 'Classicality produces rigidity; Romanticism encourages affectation;—Purity and Vigour . . . equally enslave. . . . The romantic is to the classical, what a comet is to a constellation—what a volcano is to an iceberg—what the Hartz mountains are to Parnassus. . . . The one is a chastely formed vestal . . . the other a female of exuberant charms . . .'. But by 1841, Emerson at least had become a little sceptical: 'the vaunted distinction between Greek and English, between Classic and Romantic schools, seems superficial and pedantic'. British writers had on the whole been less eager to differentiate. In an article on Schiller in 1831 Carlyle could write thankfully: 'we are troubled with no controversies on Romanticism and Classicism'. And in 1867 this reluctance to separate classic and romantic elements within the creative process was summed up in one of the sacred texts of art history: Walter Pater's essay on Winckelmann.

Pater christened Winckelmann 'the last fruit of the Renaissance'. But everything he wrote about him emphasized the fact that Winckelmann's contribution was really a Romantic rejuvenation of the classical tradition. Winckelmann called in Greece to redress the outworn dominance of Rome. The key to his influence lay firstly in an accident of timing—never was a book more opportune than the *Reflections*—and secondly in the magnetic force of his own enthusiasm. Having thrown off the shackles of German Protestantism, he rejoiced in the sensuous paganism of ancient art. 'Enthusiasm—that', wrote Pater, 'was the secret of his divinatory power over the Hellenic world.' And it was this burning passion—transmuted into quite a different form—which Goethe inherited: Goethe, the youth of nineteen who in the fateful Summer of 1768 awaited at Leipzig the arrival of the great man, and received only the news of his death. The reluctant prophet of Romanticism and the self-appointed apostle of Neo-Classicism never met. But their minds were never far apart. In a room in Oxford, overlooking Radcliffe Square—that grand conjunction of Gothic and Classic—Pater wrote their joint epitaph: 'that note of revolt against the eighteenth century, which we detect in Goethe, was struck by Winckelmann. Goethe illustrates that union of the Romantic spirit, its adventure, its variety, its deep subjectivity, with Hellenism, its transparency, its rationality, its desire of beauty—that marriage of Faust and Helena, of which the nineteenth century is the child. . . . Goethe illustrates, too the preponderance in this marriage of the Hellenic element; and that element, in its true essence, was made known to him by Winckelmann'.

Of course Classic and Romantic represent different states of mind. Authority and freedom, order and disorder, tyranny and anarchy, moderation and excess, ideal and real, fact and fantasy, finite and infinite, clarity and obscurity, regularity and irregularity, sophistication and innocence, reason and imagination, logic and faith, calculation and spontaneity, form and spirit, common sense and uncommon sensibility—these are the traditional polarities. They are different states of mind—but different states of the same mind, as interdependent as the male and female principles. After all, as Wordsworth pointed out,

> . . . Imagination, . . . in truth,
> Is but another name for absolute power
> And clearest insight, amplitude of mind,
> And Reason in her most exalted mood.

F. L. Lucas summed it all up: the whole of life is 'an eternal tight-rope walk. Balance is essential. To the question "Classic or Romantic?" the answer is surely "Both" '. 'Classical and romantic', wrote Sir Herbert Grierson, '—these are the systole and diastole of the human heart in history. They represent on the one hand our need of order, of synthesis, of a comprehensive yet definite, therefore *exclusive* as well as inclusive, ordering of thought and feeling and action; and on the other hand the inevitable finiteness of every human synthesis, the inevitable discovery that, in Carlyle's metaphor, our clothes no longer fit us, that the classical has become the conventional, that our spiritual aspirations are being starved, or that our secular impulses are "cribb'd, cabin'd, and confined"; and the heart and imagination bursts its cerements and reaches out, it may be with Faust after the joys of this world . . . it may be with Rousseau and Wordsworth and Shelley after a "return to nature", a freer, juster, kinder world . . . it may be after "a past that never was a present", "the glory that was Greece" . . . or it may be the ages of faith, the Gothic Rose . . .'. The artistic achievements of every age are thus but the off-spring of this endless antiphony.

Poetry and architecture at the end of the eighteenth century were in fact both engaged in the same romantic pursuit of classic forms. Mario Praz concludes: 'The self-same urge to adjust to the eternal truths of nature drove Wordsworth to reform the language of poetry and the neo-classical architects to purge the language of forms of its baroque "artificialities": in both cases, seemliness and appropriateness of sentiment (*Stimmung*) were the dominant criteria; the style seems to base itself, in Goethe's words, "on the deepest foundations of knowing, the essence of things". Seen from this point of view the old antithesis between classical and romantic loses its meaning, and both the one and the other appear to be pursuing ends that are in substance identical; Gothic taste and Greek taste seem to be merely contingent characteristics'. Nature and nature's laws; geometry in a pastoral wilderness: landscape and architecture in the age of Romanticism. Megalomania and melancholia—utopianism and nostalgia—these were a powerful combination, suffusing Greek and Gothic alike. Hence the ease with which William Beckford, that arch-Romantic, moved from Neo-Gothic Fonthill to his Neo-Classic Lansdown Tower (Plate 143). Hence the double magnetism of Paestum (Plate 12): an image of classic logic in design and a vision of romantic decay. And hence the architectural paradise of Soane or Gandy, Gilly or Ledoux: 'an ideal . . . region', as Praz describes it, 'in which classicism became, romantically, the material of dreams . . . a stereometric universe of huge flat walls, rotundas, Doric columns, powerful arches, funeral pyramids'—all set in sylvan Arcady (Plates 41, 173, 174, 177, 235, 243).

Byron himself was a Romantic-Classic hybrid. His way of life was self-consciously romantic. But his literary mannerisms remained firmly cast in a classic mould. A romantic hero in a classic land, his attitudes were gloriously ambivalent. He revelled in the paradox of his own style: in form classic, in feeling romantic

> Which some call fine, and some call frantic;
> While others are or would seem *as* sick
> Of repetitions nicknamed Classic.

The Greek Revival: Classic and Romantic

> For my part all men must avow
> Whatever I was, I'm classic now.

George IV echoed this same ambivalence when he presented Sir Walter Scott with a full set of Montfaucon's antiquities. And several of the most romantic monuments to Scotland's Robbie Burns were modelled on that classic cliché, the Lysicrates Monument. After all, Gray's poems were illustrated by Blake. Friedrich painted at Agrigentum. And Napoleon was both the ultimate Romantic hero and the greatest patron of Neo-Classicism.

Translated into formal terms, classic and romantic impulses sustained both the major traditions in European architecture. That was recognized in the 1820s. 'A Doric temple', wrote James Elmes, 'differs from a Gothic cathedral, as Sophocles does from Shakespeare'. 'The principle of the one', Hazlitt concluded, 'is simplicity and harmony, that of the other richness and power. The one relies on form and proportion; the other on quantity and variety, and prominence of parts. The one owes its charm to a certain union and regularity of feeling, the other adds to its effect from complexity and the combination of the greatest extremes. The classical appeals to sense and habit, the gothic, or romantic, strikes one from novelty, strangeness and contrast. Both are founded in essential and indestructible principles of human nature'.

In other words, the interaction of classic and romantic is an antiphonal process, a perpetual aesthetic dialogue between complementary creative principles. In the early and mid-eighteenth century first Rococo and then Neo-Classicism infused classic forms with romantic feelings— 'pollinating scholarship', as Christopher Hussey put it, 'from the flowers of sentiment and imagination'. As the eighteenth century moved towards the nineteenth, the romantic impulse moved into its most dominant phase: it came to comprehend both Classic and Gothic traditions. Hence the collective label 'Age of Romanticism', an age in which the poetic replaced the academic.

The academic idea, established by the Renaissance, was of course an ideal—the ideal of the Ideal: the unities of drama, the orders of architecture, the beauty of nature, the perfection of the antique, nobility of subject in painting and sculpture, mathematical harmony in architectural design. Such classic qualities—order, harmony, precedent, unity, perfection—appeal to the intellect rather than the passions, to reason rather than imagination, to the school rather than to individual genius. In painting, for example, classicism favoured line drawing—susceptible to precise calculation—rather than colour, based as it must be on individual perception. Similarly, classicism favoured nature idealized in antique form, rather than nature natural:

> What Nature *could*, but *would not* do,
> And Beauty and Canova *can*.

Classicism was concerned with the abstract rather than the concrete, the conceptual rather than the specific. And above all classicism was a moral principle, didactic not indulgent. It derived from the observation and formulation of rules. Hence its fullest expression in the aesthetic legislation of Louis XIV's French Academy.

One modern critic, the late F. P. Chambers, has supplied a memorable description of the triumph of romanticism over classicism in the late eighteenth and early nineteenth centuries. 'Classicism was a philosophy of causes, romanticism a philosophy of values; classicism reasoned, romanticism imagined. Classicism stood for an ideal of beauty, romanticism for a real beauty; classicism for beautiful nature, romanticism for every mood and aspect of nature; classicism for tyranny, romanticism for the free expression of individuality. Mathematics was the starting point of academic art. . . . But romanticism started from observation. . . . It asked for no abstract of line and draughtsmanship, but watched the forms and colours of nature. It preferred asymmetry and the "picturesque" to the regularity of academic geometers. . . . Art should be felt, not judged. Orders destroyed architecture, precepts destroyed painting, unities destroyed drama . . .'. Or, as Keats put it, with a splendidly anti-Newtonian flourish, 'philosophy will clip an angel's wings'. Hence the Romantic escape from the cultural bonds of the Ancien Régime into a purer world of imagination and feeling, a distant world beyond the cultural watershed of the Renaissance. 'When art languishes', wrote Victor Hugo, 'a return to nature is prescribed'—that is, a retreat from sophistication to innocence. 'Men probed deeper into the classic idea', Chambers concluded, 'or rejected it altogether; those who had probed into it discovered Greece, those who rejected it discovered the Middle Ages'. That was the choice available to the *avant garde* towards the end of the eighteenth century.

And the choosing of either alternative stemmed from the same Romantic impulse.

✳   ✳   ✳

Those who chose the road to Greece made their way by either of two routes: one English, the other French; one pragmatic, the other programmatic.

The English archaeological tradition was essentially empirical. Wood's *Balbec* and *Palmyra* volumes set the tone: 'It shall . . . be our principal care to produce things as we found them, leaving reflections and reasonings upon them to others. This last rule we shall scrupulously observe in describing the Buildings, where all criticism on the beauties and faults of the Architecture is entirely left to the reader'. Stuart and Revett's *Antiquities of Athens* took up a similarly uncommitted standpoint: 'Architecture is reduced and restrained within narrower limits than could be wished, for want of a greater number of ancient Examples than have hitherto been published; . . . every such Example of beautiful Form or Proportion, wherever it may be found, is a valuable addition to the former Stock; and does, when published, become a material acquisition to the Art. . . . It will certainly be a study of some delight and curiosity, to observe wherein the Grecian and Roman style of Building differ; for differ they certainly do; and to decide, by a judicious examination, which is the best'. In short, Stuart and Revett set out to break the Roman monopoly by the submission of a viable alternative—the Grecian.

During the seventeenth and eighteenth centuries, and even early in the nineteenth century, a good deal of confusion existed as to the difference between Greek and Roman, let alone between Etruscan and Hellenistic. 'Soon after the reign of Henry VIII,' wrote Horace Walpole in 1762, 'the Grecian style was introduced, and no wonder when so many Italians were entertained in the King's service'. Piling up the *non sequiturs*, he later adds that this style remained debased until 'Inigo Jones . . . stepped into the true and perfect Grecian'. William Kent's Temple of British Worthies (1735) at Stowe includes a bust of 'Ignatius Jones' and an inscription by Lord Lyttleton crediting him with the fact that he 'introduced and rivalled the Greek and Roman architecture'. Nearby Kent also erected a 'Grecian Temple' in a 'Grecian Vale'; that is, a version of the

69

Maison Carrée set in *le jardin anglais*. In 1785 we still find Thomas Warton talking of 'Sir Christopher Wren's Grecian proportions'. And as late as 1808, Humphry Repton is still confusing Greek and Roman orders. Nicest of all, as an illustration of persistent confusion, is McCann's Irish ditty on a theme from Pugin's *Contrasts* (1836):

> 'Twas Harry the Eighth, that nasty baste,
> That introduced the Gracian.
> When they denied the truth outright
> Of Transubstantiation,
> They built them in the Composite—
> That great abomination.

In other words, to the seventeenth and eighteenth centuries Grecian was usually a synonym for classical; to the eighteenth and early nineteenth centuries, often enough, Grecian simply meant Arcadian. Gradually, however, the use of a more precise nomenclature permeates downwards from the professional archaeologists. And eventually most Regency young ladies could distinguish between Roman and Grecian Doric as easily as their daughters could tell the difference between Decorated and Perpendicular Gothic.

The two men chiefly responsible for this slow process of education were of course James Stuart and Nicholas Revett. Their work formed part of a prolonged development: the pursuit of purer architectural forms, a quest which sent Inigo Jones back to Palladio, and Burlington back still further to Palladio's antique sources. Even Wren and Hawksmoor had shown some vague and misinformed interest in the Tower of the Winds: Wren at St. Bride's, and Hawksmoor at Worcester College, Oxford. Reacting against the excesses of Baroque, English Palladianism developed attitudes which might almost be described as proto-Neo-Classical. Inigo Jones himself had in 1631 designed a church—St. Paul's Covent Garden—which seems to anticipate many of the primitive virtues of later Neo-Classicism. Colin Campbell's *Vitruvius Britannicus* (1715) complained that 'the Italians can no more now relish the Antique Simplicity'. Instead he advocated judgement 'truly of the Merits of Things by the Strength of Reason'. The works of Bernini and Fontana are described as 'affected and licentious'. And Borromini is condemned for having 'endeavoured to debauch Mankind with his odd and chimerical beauties'.

Within this framework of thinking, Burlington himself is best understood, in Christopher Hussey's words, as 'the forerunner of the Neo-Classical movement rather than . . . the retrospective reviver of a mannerist style'. In 1731 Burlington's Assembly Rooms at York were modelled on Palladio's reconstruction of the Vitruvian Egyptian hall: a piece of vicarious Neo-Classicism. In 1734 Kent's entrance hall at Holkham powerfully evoked a Roman basilican prototype. And at Rokeby in Yorkshire, at least two years previously, Sir Thomas Robinson designed a Tuscan porch (Plate 81), with unfluted, baseless, primitivistic columns —first hinted at by Serlio and then recommended by Palladio in one of his less familiar passages.

The Puritan streak in English Palladianism is submerged but deeply rooted. And it was this burgeoning archaeological process which eventually canonized Athenian Stuart as in some way the spiritual heir of Jones and Burlington. Stuart's posthumous reputation expanded as the Greek Revival soared to its meridian. In 1816 his heir, Lt. James Stuart, still felt it necessary to defend his father's fame: 'When all jealousy shall have smouldered out', he wrote, 'then will "the Athenian Stuart" receive the honour so justly his due'. But by 1842 Joseph Gwilt had no doubts: 'The chasteness and purity which [Stuart and Revett] had, with some success, endeavoured to introduce into the buildings of England, and in which their zeal had enlisted many artists,' eventually superseded 'the opposite and vicious taste of Robert Adam, a fashionable architect whose eye had been ruined by the corruptions of Roman art'. And by 1847 James Elmes could state: 'no event that ever occurred in the history of architecture in England, and thence throughout all Europe, produced so sudden, decided and beneficial effect as did the works of James Stuart'.

That was overstating the case. The full impact of the *Antiquities of Athens* was slow in coming. Stuart and Revett earned themselves prominent niches in the Neo-Classical pantheon: together they laid the foundations for an architectural revolution. But there was still a long way to go. In the 1760s and 1770s the future lay with Stuart and Revett. But the present state of British architecture rested firmly in the hands of Robert Adam, the man who forestalled the Greek Revival.

Zucchi's frontispiece of 1775 to *The Works in Architecture of Robert and James Adam Esquires*, sets out allegorically the Neo-Classical basis of the

Adam style: 'A Student conducted to Minerva, who points to Greece, and Italy, as the Countries from where he must derive the most perfect Knowledge and Taste in elegant Architecture'. And the map is ingeniously arranged with Italy to the North of Greece, as if to emphasize the fact that Roman architecture was itself rooted in the previous achievements of the Greeks.

Robert Adam himself, however, never visited Greece; and brother James only got as far as Paestum. The lure was there, even the opportunity. In 1756, in a letter to James, Robert expressed a sneaking wish 'to view the Temple[s] of Athens, of Thebes, of Sparta; the field of Marathon and the Straits of Thermopyle, and though the Thought is altogether imaginary yet it is pleasing to be where harrangued Demosthenes, were fought Epaminondas and where Pericles counciled . . .'. That was the tug of Romantic Hellenism. But there was also a little matter of professional ambition. Next year, writing to Janet Adam, he remarked: 'If John would set off directly and meet me at Vicenza we would go at his expenses in a Vessel from Venice directly to the Greek Islands which is a pleasant Saill of eight days and from that we'd go to Athens. In short taking Clérisseau and my two Draughtsmen with us two, we would furnish a very tolerable Work to Rival Stuart and Rivets in three months time and return home laden with Laurel . . .'. Nothing came of the idea. Robert Adam was to be known as 'Bob the Roman' not Robert the Greek. Success might be won by a different route, without visiting Athens. Instead of going Greek this hard-headed Scot hit upon a brilliant compromise. Astutely anticipating the taste of his chosen public—no longer Palladian but not yet Grecian—he gave them a stylistic synthesis of his own creation.

Adam's method was consciously Neo-Classical: by-passing the Renaissance, he returned to ancient Rome for inspiration, to Spalato, to Palmyra and Baalbek, to Pompeii and Herculaneum, to Baia, Pozzuoli and Cumae. His style was neither Greek nor purely Roman, nor simply Renaissance, nor exclusively Graeco–Roman. In his glorious Ante Room (*c.* 1761–65) at Syon House, Middlesex (Plate 59), for example, the gilded volutes of the Ionic columns are enriched versions of Le Roy's engravings of the Erechtheion. But the necking of the capitals echoes a prototype illustrated in Cameron's *Baths of the Romans*. The necking properly belonging to the Erechtheion columns (Plate 10) is in turn transferred to the frieze of the entablature. The formidable martial trophies are borrowed from Piranesi's illustration of the trophies of Octavianus Augustus on the Campidoglio in Rome. And the ceiling follows a Palladian formula previously used at Houghton Hall, Norfolk. In the gallery (1761–*c.* 1766) at Croome Court, Worcestershire, the coffering echoes that in Constantine's Basilica and the frieze that in Trajan's Forum, or perhaps that in the Temple of Concord in Rome. Doorcases in the saloon (*c.* 1768–71) at Saltram, Devon, and in the dining-room of old Lansdowne House (1762–68) combine Greek anthemion friezes with pilaster capitals from Diocletian's Palace at Spalato. The great hall at Kedleston (*c.* 1761–70), Derbyshire, owes not a little to Palladio's illustration of the Roman Temple of Mars. And ceilings at Bowood (1761–64), Compton Verney (*c.* 1761–65), Audley End (1763–65) and Osterley (1761–80) all share a common ancestry in the reticulated cofferings of Wood's *Palmyra*. Palmyra again—this time the Temple of the Sun—inspired the coffering inside the great portico at Osterley (Plate 60). Osterley's famous Etruscan Room (1775–77) takes inspiration both from Piranesi and from antique vases. The grotesque panels at Hatchlands (1758–61) and Castle Ashby (1759) have been traced to Bartoli's illustrations of the Domus Aurea in Rome. But those at Osterley, for instance, seem closer in spirit to Raphael's *loggie* in the Vatican. While much of the plasterwork at Hatchlands appears to be consciously modelled on mid-seventeenth-century work by Algardi and Grimaldi at the Villa Doria Pamphili in Rome.

This, then, was the Adam style: a synthetic amalgam compounded of Greek, Roman, Hellenistic and Etruscan, Italian cincquecento and English Palladian. By 1772 the brothers Adam were able to boast of the abject defeat of Palladianism: 'the massive entablature, the ponderous compartment ceiling, the tabernacle frame . . . are now exploded' and replaced by a 'beautiful variety of light mouldings gracefully formed and delicately enriched', embodying 'the beautiful spirit of antiquity' diversified by 'novelty and variety'. In A. T. Bolton's words, the mood of Fragonard replaced that of Michelangelo. It was essentially a decorative revolution, grafted on to a system of planning which was equally fresh and equally personal. Ichnographically as well as iconographically the Adam style was essentially Neo-Classic: Roman baths inspired not only the details but the planning as well. And in Sir John Soane's later words 'the electric power of this revolution' was not only confined to interiors.

In their components, Adam's exterior designs seldom deviate from the Palladian canon. In their composition, however, they begin to demonstrate a novel personal aesthetic: the theory of 'movement'. 'Movement', Adam explained, 'is meant to express the rise and fall, the advance and recess, with other diversity of form, in the different parts of a building, so as to add greatly to the picturesque of a composition. For the rising and falling, advancing and receding, with the convexity and concavity, and other forms of the great parts, have the same effect in architecture, that hill and dale, foreground and distance, swelling and sinking have in landscape; That is, they serve to produce an agreeable and diversified contour, that groups and contrasts like a picture, and creates a variety of light and shade, which gives great spirit, beauty and effect to the composition'. Such were the origins of the great South front at Kedleston (finished 1765) (Plate 61), where the Roman 'triumphal arch' motif (The Arch of Constantine) is boldly manipulated in pursuit of a variety and plasticity reminiscent of that Baroque *manifestation touristique*, the Fontana Trevi in Rome (finished 1762). And it is here—as much in Adam's compositional theory as in his handling of decorative motifs—that the classic-romantic ambivalence of the Adam style is clearest. Hussey thought it posthumously Rococo. Kaufmann christened it 'frozen Baroque'. But its combination of classic sources and romantic inflections made it in fact essentially Neo-Classic.

In many ways the Adam style was indeed a transitional phenomenon. As A. T. Bolton put it, 'Robert Adam came at the ebb and flow, between the lapsing classic and the rising romantic movements, and having by temperament sympathies alive to the influence of both, his work in its results was bound to exhibit their opposing characteristics'; indeed his achievement embodies 'an element of compromise between the Classic and Romantic states of mind', a compromise which always has been characteristically British. Precisely because it was based on a stylistic compromise—the Royal Society of Arts building (1772–74), for example, combines a Palladian Venetian window with an Ionic order from the Erechtheion and a Corinthian order from the Tower of the Winds—the Adam style possessed an instant and widespread appeal. And it was a style which was sufficiently flexible to survive imitation: Thomas Leverton's superb interiors at Woodhall Park, Hertfordshire (1772–82) almost outplay the Adams at their own game.

Naturally enough, Robert Adam could hardly bring himself to praise the designs of James Stuart. 'Bob the Roman' recognized 'the great Athenian' as a potentially dangerous competitor, peddling a purer brand of Neo-Classicism. At Spencer House in London (Plate 58), Stuart had in fact produced a suite of rooms rightly famous as the first truly Neo-Classic interiors in Britain. Adam's scorn for this 'Archipelagan Architect' was therefore an obvious piece of professional jealousy. He described Spencer House as 'pityfulissimo'; the ceilings may be 'Greek to the teeth . . . but by God they are not handsome'. He dismissed Stuart's designs for Kedleston as 'so excessively and ridiculously bad' that they 'beggared all description'. And no doubt he revelled in Lord de la Warr's horror at Stuart's work for Lord Nuneham: 'God damn my blood, my Lord, is this your Grecian architecture? What villainy! What absurdity! If this be Grecian, give me Chinese, give me Gothick! Anything is better than this! For shame, my Lord, pull it down and burn it. Is it possible that any man can, by sheer impudence and speaking, so impose upon the good sense and taste of mankind?'.

It was nonsense, of course. Stuart's decorative style—the detailing inside Montagu House (c. 1775–82; demolished) or Spencer House (c. 1760–65) (Plate 58), for example—is ingenious, meticulously finished, superbly controlled and despite Adam's opinion undeniably handsome. His Lichfield House facade (15 St. James's Square; 1765; Plate 114) subtly injects Grecian forms into the Palladian system. But Adam need not have worried. England was not yet ready for the dogmatic simplicity of the Greek Revival. And even if the time had been ripe for such a revolution in taste, the dilatory Stuart was hardly the man to capitalize on his good fortune. At times he was almost an arbiter without employment. Even his finest work, the interior of Greenwich Chapel (Plate 17), was executed and partly redesigned by his assistant William Newton. Adam's successor as the Vitruvius of the day was not James Stuart but James Wyatt—the young genius who in 1772 took London by storm with that stately pleasure dome, the Oxford Street Pantheon.

Wyatt's contribution to the British classical tradition was twofold.

His early work—Heaton House, Lancashire (1772), for example, or Heveningham Hall, Suffolk (*c.* 1784) (Plate 66)—brilliant but derivative, simplified and purified the mixed 'Adamitic' inheritance. The influence of Bramante, Raphael, Peruzzi and Palladio, is still as powerful as the inspiration of antique sources. But many would agree with Horace Walpole that Wyatt 'employed the antique with more judgement', and perhaps with equal sensitivity, even if his domestic planning lacks Adam's extraordinary inventiveness. His later work—Goodwood House, Sussex (1800) (Plate 69), for example, or Dodington, Gloucestershire (1796–1813) (Plates 20, 21, 22, 65, 68)—was more stringently Grecian in detail and more rigidly Neo-Classical in composition. In his Radcliffe Observatory (Plate 163) which—after a complicated building history involving Henry Keene—he completed in 1794, Wyatt reached the half-way point in his career. Here he seems almost to hesitate at the crossroads—and not just Wyatt, but the whole of British architecture—poised between historicism and experimentalism, punctuating a Graeco–Palladian vocabulary with the language of formal geometry. It was the Radcliffe Observatory, in fact, even more than Heaton or Castle Coole, Co. Fermanagh (1790–97) (Plates 63, 67), which forced Kaufmann to a resounding conclusion: 'the Janus-faced nineteenth century was anticipated in the work of James Wyatt'.

But that is to anticipate a little. During the forty years before it really caught on—the last four decades of the eighteenth century—the Greek Revival had been developing outside the mainstream of British architecture. In this period of the movement's genesis, the key names—besides Stuart and Revett—are Benjamin Latrobe, Joseph Bonomi and Thomas Harrison. Wyatt and Soane also had a considerable part to play. Wyatt's work at Gresford Lodge, Denbighshire (*c.* 1790; demolished) and Ottershaw Park, Surrey (*c.* 1800), for instance; Soane's work at Hammels Park, Hertfordshire (1783), Langley Park, Norfolk (1786), Sydney Lodge, Hampshire (1789), Tyringham, Buckinghamshire (1792–95) and Bentley Priory, near Stanmore (1798). All these were buildings incorporating primitive Greek orders. But it is the names of Stuart, Revett, Latrobe, Bonomi and Harrison which are persistently associated with the earliest use of the Grecian Doric, fluted or unfluted. In fact the early history of the movement revolves around a mere handful of celebrated items:

Stuart's temples at Hagley (1785) (Plate 48) and Shugborough (*c.* 1764) (Plate 52); Revett's use at Standlynch, Wiltshire (*c.* 1766) (Plate 72) and Ayot St. Lawrence, Buckinghamshire (1778) (Plates 14, 15) of the semi-fluted Doric order from the Temple of Apollo at Delos (Plate 16); Latrobe's Paestum porticoes at Hammerwood (Plate 75) and Ashdown in Sussex (1793–94); Aylesford and Bonomi's remarkable church at Great Packington, Warwickshire (1789) (Plates 18, 19), as dogmatically Neo-Classical as anything by Boullée or Ledoux; and Harrison's monumental Chester Castle (1785–1820) (Plates 171, 172, 175), with which the Greek Revival comes of age.

Benjamin H. Latrobe, of course, is a figure of international rather than national significance. He emigrated to Virginia in 1796 and lived to transform American architecture. In Sir John Summerson's words, at the Bank of Philadelphia in 1798 he 'married English Neo-Classicism to Jeffersonian Neo-Classicism [and] . . . from that moment, the classical revival in America took on a national form'. The American Greek Revival, indeed became much more of a vernacular style than its English proto-type. There too, it possessed political connotations—images of New World democracy—which were less readily applicable to Britain.

Still, from the 1760s onwards, Greek Revivalism is a continuous and expanding theme in British architecture and decoration, gathering swift momentum after the turn of the century. Among the best examples of the Graeco–Palladian synthesis of the 1760s and 1770s are the engravings in Stephen Riou's *Grecian Orders* (1768). After discoursing elegantly on the superiority of Greek to Roman architecture, he supplies a number of prototypes of his own making: a 'Doric colonnade' composed of paired columns; a 'Doric arcade' of arched formation; an 'Ionic portal' with unfluted columns; an 'Ionic colonnade with pedestals and podium'; a 'Corinthian portal' and 'Triumphal Arch' of Hellenistic origin; 'Doric windows', 'Ionic windows' and 'Corinthian windows', all with their 'appropriate entablatures'; 'Ionic Venetian windows'; a Hawksmoorian 'Church after the Manner of an Antique Temple'; and 'A Grand Machine for Fireworks', a monumental square in Whitehall, a City street, a palace and an octagonal 'Hunters' Hall'—all of which combine Greek and Roman orders, Palladian plans and occasional Rococo features. The Greek Revival was never wholly Greek.

Part of the explanation lay in the nature of the available archaeological works. Only a purist could afford to limit every aspect of interior design to authenticated Grecian sources. And except in the first two decades of the nineteenth century—the decades of 'Greekomania'—there was at no time a complete embargo on the use of Renaissance precedents. Even Piranesi was not forgotten during the Regency—witness the various editions of C. H. Tatham's *Etchings*. 'It was not', Tatham observed in 1799, 'so much the object of Le Roy and Stuart to give specimens of ornament, as of the component parts peculiar to the Grecian Orders; so that the productions of Piranesi stand almost alone in that class of Ornamental Architecture, in which students are equally in need of a guide, because in that they are most of all liable to err, by following the suggestions of their own imaginations'. Tatham's examples, mostly taken from specimens in the Vatican Museum, epitomize that rich synthesis of Greece, Rome and ancient Egypt which constituted the Regency interior. Among architects Brettingham, Bonomi, S. P. Cockerell, Dance, J. M. Gandy, Hope, Holland, Hardwick, Jupp, Lewis, Lapidge, Mylne, Plaw, Soane, Saunders, Wyatt and Yenn all subscribed. To say nothing of craftsmen, patrons and pundits. Tatham's own architectural designs—his naval memorial competition scheme of 1799 for instance, with Britannia atop a Doric column rising triumphantly from the prow of a ship—were very much less successful.

For the handling of the Regency synthesis with real fluency and grace, we must look not to Tatham, but to Tatham's master, Henry Holland. Only occasionally, however, as in his exquisite sculpture gallery at Woburn Abbey (1801–03) (Plate 71), does Holland pursue the Grecian mode in all its rigour. In his finest work, the interiors of Carlton House (1783–85), Grecian elements form no more than one aspect of his eclectic technique.

Still, the progress of English architecture towards the ideal of Grecian purity was regarded with a good deal of satisfaction by its practitioners during the Regency period. James Elmes, in his *Lectures on Architecture* (1823), summed up the situation as follows:

> The style called the classical, which is more properly the Italian, was introduced into this country by Inigo Jones and his followers of the Palladian school, and was continued by the illustrious Wren, and, with

various degrees of talent by Vanbrugh, Gibbs and Kent. The art was then all but lost in the dark and tasteless days of George the First and Second, till it revived under George the Third, in Chambers, Wyatt, and Stuart; and appears now, like its sister art of painting, still in its *progress* towards a great and glorious meridian of perfection. . . . Had the highly-gifted Wren visited and studied the Parthenon . . . [he] would have become . . . one of the greatest architects whom the world ever knew: but what may be excused in him, and in his day, cannot be excused at the era of 1821. The eye of refinement should not now be satisfied with the clumsy ponderosities of the Roman school, or even with the better taste of Chambers, who may be called the *Palladio riformato* of his time. . . . He read his Vitruvius in English, and, I fear, from a bad translation. The first instance . . . of a regularly bred and genuine architect was the classical and scientific Wyatt . . . Wyatt . . . was richer and more learned in his art than either Jones, Wren, or Vanbrugh. Equally inventive, and with as fine a taste as Jones; less scientific than Wren, but more admirable in his details than any preceeding English architect; he is at the head of our best school, from which has emanated all the finest works of the present day.

Soon after his death, therefore, Wyatt had been posthumously canonized as one of the founding fathers of the Greek Revival. The Adam revolution had been rejected. That it was rejected so quickly was largely the result of persistent propaganda in the form of didactic architectural writing.

The new knowledge of Greek architecture was popularized among surveyors and builders by means of derivative works like Aikin's *Doric* (1810), Nicholson's *Instructor* (1804), Billington's *Director* (1834), Middleton's *Miscellany* (1799), and Richardson's *Capitals* (1793). Peter Nicholson's *Student's Instructor* was particularly valuable. It set out to supply directions for 'drawing and working the Five Orders of Architecture; fully explaining the best Methods of striking regular and quirked Mouldings, for diminishing and glueing of Columns and Capitals, for finding the true Diameter of an Order to any given Height, for striking the Ionic Volute circular and elliptical, with finished Examples, on a large Scale, of the Orders, their Planceers, etc.'. Such books sold well in Josiah Taylor's Architectural Library in High Holborn. They were designed for craftsmen rather than scholars, and were cheaply but clearly printed: by 1817 volumes of Stuart and Revett were selling for seven guineas apiece; Nicholson's *Instructor* was priced at ten shillings and sixpence.

Nicholson did for Thomas Harrison what Tooke's *Pantheon* supposedly did for Keats: it provided a simple key to the mysteries of antique lore. And those for whom even Nicholson was too much were not forgotten. If Stuart was the primary source of the Greek Revival, and Nicholson the secondary fount, there were also tertiary springs as well. Taylor's extensive catalogue included the following choice item: 'A *Geometrical View of the Five Orders of Columns in Architecture*, adjusted by aliquot Parts; whereby the meanest Capacity, by Inspection, may delineate and work an entire Order, or any Part, of any Magnitude required. On a large Sheet, One Shilling'. Carpenters, plasterers, smiths, upholsterers and bricklayers—each had a choice of Grecian manuals and broadsheets. Pattern books did not go out with the Palladians.

Such, then, was the early progress of the Greek Revival in England along the pragmatic path of archaeology. This English approach was one aspect of the Neo-Classical mind: broadening the stylistic framework by the accumulation of archaeological evidence; replacing Renaissance assumptions by a wider range of choice. But there was another aspect as well. In architectural terms, the Romantic rebellion brought in its wake a new wave of historicism, eclecticism and experimentalism—that is, the selection of historical styles and motifs according to archaeological precedent, and their combination in accordance with new theories of composition. There was, therefore, a need for explanation as well as accumulation; a determination not just to observe, but to rationalize as well, to hammer out a coherent aesthetic philosophy from a welter of Neo-Classical alternatives. And that philosophy was only English by adoption.

This other route to Athens—the programmatic, rationalist route—was partly Italian in origin but largely French in fulfilment. The Italian side began in the first half of the eighteenth century with the theories of a Venetian Franciscan, Carlo Lodoli, 'the Socrates of Architecture'. As transmitted by his interpreters Memmo, Algarotti and Milizia, Lodoli has come down to us as the apostle of a new functionalism, the prophet of a new rational approach which would sweep away the whole Vitruvian system of representational design, proportional harmony and expressive ornament. Instead of the sensuous forms of Serlio, Alberti, Colonna and Guarini, he put forward a single new criterion of excellence: reason. Henceforward the best architecture must be that which best expresses the purpose of a building, the elements of its structure and the nature of its materials. Here was the germ of an architectural revolution—from the formal to the functional, from the sculptural to the skeletal. But it remained only a germ. Until almost the end of the eighteenth century, Italian architecture remained obstinately Baroque in its premises despite the assaults of Lodoli's Socratic mind. It was not until the 1790s that Valadier began to produce designs which combined Lodolian logic with Piranesian drama. The triumph of the new theories occurred not in Italy but in France.

It all began with the pursuit of pure forms. The essence of the Neo-Classical faith was a belief that architectural design was subject to eternal laws, and that these laws, based on the immutable laws of nature, could only be recovered by the scientific exploration of antiquity. 'Study the antique', wrote Diderot, 'in order to learn to look at nature'. In its notice of Sayer's *Ruins of Athens* (1759), the *Critical Review* explained these assumptions at some length:

> The ruins [of ancient Greece] must be generally admired so long as mankind retains a taste for magnificence, order, and regularity in building. They have this advantage over the ruins of the famous Palmyra, that they are the precepts of Vitruvius reduced into practice; precepts that are founded upon eternal laws, and coeval and coexisting with the ideas of beauty itself. . . . This work may be justly considered as an attempt to restore architecture to its ancient dignity, and of enabling the beholder and reader to attain to the correct sublime in that noble art, after its having been so long mistaken. After all, we have certain reasons for declaring that *Le Roy's* plans are far from being correct; that his imagination has in some places run riot; that, in others, his drawings are faulty, his proportions false. . . .

First, then, rediscover the purity of the antique. Next, via the antique, return to first principles in architectural design. It was a process epitomized in Canova's description of the Elgin Marbles: 'the truth of nature united to the choice of the finest forms'. An impressive slogan. But even if agreement could be reached among archaeologists as to what were the finest forms, philosophers were unlikely to find an acceptable definition of the truth of nature. If there was any such agreement in architectural circles during the later eighteenth century, it took the form of the aesthetic credo formulated by a French Jesuit, the Abbé Marc-Antoine Laugier.

Laugier's doctrine was expressed in two works: his *Essai sur l'architecture* (1753) and his *Observations sur l'architecture* (1765). In both architectural beauty is equated with structural truth, truth with reason, and reason with the laws of nature. This quest for architectural verities begins with the enunciation of his celebrated Arcadian parable: 'On the banks of a quietly flowing brook the savage notices a stretch of grass; its fresh greenness is pleasing to his eyes, its tender down invites him; he is drawn there and, stretched out at leisure on this sparkling carpet, he thinks of nothing else but enjoying in peace the gifts of nature; he lacks nothing, he does not want for anything'. Presently, however, rain and wind drive our noble savage first to seek refuge in a cave and then to construct for himself a rough dwelling. Hence the paradigm of the Primitive Hut, 'the model upon which all the magnificences of architecture have been imagined'. 'Suddenly,' wrote Laugier, 'I saw a great light'. Alone among the arts, architecture not only took its inspiration in nature but in nature ordered and elaborated by the processes of reason.

It was not a novel doctrine. Nor was Laugier by any means the first to make use of the analogy of the Primitive Hut. Vitruvius himself had said as much; François Blondel was only his most immediate predecessor in this respect. And Laugier's most effective forerunner, the Abbé Cordemoy, had in his *Nouveau Traité* of 1706 anticipated a good deal of the rationalist argument. But Laugier was the first to turn this Arcadian parable into the basis of a coherent aesthetic philosophy. 'Take note of this', he cries, 'never has a principle been more fertile in its effect. From now on it is easy to distinguish between the parts which are essential to the composition of a work of architecture and those which necessity has introduced and caprice added to them. Let us never lose sight of our little rustic hut!'.

It was Laugier's 'principle' which gave substance to the Greek Revival. It was Laugier's doctrine which translated an antiquarian pursuit into a viable architectural programme. In the first place, the Grecian orders were held to symbolize the natural origins of architecture. The Primitive Hut was regarded as the standard of architectural purity. And subsidiary decorative features were believed to stem from similarly natural sources. 'Some drops of rain', explained Thomas Hope—very much in the Laugier manner—'distilled from the ends of the rafters that projected over an architrave, so pleased an architect that he added them as ornaments to his Doric triglyph: a few ram's horns, suspended from the top of a pillar, so struck the imagination of another, that he formed out of them the . . . Ionic capital . . . ; and a wild acanthus, accidentally lodged on the top of an ancient sepulchral cippus, and with its foliage embracing a basket placed on the pillar, and compelled to curl down by the tile that covered the basket, so charmed a third (Callimachus of Corinth), that, without altering essentially the other parts of the Ionic combination, he substituted it as a new capital'.

Such traditional forms of ornament—residual symbols of primitive functions—were not, however, to be regarded as sacrosanct: the Greeks had 'sense and taste enough not to burden themselves in the pursuit of beauty by trammels of their own creating. . . . In the cella of the Parthenon, the Doric frieze appears without its triglyphs; in the portico of the Temple of Erectheus, the Ionic wants its dentils; and in . . . the choragic monument of Lysicrates, the capital wants its smaller set of volutes. In other buildings we see the characteristics of two different orders in indissoluble wedlock . . . and the Doric of the Temple of Neptune at Corinth, and the same order of the Temple of Juno at Nemea, differ as much in their proportions as the statues of the Farnese Hercules and of the Belvedere Apollo'.

So, to critics of the Laugier school, every detail of the Grecian orders stemmed from a functional source. But those details were not on that account to be regarded as canonical. New circumstances would surely produce new Orders—that is, not just new mouldings but new systems of expressive ornament. What had first to be purged away, however, was the accumulated dross of two thousand years of sophistication. The systematic corruption of Baroque must be destroyed. Palladio must be forgotten. Baroque architects had aimed at plasticity in design and comprehension in plan. They made use of antique elements decoratively rather than functionally. Neo-Classical architects repudiated these Renaissance practices. They aimed at rigidity in design and disparity in plan. They demanded the truthful use of classical orders: their columns at least *appeared* to support something. Thus, within the context of the classical tradition, Laugier justified and disciplined every use of every order according to the doctrine of 'apparent utility'. Even the slightest moulding had to pass this same rigorous test. Hence the characteristic economy and reticence of any truly Neo-Classical design.

Laugier's purge was summed up in Piranesi's parody: 'I shall destroy everything: no wall, no column, no pilaster—tabula rasa!'. Even the Abbé himself had foreseen the likely consequences of his own logic: 'Architecture would be reduced to almost nothing since with the exception of columns, entablatures, pediments, doors and windows I take away all the rest'. He was even reluctant to admit the necessity of walls! But in the eyes of his followers the shock which Laugier administered to the body of architectural thinking was nothing less than an aesthetic catharsis. As Milizia put it: 'The rules set out . . . are more negative and destructive than positive and constructive. This is only as it should be. To clear a piece of ground overgrown with wild thorns, one needs iron and fire. The ills of architecture arise out of over-abundance. Therefore, in order to perfect architecture, one must rid it of those superfluities and tear out those frills with which stupidity and caprice have disfigured it. The simpler architecture is, the more beautiful it is. It would be about time now, after some twenty centuries, that it were purged of every defect and thus reached perfection'.

Laugier's *Essai* is best understood as the climax of French rationalist thinking in architecture, a tradition gradually developed during the previous century, most notably by Fréart, Perrault, Frémin and Cordemoy. It was a tradition concerned less with form than with explanation, and less with function than with reason. Laugier has been correctly described as a rationalist first and functionalist second. That distinguished him from Lodoli. Laugier's parable of the Primitive Hut, and its explanatory function—stone imitating wood—would not have satisfied 'the Socrates of architecture'. Lodoli condemned all imitative forms and adumbrated for the first time the theory of material expression: building materials must express their own nature and no other. Still, Lodoli was largely forgotten; Laugier became the patron saint of Neo-Classicism, the man who broke up the Baroque.

'Neo-Classicism', Summerson concludes, 'involves . . . far more than text-book theories. It involves archaeological investigation on the one hand and a release of imaginative invention on the other; it involves the puritanism of the English Palladians and the vertiginous romancing of Piranesi. But at the centre of it all is the Cordemoy–Laugier thesis of architecture as a totally rational system. . . . The germ of thought released by Cordemoy into the Renaissance–Baroque world of 1706 multiplied itself into a force which survived the extinction of that world and, in the long run, re-orientated architecture in a way which made the uneasy revolutions of the nineteenth century inevitable, and the conclusions of the twentieth century possible'.

Laugier's *Essai*—the fulfilment of Cordemoy's tentative initiatives—was perfectly timed and perfectly presented. He told people what they wanted to hear, and in a voice that made them listen. His influence gathered strength as the century progressed. And as Dr. Herrmann puts it, 'the amount of ink spent in order to refute Laugier'—by Briseux, Frézier, Blondel and others, 'was proof that he had succeeded'. In England, his influence was widespread though often unacknowledged. Soane gave copies of the *Essai* to his pupils; and one of them—Sir Robert Smirke—produced an unpublished treatise which paraphrases the rationalist philosopher point for point. Pugin infused Laugier's principles into the very heart of the Gothic Revival. In fact the shadow of the *Essai* stretches all the way from the birth of the Greek Revival to the origins of the Modern Movement. Summerson calls Laugier 'the first modern architectural philosopher'. And certainly his principles are as logically valid today as they were more than two centuries ago—masonry columns have merely been replaced by piers of steel and concrete. But how exactly were Laugier's principles absorbed by the Greek Revival?

During the 1750s, Algarotti—as a reluctant apologist of Lodoli—had suggested one way of squaring functional theory with classical tradition: go back for inspiration to the Greeks. Only by 'drinking from the most pure fountains of Greece' could the great dilemma be resolved. Greece seemed to offer a solution to the great conundrum: the need to express new rational ideals in the only architectural language available—the language of inherited forms. But before this solution could be universally adopted, a battle had to be fought. The incubus of the Renaissance had yet to be shaken off.

This battle between Greece and Rome—a battle for the hearts and minds of European architects—centred on two famous literary duels: Piranesi *versus* Mariette and Chambers *versus* the Dilettanti.

G.-B. Piranesi's attack on the primacy of Greece was contained in two celebrated works: his *Della Magnificenza ed architettura de' Romani* (1761) and his *Parere su l'architettura* (1765). In the first of these he criticized Grecian architecture as insufficiently monumental and excessively ornamental, pillorying plates from Le Roy in order to prove his case. In the second he shifted his ground, defending the inventiveness of Roman art against the imposition of any rigid system, Greek, Vitruvian or Palladian. P.-J. Mariette's reply in the *Gazette litteraire* for 1764 has now been overshadowed. But at the time it represented a whole tradition of French thinking: the concept of an absolute beauty based on natural order, an aesthetic system brought to perfection by the Greeks, debased by the Romans and recoverable only by a combination of archaeology and systematic law.

In England the controversy was equally vehement, but rather one-sided. With the exception of Sir William Chambers, no major late eighteenth-century architect maintained the full apparatus of Renaissance theory against the growing tide of Grecian taste. Isaac Ware opposed not the style as such, but the dangers inherent in its reproduction. James Paine doubted the value of the new archaeology, but thought that all those learned folios might at least supply some useful ornaments. It was the lesser men who clung to Palladian tradition. Writing in 1823 James Elmes remembered how many architects had hated 'the new-fangled "Doric" without a base, as much as they did a shirt without ruffles, or a wig without two good portly curls over each ear, and half a yard of tail behind; scorning its simpler flutes without fillets, which they compared to ribbed stockings'. Instead, they even preferred 'the rusticated and twisted columns of Batty Langley . . . [they] lamented the shocking innovations of Wyatt and Soane, the more dreadful importations of Stuart, and were nearly going into a fever when the portico at Covent Garden Theatre was opened'.

Chambers' implacable hostility to the Greek Revival, however, was based on something stronger than mere conservatism. The precision and elaboration of the Dilettanti volumes seemed to him both unnecessary and unjustified. When the *Antiquities of Ionia* appeared in 1770, only two years after Major's *Paestum* and Riou's *Grecian Orders,* he vented his rage in an explosive letter to Charlemont:

> The dilettanti book is published, and a cursed book it is, between friends, being composed of some of the worst architecture I ever saw; there is a degree of madness in sending people abroad to fetch home such stuff. I am told this curious performance has cost the society near three thousand pounds; such a sum well applied would be of great use and advance the arts considerably, but to expend so much in order to introduce a bad taste is abominable.

Chambers' antagonism was, moreover, not only splenetic but well argued—notably in the third edition (1791) of his *Treatise on Civil Architecture*, and in a series of notes probably compiled in 1768–71, soon after the appearance of the second edition.

In the first place he dismissed the static concept of absolute beauty in favour of the idea of artistic progression. The Romans, he believed, improved on the achievements of the Greeks, just as the Greeks themselves surpassed the Egyptians.

> In the Constructive Part of Architecture, the Antients were no great Proficients. I believe many of the Deformities which we observe in the Grecian Buildings must be ascribed to their Ignorance in this Particular such as their Gouty Columns their narrow Intervals their disproportionate Architraves their Ipetral Temples which they knew not how to cover and their Temples with a Range of Columns running in the Center to support the Roof contrary to every Rule both of Beauty and Conveniency . . . Architecture is a creative Art and that of a very complicated kind[;] the hints which it collects from Nature are rude and imperfect[;] a tree is the Model of a Column a basket and a Dock Leaf those of a Capital[,] and a hut is the Original of a Temple, the precise form, the exact Proportion, and degree of Strength, with a thousand other Particulars are left to the Determination of the Art and can only be attained by a number of Experiments and a long Series of Observations not easily made but in times of profound Peace in Countries where Wealth abounds and where Splendour prevails.

After all, primitive buildings were only to be expected in a society such as that of the ancient Greeks, politically fragmented and economically undeveloped. He concludes:

At first sight, it appears extraordinary that a People so renowned for Poetry, Rhetoric, and every sort of Polite Literature and who carried Sculpture farther than any of the antient nations should be so deficient in Architecture[;] yet upon Reflection many Reasons will suggest themselves to us why it naturally should be so. Greece a Country small in itself was divided into a Great Number of little States none of them extremely powerful populous nor Rich so that they could attempt no very considerable Works in Architecture neither having the Space nor the Hands nor the Treasures necessary for that Purpose . . . if we recollect at the same time that whilst divided into many Governments Greece was constantly haressed with domestic Wars and from the time of its union under Philip always in an unsettled State and that an uncommon Simplicity of Manner prevailed amongst the Grecian Nations and that the Strictest Maxims of Equality were jealously adhered to in most of their States, it will be easy to account for the little Progress the Grecians made in Architecture. . . . [Besides] what little Magnificence the Grecians then displayed in their Structures was confined to public Buildings which were chiefly Temples in which there appears to have been nothing very surprizing either for Dimensions or ingenuity of contrivance. Greece almost constantly the Theatre of War[,] abounded not like Italy in magnificent Villas where the richest Productions of the Pencil and Chizel were displayed, their Roads were not adorned with Mausoleums to commemorate their Heroes, nor their Towns with Arches to celebrate their Triumphs, the Grecian Theatres were trifling compared with those of Italy[,] the Numachia and Amphitheatres unknown amongst them as were also the Thermini in which the Romans displayed so much splendor.

In the second place, the Grecian buildings which archaeologists so much admired seemed to Chambers intrinsically unremarkable:

It hath afforded, Occasion of Laughter to every intelligent Architect to see with what Pomp the Grecian Antiquities have lately been ushered into the World and what Enconiums have been lavished upon things that in Reality deserve little or no Notice. . . . The celebrated Lantern of Demosthenes or Choragic Monument of Lysicrates or the Temple of Hercules with all its other names is in Reality not quite so large as one of the Centry Boxes in Portman Square[;] its Form and Proportions resemble those of a silver Tankard excepting that the Handle is wanting . . . this Monument was erected in the Days of Alexander the Great when the Grecian Arts were at the highest Pitch of Excellence so that we may look upon this Building as a Cryterion of the Grecian Taste in Architecture when its utmost Perfection which as the learned Architect will perceive bore a very

88

exact Resemblance to the Taste of Boromini universally and Justly esteemed the most licentious and Extravagant of all the modern Italians.

The celebrated Temple of the Winds or Tower of Andronicus Cyrrhestes to vulgar Eyes resembles exactly one of the Dove houses usually erected on Gentlemens Estates in the Country of England, excepting that the Roof is somewhat flatter and there is no Turret for the Pigeons to creep in and fly out at. . . . Indeed none of the trifles now existing in Greece although so pompously described and Elegantly represented in Several late publications seem to deserve much notice—either for Size or taste of Designs nor are they in any way calculated to throw new lights upon the Art or to contribute in the least towards its advancement, not even those said to be erected by Alexander[,] the famous Parthenon or Temple of Minerva built in the Acropolis of Athens, during the Government of Pericles when the Grecian Arts flourished most was no very surprizing Work although it excited the Murmurs of all Greece and had for its Architects Phidias, Callicrates and Ictinus, the Onions and Radishes distributed to the Workmen during the Building of one of the Pyramids amount to twice the Sum expended upon this whole temple[;] many of our Parish Churches are much more considerable Buildings and by a very exact Calculation I find St. Pauls of London just three and forty times as large exclusive of a fraction of 247,384598; with Regard to the Stile of its Architecture it is too imperfect to deserve a serious Criticism.

We find indeed in antient Writers very pompous Descriptions of the Ephesian Temple of Diana and of several Other Temples of Greece but they are in general stuff and with so many absurdities that little faith ought to be given to them[,] and if the Grecian Architecture was imperfect in the Days of Pericles and Alexander surely it must have been much more so four or five Hundred Years before about which time the Ephesian Temple may be supposed to have been built.

Such criticisms, with their built-in Renaissance assumptions, missed the whole point of the Neo-Classical revolution. Primitivism, simplicity, purity—these were now the cardinal virtues, prized far above novelty, variety, flexibility or sophistication. Chambers was incapable of appreciating such an aesthetic somersault. By the time of his death in 1796 he had become a stranded colossus, a giant laggard from the age of Palladianism. 'They might', he believed, 'with equal success oppose a Hottentot and a Baboon to the Apollo and the Gladiator as set up the Grecian Architecture against the Roman[;] the *Ton* in anything is not so easily given and it would be absurd to suppose that Monsieur or Mr. such a one should turn the torrent of Prejudice in any particular Branch of Art as it would be to imagine that a Peasant could set the Fashion of a dress'. What Chambers never realized was the fact that such inversions of taste lay at the heart of Neo-Classical thinking. Peasants would indeed 'set the Fashion'. Gray summed it all up when he dismissed Stuart's conventionally genteel subscription list as 'the fine *Lady* part' of the project: 'What business have such people with Athens?'. The pursuit of primitive forms was a serious business.

These, then, were the two major routes along which the Greek Revival progressed: Anglo–French archaeology and Franco–Italian rationalism. It was the interaction of these two traditions which stimulated and controlled Neo-Classical design in architecture. The High Victorian battle between historicism and modernity had already been fought out once before—during the Regency. And in both cases the result was the same: first an uneasy compromise based on the mimetic principle of creative imitation, and then the triumph of scholarship over invention.

From the start it was realized that archaeological precision was something of a mixed blessing. In 1767 Berkenhout had 'purposely omitted' detailed measurements of Paestum. 'It may not be amiss to observe', he wrote, 'that the great degree of accuracy which has been used in measuring the remains of ancient Greece and Rome, has contributed much less to the improvement of architecture than may at first be imagined. It prevents the mind from taking in the whole together, and from attaining to that sublimity and grandeur of style which the ancients possessed in so eminent a degree. Nor were the ancients themselves so exact; we hardly find any two columns or intercolumniations, precisely the same in any of their buildings. Besides, those who have pretended to the greatest accuracy, have often been extremely inaccurate; Desgodetz, for instance, who was so careful in measuring the different diameters of the Pantheon, has committed a number of mistakes in the measurements of the Temple of Vesta at Tivoli, the columns of the Campo Vaccino, and many others'.

Certainly the precision of much Greek Revival architecture was something of a fiction. Stuart and Revett's first volume (1762) gave the radius of the columns of the Poihele Stoa as 1 ft. 5·65 in. Henry Holland's portico at Carlton House was reported to have 'precisely the same' measurements. And when those celebrated columns were re-used in the side porticoes of the National Gallery, William Wilkins claimed to have copied them exactly in the columns of his great central portico. But in fact the columns of the Poihele Stoa measure 1 ft. 3·325 in. in radius. And when in 1968 the Ministry of Public Building and Works undertook a precise measurement of the National Gallery, the radius of Holland's columns just below the capital was found to be 1 ft. 3·55 in., as against 1 ft. 3·39 in. for Wilkins's columns in the central portico. Stuart and Revett, Holland and Wilkins, were all wrong—at least by the most rigorous scientific standards.

Archaeological precision, however, was not only an illusion. It could also be a snare. The ablest Greek Revivalists realized there was no future in pure copying. And the lesser men in any case lacked the necessary learning. But the ideal of accuracy hovered threateningly on every Neo-Classicist's mental horizon. The glories of the Acropolis represented both inspiration and limitation. Fortunately for Greek Revivalism in Britain, however, archaeological accuracy was consistently subordinated to the compositional demands of two very different aesthetic philosophies. Greek Revival architecture was doubly the product of classic and romantic impulses. The rediscovery of Greece was a romantic quest for Arcadia; rationalizing the archaeological discoveries which flowed from that quest was nothing less than a classic attempt at reorganizing the rules of architectural design. And the composition of British Greek Revival buildings was controlled by a similar duality of inspiration summed up in the aesthetic philosophies of the Sublime and the Picturesque.

Edmund Burke produced his *Philosophical Enquiry into the Origin of our Ideas on the Sublime and the Beautiful* in 1757. Its argument, lucidly articulated, was founded on a simple observation: the basic forces of human nature were love and fear, the instincts which inspired propagation and self-preservation. Our aesthetic response to any object must therefore be conditioned by one or other of those instincts. Objects were described as beautiful which inspired a loving appreciation of eternal harmony. Objects inspiring awe were sublime. But as the eighteenth century progressed, the concept of the Sublime became, appropriately, hazier and hazier. Many would have agreed with Sir Martin Archer Shee who in 1809 dismissed the Sublime as 'the insane point of the critical compass. . . . Those who talk rationally on other subjects, no sooner touch on this, than they go off in a literary delirium; fancy themselves, like Longinus, "the great sublime they draw", and rave like methodists of inward lights, and enthusiastic emotions, which, if you cannot comprehend, you are set down as un-illumined by the grace of criticism, and excluded from the elect of Taste'.

One of the clearest definitions of the sublime qualities inherent in ancient Greek architecture came from an ex-pupil of Chambers and a convert from Palladianism, Willey Reveley. In the third volume of *Antiquities of Athens* (1794) he defended pure Doric forms in terms which were entirely Burkean:

> The awful dignity and grandeur of this kind of temple, arising from the perfect agreement of all its various parts, strikes the beholder with a sensation, which he may look for in vain in buildings of any other description. . . . There is a certain appearance of eternal duration in this species of edifice, that gives a solemn and majestic feeling, while every part is perceived to contribute its share to this character of durability. . . . The Grecian Doric is by many indiscriminately censured for clumsiness. But those who are so ready to condemn it should first recollect, that it was applied only where the greatest dignity and strength were required. It happens in this, as well as in every other part of ornamental architecture that the judicious application makes all the difference between the censure or praise it deserves. . . . Let those who prefer the later Doric indiscriminately, and entirely reject the Grecian, try whether they can, with their slender order, produce the chaste and solid grandeur of the Parthenon, or the still more masculine character of the great temple of Pesto . . .

Simplicity, strength, vastness—these were the characteristics of the Sublime. So also was an element of the terrible: as when young Robert Adam, watching a nocturnal firework display in Rome, described the scene as 'horribly antique and pleasing'. But Sublimest of all was the quality of timelessness, of mute stones triumphing over time and tempest, shaming the transient achievements of mere mortals. Sir Christopher Wren had put it in a nutshell long before: 'architecture aims at eternity'. The Greek Revivalists came closer still to capturing that elusive mirage.

Paestum, of course, represented the Sublime ideal. Lusieri, for example, spent the bulk of his active life in Athens. But his heart remained at Paestum. There, he believed, 'the Doric order attained a pre-eminence beyond which it never passed; not a stone has been there placed without some evident and important design; every part of the structure bespeaks its essential utility'. Only the stern Doric temple at Aegina represented a style equally pure and equally correct: 'of such a nature were works in architecture, when the whole aim of the architect was to unite grandeur with utility; the former being founded on the latter. All then was truth, strength and sublimity'. By comparison, even the Parthenon fell short of this ideal: the very perfection of its sculptures seemed not an echo of some heroic Arcadia but the product of decadent virtuosity in the golden days of Pericles.

Sublimity was clearly a major component in Greek Revival design. Still more potent, however, was that corpus of ideas summed up under a convenient umbrella label: 'The Picturesque'. Every age interprets its Hellenic inheritance in a slightly different way. The Romantics even managed to separate Greece from the stereotypes of the classical tradition: their vision of Hellas was a remote Arcadia, primitive, innocent and pure. 'Few things', as F. L. Lucas pointed out, 'are more romantic than "classical" mythology . . . [That] earlier Hellas breathes a fragrance of young romance which was one day to intoxicate Keats, even when he found its blossoms pressed and dry in the *hortus siccus* of Lemprière'. Even the weight of the classical tradition could not cloud the romantic dream world of Olympus and Parnassus. And British Romantics in particular formulated that sweet Arcadian dream principally in terms of their own philosophy of the Picturesque.

The theory and practice of the Picturesque, as developed during the eighteenth century by Charles Bridgeman, William Kent, 'Capability' Brown, William Gilpin, Richard Payne Knight, Sir Uvedale Price and Humphry Repton, was essentially a system of visual values fusing architecture with nature in a series of scenic entities. For Payne Knight every 'stately mansion' should be 'well mixed and blended in the scene':

> . . . mixed and blended ever let it be,
> A mere component part of what you see.

The Picturesque formed an intermediate category between the Beautiful and the Sublime—Uvedale Price, for instance, thought Paestum (Plate 12)

Sublime, the Erechtheion (Plate 4) Beautiful, and the Lysicrates Monument (Plate 54) and Tower of the Winds (Plate 13) Picturesque. Because of its intermediate status, the term Picturesque came to be applied to scenes which were neither harmonious enough to be truly Beautiful nor sufficiently terrifying to qualify as Sublime. Such scenes were characterized by irregularity, variety, contrast and surprise. And these qualities became in turn the British contribution to Neo-Classical composition. Indeed the visual philosophy of the Picturesque forms a single continuous thread which links the three main stages of Neo-Classical architecture in Britain: first Roman and 'Etruscan'; then Greek and Hellenistic; and finally Graeco–Roman.

The whole concept of the naturalistic landscape was pictorially based. Hence the fact that the Picturesque tradition was initially not Grecian in inspiration but Italian: the landscape of the *campagna* filtered through the golden haze of Claude and Poussin and transmuted empirically into *le jardin anglais*. Stourhead (1741 onwards) was recognizably Claudian. Stowe (1713 onwards) less obviously so. Despite its Grecian Temple and its Grecian Valley, its grassy contours are essentially English. What is dimly visible at Stowe, however, is the Arcadian ideal, even if only nominally, a kind of aesthetic yardstick against which naturalistic landscapes might be ideally matched. When Neo-Classicism switched from Roman to Greek, the Arcadian mirage seemed appreciably closer. At Shugborough in Staffordshire 'Athenian' Stuart decorated a Rococo landscape by Wright of Durham with a whole series of Grecian souvenirs: the Arch of Hadrian, the Theseion in miniature, and the Tower of the Winds, all set just a little incongruously in wooded English parkland (Plates 49–53, 55, 57). It is this element of incongruity which has to be explained away if we are to enter into the minds of the Greek Revivalists.

The effort is worth making. First comes the concept of simplicity. The affectation of rusticity is a recurrent symptom of the Romantic neurosis. Sir John Soane described his rustic dairy at Hammels Park, Hertfordshire (1783) (Plate 76), as 'roughcasted . . . the roof . . . covered with reeds; the pillars are the trunks of trees, with the bark on, decorated with woodbines and creepers'. At Shugborough, Samuel Wyatt's Ionic colonnade is composed of columns each actually made of single oak trees covered with slate and painted. Laugier's doctrine of the

Primitive Hut was a therapeutic purge for English Palladianism. But it also produced some rather comic results. Then there was that sweetest of Arcadian sensations: melancholy. Grecian ruins were less frequently used in landscape settings than Gothic. But in 1826 at Virginia Water near Windsor, Wyatville incorporated genuine fragments from Leptis Magna in a lakeside feature known as the Temple of Augustus (Plate 79). The result is worthy of Hubert Robert—'Robert des Ruines'. Shugborough actually contains a so-called Shepherd's Monument (Plate 49) inscribed 'Et in Arcadia Ego'. And a whole genre of funeral monuments stemmed from the same associations: schemes for mausolea by Soane, Gandy or Wightman for example (Plates 33, 35, frontispiece)—gaunt and heroic, midst gloomy cyprus shade; or Richardson's pious rendering of the Soane family tomb against a background closer to Mount Olympus than to St. Pancras (Plate 41). Benjamin Green's Penshaw Monument, Co. Durham (1830)—'an apparition of the Acropolis under hyperborean skies'—is merely the most striking example of a long funereal tradition.

At West Wycombe Park in Buckinghamshire, Nicholas Revett's 'Music Room' or temple by the lake (1778–80) (Plate 77) comes very close to a satisfying conjunction of English landscape and Grecian architecture, Neo-Classicism and the Picturesque, even if it is in fact no more than a delicious scenic conjuring trick. But the most heroic attempt to recreate the Arcadian vision occurred at Grange Park in Hampshire (rebuilt 1804 onwards) (Plates 96, 97). Here through the sympathetic eyes of W. A. Nesfield (Plate 92) we can begin to understand Wilkins's dramatic evocation of the Theseion in a romantic Reptonian landscape. C. R. Cockerell certainly recognized its Arcadian flavour. 'Nothing', he wrote, 'can be finer, more classical or like the finest Poussins. It realizes the most fanciful representations of painters' fancy, or the poet's imagination. . . . There is nothing like it on this side of Arcadia'. He found 'the sunshine upon the building, as clear a sky, the lights and shades and reflections, as in Greece. The rooks and jackdaws in the lime tree avenue sailing and cawing in the air brought home the recollections of the Acropolis, the buzzing of the blue flies and the flowers something of the aromatic scent of thyme . . .; the gravel walk beneath . . . the slope . . . to the water and tufted trees finer . . . than ever grew on the banks of the Ilissus'.

The Romantic landscape was not photographic but imagistic. Burne-Jones defined it as 'a beautiful romantic dream of something that never was, never will be—in a light better than any light that ever shone—in a land no one can define or remember, only desire'. It was indeed both vanished paradise and utopian dream, a Keatsian landscape of imagination, revealed only to the inward eye by magic casements opening out on faery lands forlorn. And often enough, in a world still nourished on the classics, its inspiration was the legend of Arcadia: a Virgilian compound of Theocritan Sicily and Polybian Arcady; a rocky garden watered by the rippling Alpheus and shaded by groves of pine and cyprus; a land of patriarchal simplicity, ruled by Arcas, son of Zeus and Callisto, and peopled by a race who 'lived before the moon' and worshipped daily at the shrines of Artemis and Pan. Such Rousseauesque notions were a powerful ingredient in Greek Revivalism.

The ultimate inspiration for the whole movement came directly from the relics of that lost world, the fragments scattered upon the 'holy ground' of Greece. These fragments cried out with the siren call of Count Platen's 'Antiques':

> Here have ye piled us together, and left us in cruel confusion;
> Each one pressing his fellow, and each of us shading his brother;
> None in a fitting abode, in the life-giving play of the sunshine.
> Here in disorder we lie, like desolate bones in a charnel,
> Waking, in all that can feel, deep sense of sorrowful yearning
> For the magnificent days when as all but alive we were honoured!
> Ye, too, have ye no temples, no pleachèd arcades in your garden,
> Where ye can take us, and plant us all near the unperishing heavens,
> After our sweet event, to the joy of the pious beholder?

The Greek Revivalist answered that cry. And his answer was essentially a Romantic gesture.

Appropriately, the Greek Revival in British architecture—indeed the Greek Revival anywhere in the world—began symbolically in 1758–59 with the Doric landscape temple at Hagley (Plate 48), designed by Stuart and executed by Miller. That date is sacrosanct, unless we fall back on

1757—when an illustration of the Tower of the Winds first appeared in the *Gentleman's Magazine* and Revett apparently constructed a vanished 'ornamental portico' in his brother's garden at Brandeston, Suffolk. In October 1758, in a letter to Mrs. Elizabeth Montagu, Lord Lyttleton announced the portentous news: Stuart 'is going to embellish one of my little hills with a true Attic building, a Portico of six pillars, which will make a fine effect to my new house, and command a most beautiful view of the country'. Thus the Greek Revival was launched within the context of the Romantic landscape, a launching confirmed during the next few years with Stuart's Arcadian group at Shugborough and Revett's temples and porticoes at West Wycombe (Plate 77), Standlynch (Plate 72), and Ayot St. Lawrence Church in Hertfordshire (1778) (Plates 14, 15). West Wycombe's flint-faced Tower of the Winds—half way between the Rococo and the Picturesque—dates from 1759. This association between Greek Revivalism and the Romantic landscape can be traced back to 1752 when Richard Dalton recommended the Lysicrates Monument as a garden feature. And it outlasted Wilkins's transformation of the Grange. Indeed it is perhaps the major ingredient in the first half century of the movement.

A distinction should certainly be drawn between the development of the Grecian style in England between the 1760s and the 1790s, and its propagation during the Regency period. The six years 1803–9 were crucial. Before 1803, the Greek Revival had developed as one of several exotic styles produced by the romantic impulse: the contiguity at Hagley of Stuart's Doric Temple, Miller's Gothic Ruin and Miller's Rococo interiors, is by no means accidental. After 1810, however, the Greek Revival was emancipated from its landscape setting. It was no longer merely a fashionable conceit; it was the very criterion of architectural distinction. In 1803–6 George Dance reconstructed Stratton Park, Hampshire (Plates 89, 90), using a Paestum-proportioned, unfluted Doric portico and a staircase with primitive Doric columns borrowed from Dubut's *Maisons de Ville et de Campagne* (1803). In 1804 Wilkins defeated James Wyatt in the competition for Downing College, Cambridge (Plate 184), with the help of a fighting pamphlet by the rich and influential Thomas Hope. In 1805 Wilkins defeated Henry Holland in a parallel competition for the East India College at Haileybury, Hertfordshire. Both competitions were cases of Greek defeating Roman. In 1806 Dance produced an unfluted Ionic portico in London at the Royal College of Surgeons, Lincoln's Inn Fields. In the same year Wilkins designed a giant Doric portico for Osberton House, Nottinghamshire, the first full-scale, pure Grecian portico in British domestic architecture. By 1809 Wilkins's Theseion portico at Grange Park had put nearby Stratton in the shade, and the Parthenon columns of Smirke's Covent Garden Theatre (Plates 180, 181) had become the talk of the capital. Thenceforward the fashion swept the country. Within twelve months, William Stokoe had carried Covent Garden as far north as Newcastle-upon-Tyne in the shape of his sturdy Doric Moot Hall. In buildings as different as Barry's Manchester Institution—a building with debts to both Dubut and Schinkel—now the City Art Gallery (1823), the Inwood's exquisite St. Pancras Church (1819–22) (Plates 26, 28) and Smirke's monumental British Museum (1823–47) (Plate 189), the Greek Revival reached its culmination in England. And the work of prolific provincial architects like Haycock of Shrewsbury, Foulston of Plymouth, Foster of Liverpool, Mountain of Hull, and Lane and Goodwin of Manchester ensured the spread of the new style throughout the country during the later 1820s and 1830s. As C. R. Cockerell sarcastically put it in 1815, 'Greek is the fashion and all noodles are ashamed of being out of the fashion'.

The extent of the Greek Revival's supremacy can be gauged by its dominance over one particular building type: the public building for legal, administrative or cultural purposes. During the controversy relating to the style of the New Houses of Parliament in 1836, W. R. Hamilton catalogued the triumph of Grecian: 'the Courts of Justice at Newcastle, Chester (Plates 171, 172, 175), Gloucester, Hereford, Perth (Plate 194); the Council House at Bristol (Plate 193); the High School at Edinburgh (Plates 233, 239); the Bank (Plate 246), Exchange and County Hall at Glasgow; the Custom House at Liverpool; the Town Halls at Manchester and Birmingham (Plate 222); the Post Office, St. George's Hospital, the London University (Plate 186), King's College, Covent Garden Theatre (Plates 180, 181), the National Gallery (Plate 229), the Mint, the Trinity House, and the British Museum (Plate 189) in London. . . . To those . . . may be added the . . . literary, scientific, and other public Institutions in Westminster, and in many of the provincial towns, the Post

Office and Custom House in Dublin. The University Library (Plates 185, 187, 188), and Fitzwilliam Museum at Cambridge are projected in the same style. I have heard of none that are Gothic, except the [County Courts] at Lincoln and Lancaster'. And both of those, Hamilton might have added, were designed by committed Greeks, Sir Robert Smirke and Thomas Harrison.

So the Greek Revival became respectable and scholarly two generations sooner than the Gothic. By the 1840s when the Gothic Revival was beginning to move into its dominant, High Church phase, the Greek Revival was almost over—in England, if not in Scotland. Regency architects adopted it with greater speed and accuracy than they did the Gothic —with greater speed because of the strength of the Hellenist fashion and with greater accuracy both because of the mass of archaeological publications and because Regency architects were in any case natural classicists, trained in the Georgian tradition.

But however academic it became, Greek Revivalism never entirely shook off its Romantic origins. 'A piece of Palladian architecture', wrote William Gilpin, 'may be elegant in the last degree. The proportion of its parts—the propriety of its ornaments—and the symmetry of the whole may be highly pleasing. But if we introduce it in a picture, it immediately becomes a formal object, and ceases to please. Should we wish to give it picturesque beauty, we must use the mallet instead of the chisel: we must beat down one half of it, deface the other, and throw the mutilated members around in heaps . . .'. Greek Revivalists scarcely went to such extremes, but they did attempt to break up the rhythmic unities of Palladianism in favour of a loose agglomeration of parts. And in that respect their designs were both Neo-Classical and Picturesque. Occasionally they might also be Sublime. Thomas Harrison's mighty Propylaeum (1810–20) (Plate 175) at Chester Castle, for instance, manages to combine direct antique inspiration—the Temple of Philip at Delos and the so-called Temple of Augustus at Athens—with the primal simplicity of the Sublime and the variety of light and shade associated with the Picturesque.

Picturesque philosophy had in fact a double impact on the classical tradition in British architecture. In the first place its emphasis on the conjunction of architecture and landscape gave added impetus to the Romantic pursuit of the Arcadian vision. In the second place its emphasis on variety and irregularity hastened the disintegration of Baroque unities. As Dr. Syntax proclaimed:

> The first, the middle and the last
> Of *picturesque* is bold *contrast*.

And these contrasts could be expressed just as powerfully whether their forms were geometrical or naturalistic.

It was Emil Kaufmann who first explained the transition from Baroque to Neo-Classicism. He summed up the yardsticks of Baroque composition under five headings: 'symmetry, proportionality, unification, integration, and gradation'. At the same time he identified five prime characteristics in Neo-Classical composition. Those have been summarized by Mario Praz as follows: 'the predilection for elementary geometrical forms: the isolation of a building from the space surrounding it; the replacement of the principle of symmetry (analogous to that of the human body, according to the well-known axiom of Vitruvius) by a principle of compensated symmetry in which the separate parts possess an autonomy of their own; the search for unity through the spatial disposition of the separate elements so as to create a tension on the surfaces; and, finally, regard for the properties of the material (subordinated to design by the architects of the Renaissance and the Baroque)'. This, as Kaufmann put it, is 'what was going on below the pseudoclassical surface'.

Such subterranean changes can in fact be interpreted as Romantic elements in Neo-Classical design, breaking through the classic crust of the antique. They are there beneath the surface in the burgeoning romanticism of Rococo—James Paine's Stockeld Park, Yorkshire (1758–63), for instance. They are fully present—conspicuously so—by 1790, in George Steuart's extraordinary church of St. Chad, Shrewsbury (Plate 23). There the flowing currents of Baroque tradition have been shattered by the syncopated rhythms of Neo-Classicism. The result is an uneasy partnership of abstract geometrical shapes and elongated classic forms. The offspring of this tense marriage, a marriage between geometry and archaeology, was in fact the movement we know as Neo-Classicism. And within that movement, absorbing the romantic elements of the Picturesque and the Sublime into an evolving classical tradition, the Greek Revival found its happiest expression in the Arcadian setting of a naturalistic landscape.

One tiny building—a folly rather than a building—sums up several of these interlocking themes: Jeffry Wyatt's Nant-y-Bellan Tower in Wynnstay Park, Denbighshire (Plate 78). Built about 1800 for Sir Watkin Williams Wynn as a military memorial, it also incorporated miniature living quarters for a solitary Irishwoman named Lucy. Its antique prototype was the tomb of Caecilia Metella on the Via Appia in Rome. Its composition, however, is dogmatically geometrical. And its setting is quintessentially Picturesque. Or rather it was—for in recent years dereliction has become decay, and its ruined aspect is no longer Picturesque but dramatically Sublime.

On a much grander scale, Wilkin's design for the National Gallery in London (Plate 229) reflected something of the same ambivalence. His details were Neo-Classical. But his composition took the form of Palladianism diversified by a conscious pursuit of the Picturesque. As a Greek Revivalist he was not impressed by James Gibbs's Roman portico of St. Martin-in-the-Fields (Plate 229): 'I should have passed a great many years of useless study if I could not design something very superior to that'. But this pursuit of archaeological purity was limited only to matters of detail: the building's silhouette is manipulated with self-conscious bravura. The architect believed that 'breaking the horizontal skyline' would 'greatly improve the general effect'. Sculpture was employed for the same purpose—although not as extensively as Wilkins desired. Baily's Britannia from Marble Arch was transformed into Minerva and placed between two trophies on the East front in such a way that it would 'break the horizontal line of the top of the balustrade, so as to make the centre culminate . . . in a triangular form so much desired by lovers of picturesque effect'. Finally, the whole approach to the National Gallery, down Whitehall and across Trafalgar Square, was conceived by Wilkins in Picturesque terms. He would have preferred a fountain to Nelson's Column. 'Although it may seem objectionable', he wrote, 'as interfering with the portico in the approach from Whitehall to Charing Cross, it will add to the picturesque effect, by making a new combination at almost every pace as we advance from the South. I am not at all in favour of viewing the portico under the same aspect for a long extent of distance'.

In other words, landscape theory had invaded townscape design. The landscapists' convention of the moving spectator is called in to justify the

parallactic effect of serried columns. Even in an urban area as monument-
ally formal as Trafalgar Square, Neo-Classical design is permeated by
Picturesque theory. Once again the classic and romantic principles turn
out to be complementary rather than conflicting.

Both themes—classicism and romanticism—can be traced in the composition and setting of most Greek Revival buildings, not only in Eng-
land, but in Wales, Ireland and Scotland as well. Wales and Ireland have
a smaller share of Greek Revival monuments than England and Scotland.
But they boast several examples which are by no means insignificant.
Brecon Shire Hall (T. H. Wyatt, 1842) and Bridgend Town Hall (David
Vaughan, 1843; demolished) are both impressively and austerely Doric.
But the precise Erechtheion Ionic of Clytha House (Plates 135, 136)
near Abergavenny, built during the later 1830s to designs by Haycock of
Shrewsbury, fits happily into a rough landscape adorned with Gothic
features. And several of Thomas Harrison's most Sublime designs—the
Anglesea Column at Plas Newydd (1816–17); the Holyhead Memorial
Arch (1842); and—in diminishing scale—the portico of Glan-yr-Afon,
Denbighshire (1812)—are by no means out of place in their picturesque
Welsh setting. The Court Houses at Dundalk (Edward Park and John
Bowden, 1813–18) (Plate 216) and Waterford (J. B. Keane, 1849), Cork
Prison (1818) by George and James Pain (Plate 203), the Roman Catholic
Pro-Cathedral in Dublin (John Sweetman, 1816–25) and the church of
St. Patrick, Cork (G. R. Pain, *c.* 1835), are all sublimely Greek by any
standards. The Dundalk portico in particular was a dogmatic recreation
of the Theseion. Sir Walter Scott thought it outdid anything in Edin-
burgh. But the reticence of Francis Goodwin's Lissadel, Co. Sligo (1834)
fits easily into the soft contours of its surrounding landscape. And the
Banqueting House (*c.* 1780) at Mount Stewart, Co. Down (Plate 47) on
the shore of Strangford Lough is not only 'Athenian' Stuart's finest evocation of ancient Greece, but a near-perfect fulfilment of the whole
Arcadian dream.

One English building above all symbolizes the different strands which
together made up the Greek Revival: the Lansdown Tower, Bath (Plate
143). Designed in 1825–6 for Beckford of Fonthill by a local architect,
H. E. Goodridge, its style, its setting and the circumstances of its construction defy any suggestion that Neo-Classicism can be separated from

Romanticism in any meaningful way. In fact its combination of Picturesque irregularity with abstract geometry and archaeological detail make
Goodridge's design worthy of very close study. Its wood and cast-iron
turret manages to echo both the Tower of the Winds (Plate 13) and the
Lysicrates Monument (Plate 54). But the rest of the detailing is Franco-
Italian in origin. And by uniting eclecticism with abstraction Goodridge
actually manages to anticipate the later triumphs of 'Greek' Thomson.

Even as late as 1844 the structure and contents of Lansdown Tower
were thought worthy of publication in chromolithograph. The letterpress
—by the man responsible for much of the interior decoration, Edmund
Francis English—eventually gave up the unequal task of description: 'no
language can do justice to an object so unique, to a *bijou* so exquisite, as
Lansdown Tower'. Certainly, Beckford's last folly was a unique combination of Classic and Romantic, Greek and Italianate, Picturesque and
Sublime. Approached via a grotto and a cottage, through gardens irregular
and mixed, it looked out across the city of Bath, over a landscape worthy
of the *campagna*.

> Although the resources of art are put into abundant requisition, there is no
> trace of cultivation—nothing either park-like or formal—all is kept, as
> much as possible, in subjugation to the modesty of Nature. Among the
> boundaries of the grounds there is a rugged and rocky prominence ex-
> cavated in several places in remoter times; it may have been for the ex-
> traction of building materials, or, possibly, to serve as rude habitations for
> our uncivilised forefathers. . . . One evening the writer accompanying
> Mr. Beckford through the grounds . . . was anxious to learn what recon-
> ciled him so perfectly to the locality of Lansdown after the vastness of
> Fonthill, with its extensive gardens and groves of almost Oriental beauty.
> . . . Extending his arms and elevating his voice, as if excited by 'the poet's
> fire', he exclaimed, 'This!—this!—the finest prospect in Europe!' Pointing
> to the vast panoramic view around, to the countless hills near, the far
> Welsh mountains, the blue fading distance, and then to the most beautiful
> of our ancient cities, which at that moment slept beneath, enveloped in the
> rich purple mist of a summer sunset,—'This!' he repeated . . .

Here the Caliph of Fonthill designated what was meant to be his own
last resting place: a granite sarcophagus shaded by lilac branches. No
wonder Lansdown Tower, 'this wonder of wonders', lifting 'its gilded
and glittering head a hundred and thirty feet above the summit of the

hill', itself 'eight hundred feet above the Avon', became something of a mecca for connoisseurs of the Romantic. And today, overgrown and derelict, it portrays to perfection that conjunction of Neo-Classicism and the Picturesque which was the product of the Romantic age in British architecture.

But it was in Edinburgh, 'the Athens of the North', that Romanticism in Britain found its ultimate architectural expression: Neo-Classic and Neo-Gothic, Picturesque and Sublime. Neither Wales nor Ireland produced a native Greek Revival tradition. Things were very different in Scotland. Here the dissemination of the style was less rapid than in England but much more complete. Perhaps grey stone columns suited the chilly northern temperament. Perhaps the Grecian style expressed religious hostility to the liturgical enthusiasm of High Anglican Gothic. Either way, north of the border the fashion enjoyed an Indian Summer which lasted beyond the High Victorian period. The incipient Hellenism of David Hume, Lord Kames, Allan Ramsay and Gavin Hamilton was amply fulfilled.

The story begins with the Glasgow Courthouse (*c.* 1807–14) by the shadowy William Stark. This building boasted a giant Doric portico (Plate 182) which certainly rivalled and probably antedated Smirke's Covent Garden. During the next three decades David Hamilton fully maintained the Glaswegian tradition of Greek Revivalism. And Archibald Simpson became the principal creator of classic Aberdeen. His greatest houses Strathcathro, Angus (1827) (Plates 155, 156) and Park (1822) and Crimonmogate (1840), Aberdeenshire, place him among the first rank of Neo-Classicists. But the biggest opportunities occurred in the New Town of Edinburgh. For this indeed was 'the Athens of the North' —a title invented by the painter 'Grecian' Williams in the early 1820s—a capital city in a setting which combined the variety and incident of the Picturesque with the scale and grandeur of the Sublime. Archibald Elliot set the pace with his use of the Ionic order at Waterloo Place (1815–19) and County Hall (1816–19). William Burn proved himself an apt pupil of Smirke with his Doric New Academy (1822–24) and John Watson's School (1825) and Hospital (1835). Thereafter the stage is dominated by two architects, Thomas Hamilton and W. H. Playfair. Hamilton's heroic High School (1825–29) (Plates 233, 239), Playfair's

Scottish Academy (1822–26 and 1832–35) and National Gallery (1850–57) (Plates 235, 236, 237), and Cockerell and Playfair's unfinished National Monument (1822–29) (Plate 234), as well as several conspicuous funeral trophies, brilliantly turned Calton Hill and its environs into a Caledonian Acropolis. And in the Scottish Physicians' College (1844–46) (Plate 240), Hamilton produced one of the most exquisitely modulated facades in the whole history of the movement.

Hamilton and Playfair were the Klenze and Schinkel of the British Greek Revival. In their hands the style attained new levels of sophistication. Hamilton was a self-taught Grecian of rare skill and uncommon sensibility. He was a master of the majestic and the miniature: his giant High School (Plate 242) was the grandest monument in the Athens of the North; his tiny Arthur Lodge (1827–30) ingeniously compressed the Grecian idiom into minute domestic scale. On occasion, Hamilton was prepared to draw upon both the Roman and the Greek traditions. His Burns Monument on Calton Hill (1830–32) combines the Lysicrates formula with details from the Temple of the Sibyls at Tivoli. His Dean Orphanage (1833) manipulates Roman orders with truly Hawksmoorian panache. But Greece was his first love: he also produced Lysicrates monuments in the orphanage cemetery and on the other side of Scotland, at Alloway in Ayrshire (1818–23). And it is of course the Royal High School (Plates 233, 239), by which this half-deaf, solitary genius will always be remembered. Its classical sources are straightforward: the Theseion (Plate 94), the Thrasyllus Monument (Plate 95), the Propylaea. But its dramatic composition, elemental and essentially romantic, make it—in Sir Albert Richardson's words—'one of the most superb modern structures inspired by Athenian models'. 'Hamilton', Richardson concludes, 'ordered his masses like a giant, arranging them as an integral part of the cognate rock which forms their setting, and employing a subtle curved frontage to embody the whole grouping. . . . He disposed his principal and subordinate masses with skill and regard for the maximum effect of light and shade. His genius resulted in a building containing all the attributes of the monumental'.

Hamilton's was an uncompromising, inflexible talent. Playfair was an architectural *politique*. After training with Stark and Smirke he spent some time in France before winning the competition to complete Adam's

Edinburgh University (1817–24). His minor monuments on Calton Hill—the Observatory (1818), the Playfair Monument (1825–26) and the Dugald Stewart Monument (1831–32) (Plate 238)—embody conventional classic prototypes: the Theseion portico (Plate 94), the tomb of Theron at Agrigentum, and the Lysicrates Monument (Plate 54). But his extraordinary church of St. Stephen (1826–28), in St. Vincent Street, combines ingenious planning with a novel fusing of Greek, Roman, Gothic and Renaissance: a synthesis worthy of Hawksmoor or Vanbrugh. And the twin Gothic towers of his New College (1846)—not to mention his miniature Baronial entrance to Heriot's Hospital—suggest an architect capable of submerging his classic preferences and exploiting to the full the many faces of Edinburgh's *genius loci*. Perhaps his Scottish Academy and National Gallery buildings (Plates 235, 236, 237) are less rigorously Athenian than Hamilton's stylophilous dreams (Plate 241)—at one point he even thought of crowning his Ionic portico with Corinthian tempiettos. But their dramatic contour and massy bulk have come to symbolize the Attic dignity and civic pride of early nineteenth-century Edinburgh.

Those qualities were above all to have been represented in the National Monument on Calton Hill (Plate 234). Conceived as early as 1817, it was intended to serve partly as a memorial to Scotsmen killed in the Napoleonic Wars, partly as a permanent Valhalla. Its model was the Parthenon. Its scale and situation rivalled Klenze's most monumental creations, the Rumeshalle in Munich or the Valhalla at Regensberg. The National Monument, in fact, marked the summit of Neo-Classical ambitions in Britain. And, appropriately, the subscription list was headed by the name of Scotland's greatest Romantic, Sir Walter Scott. The foundation stone was laid in 1822 during George IV's triumphal northern tour. In 1823 the name of the designer was formally announced: C. R. Cockerell, the prince of British classicists. After a good deal of in-fighting—Lord Aberdeen and Lord Elgin had supported Cockerell against the claims of rival Scottish architects—Playfair was appointed resident architect, narrowly outpacing William Burn, Gillespie Graham and Archibald Elliot. Work began in earnest during 1824 and continued for the next four years. 'It takes twelve horses and seventy men', Playfair told Cockerell, 'to move some of the larger stones up the hill'. But by 1829 the money had run out, and work came to a 'dead halt'. Only twelve columns had been erected. Despite several later schemes—by G. M. Kempe (1843), by J. Dick Peddie (1886) and by G. Washington Brown (1918)—the temple remained unfinished. The National Monument became Edinburgh's Folly—a symbol, as Playfair put it, of 'the pride and poverty of Scotland'. 'When the sun shines', he told Cockerell a little sadly, 'and there is a pure blue sky behind [the columns] (a rare event you will say) they look most beautiful, but surprisingly small'.

In many ways 1829 marked the zenith of the Greek Revival in Britain. The year which saw the collapse of the Scottish National Monument project also saw the construction of Sir Charles Barry's Travellers' Club in London—the triumph of Italianate over Greek. Edinburgh's Folly has come to symbolize the failure of the Neo-Classic ideal. Calton Hill might even be called the graveyard of the Greek Revival—were it not for the fact that there was more to Neo-Classicism than archaeology. After the heyday of Hamilton and Playfair the centre of Scottish Greek Revivalism switches back from Edinburgh to Glasgow, to the work of Alexander 'Greek' Thomson. In a remarkable series of churches, commercial buildings, villas and residential terraces built between the 1850s and the 1870s, Thomson realized to the full the rich potentialities of the Grecian idiom. Those potentialities were compositional rather than decorative. No doubt that would have surprised many of the minor practitioners of the art. Perhaps it still surprises their critics too—concerned as they have been too exclusively with the archaeological chrysalis of the movement. We must look beneath the surface of the style. And that means, first of all, boldly grasping an art-historical nettle: historicism.

The modern museum was very largely a Neo-Classical creation. Museums, art galleries, libraries and universities are among the most prominent examples of Greek Revival architecture all over the world. They stem initially from a late eighteenth-century cultural ideal: the Neo-Classical Temple of the Arts. Such temples expressed not only the catholicity of Neo-Classical taste but the Neo-Classical concept of the unity of art and science, the indivisibility of knowledge. In fact the Temple of the Arts perfectly expressed the historicist and didactic premises of Neo-Classical thought: a reverence for the creative achievements of antiquity, and a wish to display those achievements for the education of mankind—an ambition of the Encyclopaedist. In England these ideas were summed up in Sir Robert Smirke's British Museum (Plate 189), a Grecian shrine built to house, among many other things, the Elgin Marbles.

Both the Sublime and the Picturesque found uneasy expression within this general historicist framework. Both categories were, for example, reflected in miniature in that crowded microcosm of Neo-Classical taste, Sir John Soane's Museum (Plate 170). In fact the omniverous quality of Neo-Classicism is nowhere better expressed than in that strange repository in Lincoln's Inn Fields—and nowhere better described than in George Wightwick's memoir of his old master, the 'poor dear old tyrant', in *Bentley's Miscellany* for 1853:

> . . . a very odd shell—denoting the abode of a very 'odd fish' . . . 'here's something *original* at all events!' . . . although queer, the thing is unvulgar; eccentric, but not inelegant; fantastical, but refined. Museum-like in its non-descript character and its miscellaneous and fragmented appendages —and its Gothic bits, Greek caryatids, and Italian balustrades, mingle with original forms and details, the disposition of which manifest a singular union of niggardly simplicity with gratuitous ornament. But still more extraordinary than the exterior is the interior of this Museo Curiosissimo. It is, unquestionably, the most unique and costly toy that the matured man-baby ever played withal; and doubtless much within it is of high quality, great value and deep interest: but there is a positive sense of suffocation in the plethoric compendiousness, which distends its little body to the utmost endurance of its skin, and leaves scarcely any free way for the circulation of observance. The main sitting-rooms are reasonably roomy, but all besides is decidedly hostile to the idea of that practical freedom, signified by the asserted space necessary to those who are given to the *swinging of cats*. Never was there, before, such a conglomerate of vast ideas in little. Domes, arches, pendentives, columned labyrinths, monastic retreats, cunning contrivances, and magic effects, up views, down views, and through views, bewildering narrow passages, seductive corners, silent recesses, and little lobbies like human man-traps; such are the features which perplexingly address the visitor, and leave his countenance with an equivocal expression between wondering admiration and smiling forebearance.

In its mystery and variety Soane's museum was clearly both Sublime and Picturesque. But first and foremost it was an emanation of the historicist state of mind. And it is the phenomenon of historicism which lies at the heart of the Neo-Classical dilemma. The conjunction of historicism and the Picturesque finally broke up the Palladian hegemony. Archaeology supplied a new repertoire of styles. Associational criteria loaded their use with emotional significance. And Picturesque theory demanded their subordination to the pursuit of overall compositional effects. The results were frequently novel and dramatic. But Picturesque architecture—the architecture of Romanticism—also hovered on the brink of bathos.

Given the view that architecture was basically a rather permanent form of scenery, its design might easily become geared to the concept of the moving spectator. In 1815 Ackermann's *Repository of Arts* contained an amusing article by 'Scriblerus', a parody of the Picturesque based on the fictitious casino of Mrs. Mandeville, designed by Signor Alberti to unite *all* styles: 'The back elevation corresponded . . . with the principal front. [But] the Grecian order was here substituted for the Roman Ionic, rising from a rusticated basement. The East flank exhibited specimens of the Egyptian, Chinese and Moorish styles of architecture; and the West was designed in the Saxon, Gothic, and castellated taste'. Fact, however, was just as fantastic as fiction. Castleward, Co. Down (*c.* 1762), sports classic in front and Gothic behind. Smirke's Lowther Castle, Westmorland (1806–12) combines a baronial entrance facade with a Gothic garden front. Bretforton Hall, Worcestershire (1830) confuses Greek and Gothic in a curiously *insouciant* manner. J. B. Rebecca's Castle Goring, Sussex (1791–1825) is Greek at the back and Gothic at the front, and (unbelievably) Greek *and* Gothic at the sides (Plate 80). And Edward Blore's Woronzow Palace (1837–50) at Aloupka on the shores of the Black Sea—Tudor, Gothic, Baronial and Oriental by turn—carries the Picturesque principle of multiplied aspects almost to the point of pure fantasy.

In the long run the influence of the Picturesque destroyed the fundamentals of the Greek Revival. Talbot Hamlin's conclusion is damning: 'Greek Revival architects . . . made magnificent construction the basis for monumental effect . . . [But] the whole cult of the Picturesque was designed to disintegrate building techniques and lower building standards'; structure took second place to the pursuit of *effect*; hence the separation of architecture and engineering; 'it was a schism ideally fitted to the ideals and desires of eclecticism; but it was the death of the essential qualities of the Greek Revival'.

The full impact of this new historical approach was felt only towards the end of the eighteenth century. By then the concept of a plurality of styles had taken firm hold. And with plurality went relativism—the collapse of implicit belief in the authority of any single style. In 1800 J.-G. Legrand added this explanation to Durand's *Recueil et parallèle des édifices de tout genre, anciens et modernes*: 'Persian, Indian, Gothic, Saxon, German, Italian and French styles—architects ought to draw from all these sources. Their first task is to know, their second to compare and the third to select in order to apply'. Edmund Aikin was saying much the same thing eight years later: 'the age of invention has gone by, and that of criticism has succeeded. . . . Every style of architecture lies open to our choice, and there is no *prima facie* reason why one should be preferred to another'. Thomas Hopper, that Regency chameleon, put it more succinctly in 1837: 'it is an architect's business to understand all styles and to be prejudiced in favour of none'.

The arrival of full-scale historicism in England, that is the multiplication of stylistic choice, was signalled by one extraordinary architectural performance: John Foulston's strange group of buildings at Ker Street, Devonport (1823–24) (Plate 214). Foulton was primarily a Greek Revivalist, the Nash, the Soane and the Smirke of the West Country. But at Devonport he tried his hand at something different. Here no less than five styles were presented simultaneously: a range of terraced houses in Roman Corinthian; a Greek Doric Town Hall and Naval Column; an 'Oriental' or 'Islamic' or 'Mohammedan' Mount Zion Chapel; a pair of Greek Ionic houses; and an Egyptian Library, now rather appropriately an Oddfellows' Hall. Only the Town Hall, the Column and the Library survive.

What was Foulston trying to do? He himself called it an 'experimental group', and justified his action as follows:

> it occurred to him that if a series of edifices, exhibiting the various features of the architectural world, were erected in conjunction, and skilfully grouped, a happy result might be obtained. Under this impression, he was induced to try an experiment (not before attempted) for producing a

picturesque effect, by combining in one view, the Grecian, Egyptian, and a variety of the Oriental. . . . Oriental Architecture is [thus] seen in juxta-position with Greek and Egyptian . . . the author's intention being to experimentalize on the effect which might be produced by such an assemblage. If the critic be opposed to the strangeness of the attempt, he may still be willing to acknowledge, that the general effect of the combination is picturesque . . . [And] should the critic be indisposed to admit the full propriety of thus congregating in one view, several buildings of different styles, the author trusts he has [at least] preserved himself from the abomination of having exhibited a combination of styles in the same building. [For] a mixed style must be imperfect; the particulars belonging to the different styles being [themselves] at variance, like a monstrous union of the parts of one animal with those of another.

In short, Foulston was an historicist but not yet wholly an eclectic. And he was working within the context of the Picturesque. Part of the explanation of the Picturesque variation in this 'experimental group' lies in the fact that it represents not only a conjunction of styles but a conjunction of streets. The Town Hall was aligned on the axis of Ker Street; the Naval Column on the axis of Union Street—Foulston's 'new road across the marshes'—laid out in 1812–20 as a link between the two Plymouth suburbs of Devonport and Stonehouse. Like John Nash, John Foulston was both town-planner and architect. With Edward Lockyer of Plymouth eager to play the part of John Clayton of Newcastle, Foulston was more than able to take up the roles of John Dobson and Richard Grainger. As a town-planning exercise Plymouth certainly rivalled Newcastle and Regency London, in quality if not in scale.

But whatever its urban context, the Devonport group was essentially a stylistic exercise. The *Gentleman's Magazine* commented: 'the architect appears to have aimed at an unusual expression of versatility in his designs; his object being apparently to congregate in one town specimens of every description of architecture in the universe'. An American historian recently christened this process a symptom of 'symbolic eclecticism'. After the disintegration of the Renaissance tradition under the impact of Neo-Classicism, the resources of the past were beginning to be fully exploited. Architecture was starting to flex its muscles for the High Victorian Battle of the Styles. But as yet there is no conflict. Regency architecture, in all its chameleon variety, was an architecture appropriate to the age of Romanticism. Neo-Gothic, Neo-Classic, Neo-Egyptian, Neo-Oriental: styles equally exotic, equally remote in time and place, but not yet equally assimilated or equally understood. Classical architectural archaeology was still far more sophisticated than its medieval or oriental counterparts. Hence the greater authenticity and effectiveness of Regency Greek Revival buildings when compared with their stylistic rivals. Foulston's Egyptian Library may well have pleased Napoleon's Egypt-ologist Denon—we know it did—but less indulgent critics said it re-minded them of Piccadilly rather than Thebes. Foulston's 'Islamic' Mount Zion Chapel may have intrigued the Dissenting shopkeepers of Devon-port, but it would hardly have impressed a visiting Moslem.

No, the significance of Foulston's 'experimental group' lies not in its authenticity, but simply in its variety, its voracious historicism. It con-stituted a series of stylistic signposts, a collective portent of much style-mongering to come. George Wightwick, Foulston's successor as the West Country's leading architect, commented: 'the spectator will, no doubt, remark upon the singular commixture of styles, as shown in the proximity of the several buildings . . . which seem as if they had met in parliament to prefer the respective claims of their Greek, Egyptian and Oriental constituents. The assemblage, though strange, is certainly pictur-esque; and if we hesitate to recommend the repetition of such experi-ments, we are far from regretting, that in this instance they have been made'. In fact Wightwick undoubtedly envied Foulston's opportunity. In his own architectural phantasmagoria, *The Palace of Architecture* (1840), he sets out to create just the sort of fantasy Foulston was dreaming of, a veritable 'epitome of the Architectural World': Indian, Chinese, Egyptian, Greek, Roman, Romanesque, Norman, Gothic in all its forms, Tudor, Moorish, Turkish, Persian, Mohammedan, Palladian and Soanean—as well as Wightwick's own particular favourites, the Anglo-Greek and the Anglo-Italian. Moreover he dreams of moving on from historicism to full-blooded eclecticism: he actually combines all these different styles into one fantastic structure. The entrance to his dream-palace was

> a Portal of strangely compounded architecture—a *Masonic* riddle—teeming with multiplied significancy and exhibiting a kind of monstrous combina-tion, in which discordant features sought to harmonise themselves within a general outline of forced uniformity. The dark rock of India, the granite

of Egypt, the marble of Greece, and the freestone of Italy, and middle Europe, were here commingled; each compartment as distinct in form as in material, and the whole, in its conjunction, wearing an aspect which, at the same time, challenged admiration and defied criticism.

The Victorians had stronger nerves—and perhaps stronger stomachs— than the architects of the Regency.

In one way, however, early Victorian architects lacked the aesthetic courage of their immediate predecessors: they turned their backs on the search for new forms. It was one of the paradoxes of the Neo-Classical phase that the historic and the modern went hand in hand. Styles replaced style. A new relativism replaced the certainty of inherited forms. Historicism bred eclecticism. And out of this new synthetic process emerged the mirage which eventually haunted later Victorian architects: the dream of a new style.

During the Regency, several writers gave some thought to this idea, and the term 'modern style' appears frequently in popular journals. Modernism, it seemed, was essentially an abstract version of Greek Revivalism. As Aikin explained in 1808, 'the style of modern architecture is universally admitted to be founded upon what is called the antique'. Grecian buildings offered a more fruitful field for radical adaptation than Gothic: 'the builder of modern Gothic is naturally led to attempt deception; for in considering Gothic architecture, we never generalize the style and reduce it to elements capable of application to all kinds of edifices, like the Grecian, but we think of particular buildings, of castles, abbeys, or cathedrals'. In other words, Grecian sources might be translated into a modern language, abstracted, generalized, mingled and re-shaped anew. And certainly Aikin's villa projects have only tenuous links with antique prototypes.

This same process was most successfully maintained by at least one leader of the profession, Sir Robert Smirke. His 'Graeco-cubic' style— as at Covent Garden Theatre (1809) (Plates 180, 181) and in several country houses, notably Kinmount (1812), Luton Hoo (1816, much rebuilt), Whittinghame (1818) and Normanby Park (1821) (Plate 142)—was usually labelled 'modern' by popular critics. But this 'new Square Style' as Pugin christened it was essentially a negative performance—creation by subtraction: the elimination of superfluous ornament and the reduction of architecture to a series of geometrical shapes. Regency critics called it 'chaste'. Victorians called it 'insipid'. There was another, and harder route: the *positive* creation of a new style.

That was the dream which haunted Sir John Soane. In his work the uneasy marriage of historic and modern gave birth to truly prodigious offspring. Compared with Smirke or Wilkins, commented one journal, his works seem 'like the Arabian Nights' Entertainments opposed to Cocker's Arithmetic'. But despite his ingenuity, despite his essentially Neo-Classical attitudes, Soane never really shook off the compositional framework of his Palladian inheritance. As late as 1835 he could still describe with unwearied enthusiasm a re-vamped student exercise of 1779 for a royal palace in Hyde Park (Plate 177), a veritable feast of Roman and Renaissance—

> In composing this design, I laboured to avail myself of the advantages arising from the contemplation of the remains of the great works of the ancients, as well as the observations and practice of the moderns. With those feelings, I endeavoured to combine magnificence with utility, and intricacy with variety and novelty. Vignola's celebrated palace at Caprarola suggested the general outline of the plan; and the villa of Adrian at Tivoli, the palace of Diocletian at Spalatro, the immense remains of the imperial palace of the Caesars in Rome, the baths of the Romans, and the interior of the Pantheon, with its superb portico by Agrippa—exemplars of magnificence, intricacy, variety and movement, uniting all the intellectual delights of classical Architecture—were objects calculated to call forth all my best energies. The portico is copied from that of the Pantheon: in the centre of the building is a dome, under which is another, of a smaller diameter, leaving a space for the admission of light, after the manner of the *lumière mystérieuse*, so successfully practised in the great church of the Invalids, and other buildings in France.

Kaufmann comments tartly: 'The architect is right. There is almost everything in his project except John Soane'. Soane's greatest triumphs of invention were in fact reserved for interior design. In the decorative field—that is, in the surface expression of space and volume—his sheer virtuosity had no equal among contemporaries. Most spectators were both puzzled and horrified. One reacted to the Dulwich mausoleum-cum-picture gallery with incredulity:

> Now for the Picture Gallery! . . . What a thing! What a creature it is! A Moeso-Gothic, semi-Arabic, Moro-Persian, Anglico-Norman, a what-you-will production: It hath no compeer, there is nothing like it above the earth, nor under the earth, or about the earth. It has all the merit and emphatic distinction of being unique.

Here indeed was a strange presentiment of the 'morbid grace' of *art nouveau*, a similar portent of a greater architectural revolution to come—but in this case a portent which failed to produce the expected cataclysm. Historicism was not so easily absorbed. The Modern Movement was strangled at birth in the early nineteenth-century, and had to wait nearly one hundred years to be born again of steel and glass. Soane was essentially a late-eighteenth-century figure. He fits uneasily into the categories of twentieth-century functionalism. His handling of exterior orders is posthumously Baroque. His delight in the syncopated silhouette is essentially Picturesque—so is his concern as an interior designer with the interplay of sunlight and shadow and reflected space (Plates 166, 167, 168, 170). And his obsession with death and destruction—transmitted through the pathological imagination of Joseph Gandy (Plates 33, 34)—can only be understood in terms of the Sublime. Even Wightwick had to admit that his master occasionally overstepped the mark and wallowed in 'the madness of architecture'; and his final judgment on Soane could hardly be bettered:

> The buildings he has left behind him, as monuments of his professional skill and artistic feeling, are certainly the most unconventional that have been erected in our day. . . . He had neither the feeling of the Greek for simple majesty, nor that of the Roman for scenic grandeur, nor that of the Goth for picturesque effect, nor that of the schoolmen for precedent; but, on the contrary, he seems to have taken from each a kind of negative hint that operated in the production of a result, just showing that he had observed them and *used* them with a perfectly independent and exclusive regard for his own peculiar and personal distinction. The consequence has been that, if any one shall ask, 'In what style is such, or such, of his buildings?' the answer would be, 'It is . . . Soanean'. . . . But, though the most original of modern architects, it does not follow that he was supreme in power. . . . He had more fancy than what deserves the name of genius;

and even his fancy was limited, for he repeated himself till he became as it were the passive slave of his own mannerism. He had pliant ingenuity, not productive invention; the creative exhausted, he could but rearrange; his refinement tended towards littleness; he could not be vulgar, but he was impotent to command the homage of popular admiration. . . . However . . . with exemplary boldness, he struck effectively at the tyranny of precedent. . . . If there be little of his external architecture that is worthy of unqualified approval, there is much of his internal design, not only to be admired, but imitated. To compensate for frivolity and fantasticism, there is more than a balance of playful grace and studied elegance. In the disposition of his floor-plans he was proverbially felicitous. . . . In fine, there was virtue in his very faults, for they were corrective of those common-place proprieties which only retard the advance of invention and originality.

Wightwick's comments on the Bank of England (Plates 166, 167, 168, 169)—in the *Library of the Fine Arts* for 1832—are also worth pondering:

The Bank of England, like the volume of Shakespeare, exhibits faults that would damn professional mediocrity; beauties that ordinary talent may worship, hopeless of effecting their equal; and a character of originality and fanciful exuberance, which renders it at once the most novel and valuable example of architecture now extant. . . . Soane has here afforded us a most valuable store of principles, the study of which will in time have the same good effect upon Athenian bias, that the existence of Stuart's work has had upon the impetus given by Palladio. When we next erect a cathedral under an injunction *not* to employ the pointed style, let the architect visit with sleepless observation the interior of the Bank, of the National Debt Redemption Office, and of Sir J. Soane's residence in Lincoln's Inn Fields. . . . He is not to be . . . imitated with servile accuracy. In the activity of his fancy, and the boldness of his daring, he sometimes hazards more than he gains, and is oft-times merely eccentric. But the spirit of a new beauty, worthy of being classed with those of the standard varieties of ancient India, Egypt, Greece, and the middle ages, pervades a great portion of his works, and will no doubt, in future times, be duly estimated to the great benefit of the nation's taste and the high honour of the author's name.

Unfortunately, despite his genius, despite his professional status, despite the foundation of his own museum, Soane left no body of doctrine; he established no school; and in the history of British architecture his achievements remain unique.

In Soane's designs we can see—more clearly perhaps than in the work of any of his contemporaries—the different strands which together made up the Neo-Classical compound, that matrix of the Greek Revival: the worship of Graeco-Roman art; the excavation and systematic analysis of antique fragments; the pursuit of the natural and the primitive; and the synthesis of nature and antiquity, historicism and modernity under the impact of emerging Romanticism.

In short, Soane viewed antiquity through the eyes of Burke and Payne Knight, Winckelmann and Piranesi. But he had more in common with Vanbrugh—'the Shakespeare of architects'—than with Ledoux. He was among the earliest to utilize pure Doric forms. But not for him the geometry and disparity of the next generation of Greek Revivalists. Sculptural integration was still his ideal. 'An edifice', he told his students, 'must form an entire whole from whatever point it is viewed, like a group of Sculpture. . . . The Ichnography of many of our Buildings consists of a series of squares and parallelograms, and the exterior is formed of discordant parts without that due connection, so necessary to constitute an entire and perfect whole'. Hence his blistering attack on young Smirke's Covent Garden Theatre.

The controversy over Downing College (Plate 184) has long been regarded as a turning point in the history of the Greek Revival. So it was. But it required a major building in the heart of fashionable London to establish the style as the dominant taste of the moment. That building was Smirke's Covent Garden (Plates 180, 181), completed in 1809 and destroyed by fire in 1856. Designed as the largest theatre in Britain, the speed of its construction and the novelty of its design set new standards in metropolitan architecture. Its seven million bricks were laid in nine months. Its giant Doric columns, their diameter of 5 ft. 6 in. said at the time to be exceeded only on the Acropolis and at St. Peter's in Rome, opened the floodgates of the Greek Revival.

But the birth of the new theatre was surrounded by controversy. A furious debate ensued; it quickly eclipsed the furore over Downing College and it still reverberates among historians. First came the praise.

One journal, *La Belle Assemblée*, called the new Covent Garden 'the best thing which has been erected for many years. . . . A building of which Athens would not have been ashamed. . . . Like every true work of art, it does not command attention by its mere mass; the effect is purely given to it by the art, the harmony, the mind of the workman. . . . Smirke . . . has lifted the mass into lightness, and like the Atlas in the fable, carries it with majesty and simplicity on his shoulders'. The building's Parthenon portico became one of the sights of the capital. Just before its opening the architect conducted Queen Charlotte and the Princesses Augusta, Elizabeth and Sophia on a tour of inspection. He did the same for the Earl of Lonsdale and Charles Long, who 'were much pleased' with what they saw. Farington noted that J. M. Gandy 'spoke handsomely' of the design, so did Henry Blundell of Ince Blundell. While Sir Thomas Lawrence was 'delighted with it', announcing that there was not 'a build-ing in so pure a taste in London'. But the most extravagant praise came from a rather curious source, an aristocratic poetaster named Lord Edward Thurlow. Thurlow is now remembered, if at all, merely because his 'damned nonsense' roused Byron's scorn—'why *would* they let him print his lays?'. In a slim volume of verses entitled *Moonlight* (1814), Thurlow inscribed a poem *To Robert Smirke Esq. On his beautiful building of Covent Garden Theatre*. His laboured couplets praise

> The wondrous genius that these walls display,
> That speak thee, Smirke, and boldly I declare
> The faultless truth, the great Palladio's heir.

And he ends by linking Smirke and Shakespeare:

> Unbounded poet! Architect divine!

Such eulogies seem to have infuriated the 'divine' architect's old master, John Soane. The two men—Soane, mercurial and crotchety, Smirke phlegmatic and businesslike—were temperamentally incom-patible. After only a few unhappy months young Smirke had left Soane's office in Lincoln's Inn Fields and completed his training under George Dance. In this way Smirke absorbed not the synthesized classicism which Soane had himself inherited from Dance's middle years, but the Grecian geometry of Dance's old age. Anyway, Soane never forgot the implied snub. In February 1810 his fourth lecture as Professor of Architecture at the Royal Academy contained a celebrated critique of Smirke's Covent Garden. He complained that the façade bore no relation to the side elevations, and he produced two large-scale drawings to support this thesis. Calcott reported that 'this attack on the work of a living artist excited instant agitation, and hissing by some and clapping by others was the consequence'. At the instigation of Smirke's father, the Academy Council formally forbade any such criticism of contemporary artists. Soane replied by suspending his lectures for almost two years. Their resumption in January 1812 was followed by a ceremonial reconciliation between Soane and Smirke at a dinner held to celebrate the Queen's birthday. 'Mr. Smirke asked me to shake hands', Soane wrote in his diary, 'and at dinner I sent to him by the waiter to say that I wished to take wine with him, which we did'. But this gesture turned out to be no more than a temporary truce. In January 1813 Soane attempted to side-step the Council's prohibition. Smirke's father countered with 'A narrative of Soane's conduct', and incited the Council to pass a declaration that the Professorship of Architecture 'was vacated'. Flaxman counselled moderation, if only to prevent a constitutional clash with the Prince Regent. And the whole affair was eventually glossed over by the General Assembly. Smirke's reputation seems to have been enhanced rather than ruined by this episode. Two years later he was appointed Attached Architect to the Office of Works. His colleagues were Nash—and Soane.

Soane's was in fact almost the only dissentient voice amid rapturous applause. Was the applause merited? Was Covent Garden Theatre really a building of such distinction? Its exterior was ruthlessly simple: a combination of flat walls, unframed openings and minimal Grecian detail. The three doorways within the portico, and the corresponding windows above them, were flanked at ground-floor level by low arcades of segmental arches and on the first floor by windows with plain shelf-cornices and sills which formed part of a moulded string course separating the two storeys. The slightly projecting wings, formed by antae, were pierced only by niches containing seven-foot figures of Thalia (Comedy) and Melpomene (Tragedy)—this permitted the resumption of the full entablature which had been interrupted on either side of the portico by basso-rilievos representing Ancient and Modern Drama. A plain cornice, parapet, blocking course and surbase moulding gave the entire composition a heavy horizontal finish. Sculptured in freestone from Flaxman's designs, Comedy and Ancient Drama were modelled by Flaxman himself. Tragedy and Modern Drama by Rossi. All four sculptured sections survive today as part of the façade by E. M. Barry which eventually succeeded Smirke's. But the most striking point about Smirke's exterior was its clean-cut geometrical massing. Some modern critics would prefer to turn Soane's criticism inside out: the different sections of the exterior design are not encumbered by an overall decorative scheme, but boldly express the major functional elements of the plan.

The interior was one of solemn richness. From the vestibule, articulated by Doric piers of red porphyry, the grand staircase rose parallel to the auditorium between granite columns of the Ionic order supporting a ceiling coved and richly coffered. The landing, dominated by Rossi's Shakespeare in yellow Siena marble, gave access to the Saloon. And above that was the Upper Saloon, a strictly Grecian apartment with crimson seats set in bays marked off by antique figures raised on pedestals, and with Paestum columns at either end of the room flanking chimney-pieces in semi-circular recesses. The remainder of the space surrounding the auditorium was occupied by various staircases, lobbies and ante-rooms leading to the gallery, and to the public, private and royal boxes. Almost half the total area of the site was given over to the stage, and to the dressing rooms, prop rooms and other apartments for management and players. There were seats for 2,800 people and standing room for another 1,400. And the acoustics, ventilation, central heating and fire precautions were the most up to date available.

How then can we sum it all up? In several ways Smirke's design was certainly revolutionary. In certain dimensions it was the largest theatre in Europe. Its tetrastyle portico introduced the pure Doric order into the metropolis. The screenwalls disguising the shallow roof were perforated by semi-elliptical openings, a novelty which seems to have remained unique. And in general terms the design embodied a crucial compositional breakthrough. Kaufmann singled it out as a key to our understanding of the whole Neo-Classical revolution. He took the clash between Soane and Smirke as a symbol of the compositional battle between Baroque traditions and the rationalist premises of Neo-

Classicism. Whereas Summerson suspected that the episodic nature of Smirke's design had been due to 'a hasty decision', Kaufmann boldly explained the basic independence of each façade as a conscious 'stylistic symptom'.

Certainly Soane and Smirke represent different generations in their architectural attitudes. They both used Grecian sources; but they used them to a different degree and in different ways. Covent Garden sums up Smirke's austere and cerebral approach to the whole business of architectural design—its chilly rationalism has none of the *bravura* of Soane's Bank of England. In its emphasis on geometrical forms, its juxtaposition of blocks independently conceived, its almost cubic simplicity, Covent Garden Theatre embodied that transition from Baroque coherence to Picturesque disparity which formed the very basis of Neo-Classicism in Britain. In that respect it was one of the most significant buildings in British architectural history. And at a personal level it was also important. Dance guided young Smirke's hand. And Smirke in turn guided three still younger assistants who would carry the Greek Revival into the 1840s: William Burn, W. H. Playfair and C. R. Cockerell. Cockerell was then acting as a junior office clerk. His father told Farington that this participation was a turning point in his career: 'his son just then stood as it were doubtfully, whether he would go right or wrong; that fixed him'.

✳   ✳   ✳

Soane and Smirke each demonstrated, in very different ways, the potentialities of Neo-Classicism. So did Nash—but he also underlined some of its basic weaknesses. John Nash was by no means a dogmatic Grecian. In fact, he was a self-confessed eclectic. 'An Ionic is an Ionic', he once told James Elmes, 'and he did not care which one his draughtsmen used'. He assured Wellington that the Marble Arch was 'a plagiarism of the Arch of Constantine'. But despite its Roman ancestry, he told Flaxman that its sculpture was 'to manifest the gusto Greco'. When an assistant queried the accuracy of his drawings for some of the Regent's Park detailing he replied, 'Never mind, it won't be observed in the execution'. Such a cavalier approach to matters of detail was all part of the Picturesque malaise. And it was this subordination of Neo-Classicism to the Picturesque which particularly provoked a thoroughbred classic like C. R. Cockerell. Regent Street he condemned for its superficiality: 'all . . . done hastily —hastily thought, hastily executed'. As for All Souls, Langham Place, he thought it only 'very good for those who know nothing about it'. Still, the planning of Regent Street and Regent's Park is by any standards a major achievement. And to Nash must go the principal credit. In old age Cockerell lived happily enough in Chester Terrace. 'Nash', he grudgingly admitted, 'always has original ideas'.

'The Regent's Park', wrote a French visitor in 1844, 'is a scene of enchantment, where we might fancy ourselves surrounded by the quiet charms of a smiling landscape, or the delightful gardens of a magnificent country house'. It is still often hard to believe that Regent's Park is in the middle of London. There are tennis courts now where the Royal Toxophilites used to practise. An open-air theatre and restaurant occupy part of the premises of the Royal Botanical Society. But the Zoo is still there, and the lake, the canal, the trees, the villas—testimony to the genius of John Nash, creator of this *rus in urbe*. More than one-and-a-half centuries after its conception in 1811, the value of Nash's scheme is more obvious than ever. In Leigh Hunt's words, Regent's Park is a blessed 'breathing-space' holding back 'the monstrous brick cancer' of the metropolis.

Today the dominant impression is of an ornamental park, surrounded by stucco terraces. This is partly due to the formal flower beds added to the Broad Walk by W. A. Nesfield in 1863, and partly to the conversion of Burton and Marnock's Royal Botanical Gardens into Queen Mary's Rose Garden during the 1930s. Nash's original idea was very different. A rival programme by Thomas Leverton and Thomas Chawner had envisaged a gridiron layout on the lines of Edinburgh or Bath. Nash replied with a plan for redeveloping the Crown's Marylebone Park estate in accordance with Humphry Repton's doctrine of 'apparent extent': an irregular landscape, terraces overlooking a serpentine lake and canal, clumps of trees camouflaging no less than fifty-six private villas, plus one villa of royal size, a *guinguette* or pleasure-house for the Prince Regent, linked to Carlton House by means of a processional way via Portland Place and Regent Street.

In preparing this scheme Nash borrowed several themes suggested by John White's abortive plan of 1809, which in turn may have derived from an anonymous plan for the redevelopment of the Eyre estate published in 1794. Another possible source was Ledoux's utopian scheme for the salt-manufacturing town of Chaux, which appeared in print in 1804. In transforming the muddy fields of Marylebone into a smart residential area, Nash's criteria were 'open space, free air and the scenery of nature'. With these he set out to attract 'the wealthy part of the public'. And with fifty-six villas, more than a dozen terraces, a circus, a barracks, a church, a suburban palace, even a Valhalla, to say nothing of attendant shops, markets and model villages, Nash dreamed up the first garden city, the ancestor of Bedford Park, Hampstead Garden Suburb and countless visionary schemes. But his employers, the Crown Lands Commissioners, were more cautious. The character of the original plan was drastically modified. The Valhalla was the first to go. Then the *guinguette*. Then the circus. In 1811 the fifty-six projected villas were reduced to twenty-six. In 1823, twenty-six became eight. J. M. Gandy's design for a monumental villa for the Duke of Wellington was never executed. An extra six villas, linked in various ways to terrace blocks, were eventually added around the periphery of the site. But no more than eight independent villas appeared in the centre of the park. And of these only four survive: The Holme, Grove House, Hanover Lodge and St. John's Lodge.

Only one of the surviving villas was designed by Nash: Hanover Lodge (1827), an undistinguished Ionic building later altered by Lutyens. Before its reconstruction by Sir Charles Barry and Robert Weir Schultz, St. John's Lodge (1817) was no more than a small Doric villa in sub-Soanic style. The other two villas, however, were both designed by the young Decimus Burton and both illustrate the Picturesque potentialities and limitations of the Greek Revival.

When James Burton the master-builder chose The Holme for his own family he chose the best site in the park. When he handed over a few of the details of its design to his eighteen-year-old son he launched Decimus on a professional career stretching from the Colosseum (1823–27) (Plate 112), Hyde Park Corner (1825; 1846) (Plates 178, 179) and the Athenaeum (1827–30) (Plate 211) to Tunbridge Wells, the conservatory at Kew and literally scores of country houses (Plates 105, 108, 134). There is nothing very novel about the decoration of The Holme, and its unexciting plan fits comfortably into the tradition of modified Palladian villa design handed down by James Paine and Robert Adam. Decimus Burton was never a doctrinaire Greek Revivalist. The columns of the Athenaeum, for instance, are Roman Doric, not Greek. And the ground plans of both the Holme and Grove House betray the persistence of Palladian inspiration. Two fine features The Holme did possess, however: a grand Corinthian entrance portico and a domed and pillared bow window overlooking the lake. From the start the setting must have possessed an almost Arcadian quality. Criss-crossed by branches and framed by lakeside shrubberies, the view across the water is still one of the most romantic set-pieces in London. Grove House (Plate 104), however—once Greenough's Villa and now Nuffield Lodge—has a quality quite independent of its setting. The simple cruciform massing of Burton's original silhouette has gone. But inside his exquisite Graeco-Roman decor survives: anthemion mouldings and allegorical friezes, plasterwork, panelling and joinery, and most of all the superb central saloon, domed and richly coffered and hung round with Corinthian columns of the Lysicrates order. Its layout is compact and rational, a paradigm of neo-Palladian planning. Its decoration satisfies even the Regency's criterion of chastity. It is, however, essentially a modified Palladian villa in a Picturesque setting. Its Grecian manners are only skin-deep. And that was a trick only too familiar to John Nash.

Nash's Regent's Park terraces—notably Cumberland Terrace (1826) (Plate 113), Chester Terrace (1825) and Sussex Place (1822) epitomize the precarious balance between Neo-Classicism and the Picturesque. Their details are vestigially Grecian; their composition is posthumously Palladian; and their dramatic impact is largely dependent on scenic conjuring tricks. C. R. Cockerell saw through the illusion: 'The architecture of the Regent's Park may be compared to the poetry of an improvisatore —one is surprised and even captivated at first sight with the profusion of splendid images, the variety of the scenery and the readiness of the fiction. But if as many were versed in the Grecian rules of this science as there are in those of Homer and Virgil this trumpery would be less popular'. More pungently, Wightwick dismissed the whole operation as 'the very harlotry of art'. He was even more caustic on the subject of Nash's Buckingham Palace. 'Is it possible', he asked in 1832, 'that the same nation which has lodged the Marquis of Buckingham in Stowe House, the Earl

[sic] of Marlborough at Blenheim, the tax-gatherers in Somerset House, her madmen in New Bedlam, and her superannuated seamen at Greenwich, should provide for the metropolitan residence of his Britannic Majesty such a gimcrack as [this]?'. Certainly Buckingham Palace was Nash's Waterloo: Cockerell said that the porticoes were just arranged 'like scaffolding'. His slip-shod technique—to say nothing of his risky business methods—caught up with him in the end. Wellington was not the only politician who vowed to 'make a Hash of Nash'. But such performances were symptomatic of a *malaise* deeper and more general than any personal weakness. English architecture in the 1830s seemed to have lost its sense of direction. The Greek Revival was almost finished. And the Gothic Revival had not yet come of age.

In the gradual break-up of Baroque unities, the Grecian style had a twofold part to play. Its planar forms smoothed away the plasticity of Renaissance modelling. And its basic rectangularity dissolved the integrated rhythms of Palladianism into a series of geometrical shapes. This was the process begun by James Wyatt and continued by Dance and Smirke. None of these architects was solely concerned with archaeological mimicry. In Akenside's words, they sought

> In matter's smouldering structures, the pure forms
> Of Triangle, or Circle, Cube or Cone.

Smirke, for instance, as Sir Albert Richardson pointed out, was 'not content with the mere transcription of Classic orders', but set out to achieve 'original combinations of primary masses'. A new style was struggling to emerge from the historicist chrysalis. And a few of the results were extraordinarily interesting.

W. J. Donthorn, for example, a dim provincial architect, produced several designs of striking originality. High House, West Acre (*c.* 1829); Elmham Hall (*c.* 1825–30) (Plate 141), Pickenham Hall (1829) and Marham House (*c.* 1825–30)—all in Norfolk and all rebuilt or demolished —were all examples of Greek Revival architecture at its most rigid and doctrinaire. They combined archaeology and geometry with a boldness worthy of the more famous 'revolutionary architects' of Revolutionary France. A house of similar calibre which still survives is Cairness in Aberdeenshire (Plates 84, 85, 86), an extraordinary place designed in the climacteric year of 1789. Its architect was James Playfair, father of W. H. Playfair, an architectural miniaturist who exercised a major talent on a series of minor commissions. On this occasion his solid geometrical forms rival in novelty, if not in scale, the sternest fantasies of Ledoux. Such was the elder Playfair's Neo-Classical commitment to all things Greek that he even called his stables Hippodromes. Cairness made few concessions to Palladianism. Neither did Francis Goodwin's County Gaol at Derby (1823–27; much altered). There the primitive Doric assumed an heroic simplicity which was almost cyclopean, and the subsidiary features of the order were entirely eliminated in favour of gargantuan geometrical masses. Cockerell visited this alarming building in 1825. 'Saw it with pleasure', he wrote; 'Goodwin . . . is truly a man of genius seizing the characteristics of a style and applying them in the most powerful manner. [Even if] he is sometimes over-charged and caricatured . . . for raciness, invention, resourse, and sometimes for grandeur [he] beats anything'. In its heyday Derby Gaol must have been almost as Sublimely terrible as Newgate. No wonder Cockerell concludes: Goodwin 'is certainly not a gentleman in his works'.

But by far the most dramatic English performance of this kind occurred at Belsay Hall, Northumberland (Plates 144–147). In the Autumn of 1804 Sir Charles Monck Bt. (previously Sir Charles Middleton) set off for Athens with his young wife Louisa and spent a protracted honeymoon there. He returned in 1806 with a son named Charles Atticus and a portfolio of architectural drawings. In Athens he had been joined by Sir William Gell. And the designs for a new Belsay—to replace an earlier house of 1614—were in fact the joint work of Monck and 'Rapid' Gell, with later revisions of detail by John Dobson of Newcastle. The house was built between 1807 and 1817, but the decoration of the interior was not entirely finished until 1830. Belsay's Grecian pedigree is impeccable. The octagonal stable belfry stems from the Tower of the Winds; the great twin columns of the portico are modelled on those of the Theseion; the oak bookcases in the library echo details from the Erechtheion, and the honeysuckle frieze in the same room is copied from the Temple of Nemesis at Rhamnos. But all these sources are at most indirect. For Belsay is more than a collection of archaeological souvenirs. Here three major factors in Greek Revivalism are represented: the Anglo-French cult of the antique; the Franco-Italian rationalist tradition; and the empirical philosophy of the Picturesque. The layout of the rooms breaks loose from the conventional villa format and follows a Graeco-Roman peristyle plan. Each section of the design is ruthlessly stripped of Renaissance trappings and strictly governed by geometrical rules: the plan is exactly 100 ft. square, and Sir Charles Monck personally worked out each proportional ratio to three places of decimals. The honey-coloured stones were cut and chiselled almost as precisely as their Grecian prototypes. Finally, the setting of the house is essentially Romantic. Nowhere else in Britain is the Romantic basis of Neo-Classicism so clearly expressed. Now that Stratton Park (Plates 89, 90) has been demolished and Grange Park (Plates 96, 97) is doomed to destruction, the Arcadian vision of the Greek Revivalists is nowhere else so faithfully preserved.

Belsay's peristyle layout was not the least of its novelties. On the whole, unlike the Gothic Revival, the Greek Revival had little effect on domestic planning. That is, perhaps, a measure of the alien nature of the style. Writing in 1864, Robert Kerr noted in his *Gentleman's House* 'the Classic revival (of the pure antique) seems to have had no effect whatever upon domestic arrangement . . . notwithstanding . . . all the fervour of the Dilettanti . . . no endeavour of any importance was made to introduce into England the elements of the plan of the Pompeian house'. Presumably he had never been to Belsay.

Belsay was too extreme for most architects, and certainly too extreme for most patrons. Predictably enough, the austerities of such a style produced a reaction in favour of purely decorative forms. At one level, this craving for ornament was satisfied by the Gothic Revival, moving into its tractarian, ecclesiological or High Church phase during the 1840s. At another level, particularly in secular buildings, the Greek Revival gave way to a recrudescence of Renaissance classicism. And here three names stand out: Harvey Lonsdale Elmes, Sir Charles Barry and C. R. Cockerell. In their hands the Grecian style was transformed into a synthetic Renaissance mode which has been variously labelled Graeco-Roman, Italianate and Neo-Grec. A comparison between Wilkins's Grange Park (1804 onwards) and Cockerell's Westminster Life and British Fire Office in the Strand (1831–32) is certainly instructive. Barry's progress from Greek to Italianate is well documented, from the Manchester Institution (1824) to the Travellers Club (1829) and Reform Club (1837) in London, and so via Bridgewater House (1847) to Shrubland (1849) and Clumber (1857). But the transition from Greek to Graeco-Roman is expressed with even greater force in the development of a single building by Elmes: St. George's Hall, Liverpool (1842–54) (Plates 225–228). Elmes's original competition designs for the Assize Courts and Concert Hall (1839–40) are conceived in terms which are categorically Greek. Yet his fusion of the two buildings in a final design (1840) of monumental strength and grandeur shows the architect already moving away from archaeological restrictions. The rich polychromy of Cockerell's later interior, modified and completed after Elmes's untimely death, exploits to the full the plasticity and power of Graeco-Roman forms.

Nash, Soane and Smirke, the all-powerful triumvirs of the Office of Works, were the three architect-princes of the Regency era. Each in a different way stimulated the reaction which set in during the 1830s against their different interpretations of the Greek Revival. Nash discredited the Graeco-Palladian compromise. Soane discredited novelty for novelty's sake. And chastity was never quite the same after Smirke had finished with it.

By the end of the 1820s the transition from Greek to Italianate had already begun. Writing in *Bentley's Miscellany* for 1854 Wightwick re-enacts the scene of 1827:

> The pure Greek mania had now reached its highest pitch under the conduct of Smirke, Inwood, Wilkins, and Gandy, as illustrated in the New Post Office, . . . the British Museum [Plate 189], St. Pancras Church [Plates 26, 28], the Audley Street Chapel, the University Club House, and the design for London University [Plate 186] then progressing. Cockerell, D. Burton, and Repton, had coquetted it between Greece and Italy; Soane, between the Corinthian of Rome, and his own fancies in the Bank of England [Plate 166–70]; while Nash had influenced the public feeling in favour of Italian Design almost exclusively. But the spirit of an important change was now at work . . . St. Pancras Church . . . was the epilogue of the Greek play. . . . The sternly cold and correct Grecian of Smirke, the commonplace Palladian of Nash, and the fanciful originalities of Soane; the unmixable peculiarities, in short, of that great triumvirate which constituted the professional strength of the Board of Works, were all to be corrected, compounded and inspirited [by Sir Charles Barry], to the establishment of that feeling and learned accomplishment, which sub-

sequently produced the Travellers' and Reform Club-houses, and led the
way to the adoption of the Italian villa, with its Belvedere tower, and
pictorial irregular grouping of parts . . .

Barry's Reform Club palazzo of 1837 certainly marked the triumph
of Italy over Greece. That was the year in which the *Quarterly Review* felt
free to dance on the grave of the Greek Revival. 'In our suburban streets',
wrote J. S. Morritt, 'we have seen salmon and smoked mackrel lying in
stately funeral under Doric pillars, and tripe surmounted with metopes,
triglyphs, and guttae of the most classical proportions. In some of our
fashionable club-houses, after every interior accommodation has been
provided for the members, a portico is superadded, apparently com-
mensurate, not so much with the building itself, as with the unexpended
residue of the subscription, and adorned, like the family picture of Dr.
Primrose, with as many columns as the artist could afford for the money'.
The Greek Revival stood indicted of incongruity and superfluity—the
very vices which Francis Jeffrey had condemned in the furniture of
Thomas Hope as early as 1807. So much for the movement's rationalist
origins. 'Athenian' Stuart had perhaps foreseen the result. Replying to
Sir Joshua Reynolds's compliment on the publication of the *Antiquities
of Athens*, he wrote: 'I undertook the labour in the hope to discover the
principles on which the ancients proceeded, and I have drawn my own
conclusions of them; but I fear, Sir Joshua, that many will be content to
copy what they find detailed in this book, without regard to the *why* and
the *wherefore* that governed either the ancients or myself'. And J. B.
Papworth, retailing the story in 1822, felt obliged to add: 'The apprehension is verified by the practice of the day. . . . The Parthenon and
temple of Minerva Polias, the Choragic monuments, the tower of Andronicus; in fact, the contents of Stuart's and Revett's *Antiquities of Athens*
are over and over again copied for any and every purpose, and with these
the public are satisfied; and so long as the error endures, any man by that
work may set up for an architect, fearless of public condemnation'. James
Elmes, father of Harvey Lonsdale Elmes, came near to writing the movement's obituary: 'we had converted Greek Architecture into the most
humdrum sort of design. Nay it seems to have paralysed our powers of
design and composition altogether, so that the only alternative left was
to escape from it by plunging *headlong* into the Gothic and Italian styles'.

And so the eclectic reaction was born. By 1840 Grecian had become only one, and in many ways the least favoured, of several alternatives. When Wightwick published his *Palace of Architecture* in 1840 the comparative plates were greeted as a once-and-for-all revelation of the practical limitations of the Grecian style. 'Though we admire Grecian architecture as far as it goes', quipped *The Surveyor, Engineer and Architect*, 'we must confess that it goes but a very little way'. The 'portico makers' had had their day. Away with 'the frippery of the antique . . . Doric . . . starved into lankiness . . . Ionic, with "cropped ear" capitals', and all the *disjecta membra* of pattern-book Grecian. 'Pie-Crust' architects—'Column drawing automata' as *Fraser's Magazine* called them—were now in disgrace. W. H. Leeds dared to suggest that, in architectural terms at any rate, pregnancy was preferable to chastity. Grecian buildings, he concluded 'may be chaste, [but] as the man said of his aunt Deborah, they are so confoundedly prim and ugly that their chastity is proof against all suspicion'.

So the rise and fall of the Greek Revival is a story of slow gestation, explosive popularity and sudden eclipse. In fact the reaction against the movement was so swift and so complete as to require some explanation. It was not just a question of fashion. The revived Grecian style carried within it the seeds of its own destruction. Several of these weaknesses were pinpointed by contemporary critics.

The two most important defectors from the movement were Sir Charles Barry and C. R. Cockerell. Barry's rejection of pure Greek Revivalism came a little later than Cockerell's, and was appropriately more dramatic and more complete. On returning to England he paid respectful visits to Revett's Ayot St. Lawrence (Plates 14, 15) and Harrison's Chester Castle (Plates 171, 172, 175). He even designed in Greek, and in the Manchester Institution produced an Ionic composition of rare sauvity and sophistication. But in 1823, according to J. L. Wolfe, while designing Grecian additions for King's College, Cambridge, 'his feeling for the Greek received a shock from which it never recovered. Downing College [Plate 184] . . . struck him as utterly poor and ineffective. He felt that a Greek portico, exalted on a rock of Attica, was a very different thing from even its exact copy in the streets of London or the gardens of Cambridge. He began to perceive that the style was comparatively cold and insipid. Polychromy had not yet been received as classical—with sculpture and painting at command, his liking for Greek architecture might have lingered for a while. But he was already convinced that, for modern purposes, the style was not sufficiently plastic. It did not admit the arch, and the use of that he found was indispensable'. Plasticity and polychromy were to be his future yardsticks of excellence—not simplicity or purity.

Cockerell's dissatisfaction with the simplicities of Greek Revivalism began in fact as soon as he started to make serious designs of his own. The triumphs of Wellington over Napoleon brought talk, in 1814–15, of a giant palace for the Iron Duke, in the manner of Vanbrugh's Blenheim. As a young architect with his name to make, Cockerell could hardly afford not to compete. But when he sat down at the drawing board, he soon realized the difficulties involved in giving new life to antique form-ulae. At first he had no doubts about the choice of style: 'As there exists no original style of architecture in the present day and as whatever style is adopted must be imitation, there can be little doubt that the Greek as the most classical and convenient should be preferred'. So the Parthenon supplied the order. But more was required than mere transcription. 'If such a design was difficult to anyone', he wrote to his father from Rome, 'you may imagine what it was to me who have never attempted anything original before. I consulted every architectural work of Europe (they are all in the library here), and I would have consulted every professional man I could get at if there had been any whose opinion was worth having. Then I composed general ideas, and finally fixed on one which pleased Mr. North [later Lord Guilford] and several other persons to whom I showed it; but when I went into detail I found the difficulties increase immeasurably, and the notions which were plausible while they were vague could not be put into execution. Plan would not agree with eleva-tion. Doors and windows would not come into their right places. I invented roundabout ways for simple ends. In fact I worked furiously and for the first time realised the practical difficulties of the profession'.

Clearly Grecian sources alone were not enough. That 'little essay' proved to Cockerell 'the folly and impossibility of close imitation'. And when he came back to England he determined to break away not only from archaeology but from Smirke's 'provokingly rational' elimination of expressive detail. 'In my first works' he wrote, 'I appealed to Smirke in all things, and nothing but seven years freedom and travel could ever relieve me from the master's spell'. Instead of Smirkish austerity he dreamed of creating a fresh style, as eclectic as Adam's but twice as expressive, joining 'the richness of rococo' to 'the breadth and merit of Greek'. Cockerell's later eclecticism, painfully matured over years of study, combined Greek, Roman and Renaissance, English, French and Italian, with rare and consummate skill. His criticisms of the Greek Revival were therefore formidably well informed.

Predictably, Cockerell disapproved of Robert Adam. 'The Adamish . . . style', he complained, 'is well called the emasculate—there is no force, no vigorous effect'. He condemned both the 'embroidery' of the Adam manner and the 'chastity' of the subsequent reaction against it. James Wyatt's renunciation of the Adam manner, therefore—and his subsequent pursuit of plain geometrical shapes—hardly endeared him to Cockerell. Commenting in 1824 on Wyatt's design for Bryanston, Dorset (1778), Cockerell complained: 'there is a cold and old stateliness which appalls and awes me. Instead of having its roots and wings attaching it to the ground it rises like a great box dropped upon the ground. I think Wyatt was the first who moulded these boxes. . . . It proves to me that Wyatt is a secondary star, first man of his day, but hardly to be counted among the genii of England.' Although he admitted that Dodington managed to be both chaste and richly decorated, in general Cockerell condemned such cool exteriors as mere 'blocks of stone'. Faced with Dance's portico at Stratton Park (1803–6), (Plate 89), he curtly noted: 'something in the Barrack fashion'. At Dance's Royal College of Surgeons in Lincoln's Inn Fields, he readily admitted the solemnity of the columns, but denied their suitability: 'the Ionic portico [is] the gravest I have seen and most severe, [but] ill-applied to the thin paper-front of a House with which it has no connection'. Wightwick was even less polite about Dance's failure to integrate portico and facade: 'The most striking instance of Attic elegance, debased by meanness of application', he wrote in 1832, 'is to be seen in Lincoln's Inn Fields, where an Ionic portico of majestic dimensions and exquisite individual beauty, is attached to a front with which it has no more legitimate connexion than the helmet of Pericles with the head of a Quaker'.

In other words, Cockerell considered both the main elements of pure Greek Revivalism—archaeology and geometry—a hindrance to architectural development. Like Sir William Chambers—whom he admired—he refused to contemplate a static concept of architectural beauty. Progression and adaptation was the rule. Grecian, he believed, must form the basis of modern design both for historical and practical reasons. 'Its intrinsic beauty of style', he wrote, 'its simplicity and cheapness and analogy to the modern system of construction and fitness of the scheme to our purpose', made it far superior to Gothic. But there was no future in copying. Even the Scottish National Monument (Plate 234) he conceived as 'a *free Translation* of the original'. And there was also no future, he thought, in the chilly rationalism of Laugier. He regretted the elimination of all 'those floating amiable forms in which the seventeenth- and eighteenth-century schools abounded'. Surely, there was room for compromise. The need now, agreed Wightwick, was to 'contemplate English desiderata through Athenian media'. Cockerell put the matter more simply: 'You begin with Greek, and as far as example leads you all is well; but the moment there is [no design to guide] your own, it is trash. What is now most essential is to appropriate the Greek style and graft it on our wants and recast it for our necessities, the Italian architects did this, particularly Palladio'. Palladio he regarded as 'the greatest modern architect'. In that respect he was unique among the architects of his generation. Gandy called 'Palladio, Vignola and other ancient masters humbugs'. Wilkins once said to Samuel Rogers: 'Sir, I have the greatest contempt for Palladio'. To Cockerell such attitudes were mere 'ignorance', worthy only of 'coxcombs'. The Renaissance, for him, was still relevant. Hence his debts as a designer to Alberti and Sansovino, to Sanmicheli and to Palladio's Mannerist phase. Hence his synthetic approach at the Ashmolean Museum, Oxford (1841–45) (Plate 223): Ionic capitals from Bassae; Vignola's cornice from the Villa Caprarola; the Hellenistic trick—elaborated by Hawksmoor at Christ Church, Spitalfields—of puncturing entablatures with bold round arches. Cockerell did not reject the Greek Revival. He absorbed it. His criticism of Grange Park was constructive not destructive. Similar thoughts struck him at Deepdene. It was the inventiveness and variety of Hope's celebrated seat which principally commended it. 'Novelty', he concluded, 'has a vast effect in architecture.

. . . The Deepdene attracts in this respect exceeding . . . if the Pompeian can be so cultivated . . . it may supersede the Templar style in which we have so long worked'.

The 'Templar style'. That was the straitjacket which imprisoned so many Greek Revivalists. Confronted with the mighty portico of Wilkins's Grange Park (Plate 97), Cockerell delighted in its Arcadian qualities, but seriously doubted its relevance. 'I am sure', he wrote, 'that the grave and solemn architecture of Temples [was] never adapted to houses, but a much lighter style, as we may judge by the vases, the object being space and commodiousness'. Predictably, therefore, he found Wilkins's porticoes at Downing College (Plate 184) 'like a string of sausages'. And as for St. Pancras Church (Plates 26, 28): 'simple Greek, Greek, Greek—radiates bad taste thro' the whole; ignorance and presumption . . . [of] Mr. Inwood attempting to impose on one an idea of his importance. . . . Mr. Inwood and his boys . . . have tormented themselves to invent du nouveau and have planned a most minute research into every moulding. Wherever their authorities ceased they have as usual [run] aground. It is anything but architecture'.

There was in fact a good deal of force in the attacks of a rabid anti-classicist like A. W. N. Pugin. Perhaps 'thrice-cooked hashes of pagan fragments' was a little harsh. But many a minor Grecian must have inwardly writhed at Pugin's parody of an architect who 'works Stuart and Revett on a modified plan, and builds lodges, cemetery chapels, reading-rooms, and fish-markets, with small Doric work and white brick facings'. In Pugin's eyes, the whole system of architectural education—such as it was—had been misdirected. At the Royal Academy he found 'pagan lectures, pagan designs, pagan casts and models, pagan medals, and, as a reward for proficiency in these matters, a pagan journey! When the mind of the youth is well infused with contempt for every association connected with his religion and country, he is next sent forth to measure temples, and in due time, he returns to form the nucleus of a fresh set of small Doric men, and to infect the country with classical adaptations in Roman cement'. No wonder he was horrified when Cockerell's Ashmolean combined Neo-Classical heresies with obvious artistic talent: 'a man who paganizes *in the Universities* deserves no quarter'. And when he visited Birmingham, and saw Hansom's gargantuan Town Hall (1832–61) (Plate

222), he despaired at what he found: secularism, philistinism, capitalism and Greek Revivalism all compounded together into a fearful vision of a new and terrifying world—'that most detestable of all places . . . where Greek buildings and smoking chimneys, radicals and Dissenters are all blended together'.

Had Pugin confined his assault on the Greek Revival to the buildings themselves, rather than to their pagan origins and secular associations, his arguments would have carried greater weight. He had in fact two well-founded criticisms: unsuitability and monotony. 'Yet notwithstanding the palpable impracticability of adapting Greek temples to our climate, habits and religion', thundered the *True Principles*, 'we see the attempt and failure continuously made and repeated; post office, theatre, church, bath, reading-room, hotel, methodist chapel and turnpike-gate, all present the eternal sameness of a Grecian temple outraged in all its proportions and character'. And his description of Decimus Burton's new town *à la Grecque* at Fleetwood in Lancashire, certainly struck home: 'Fleetwood . . . is the abomination of desolation; a *Modern Greek* town is quite insupportable. I am sitting in a Grecian coffee room in the Grecian Hotel with a Grecian mahogany table close to a Grecian marble chimney piece, surmounted by a Grecian scroll pier glass, and to increase my horror the waiter has brought in breakfast on a Grecian sort of tray with a pat of butter stamped with the infernal Greek scroll. Not a pointed arch within miles. Everything new and everything beastly'. No wonder Pugin's followers declined to be seduced by the faded charms of the Arcadian dream.

Such criticisms were particularly directed against the school of Wilkins and Smirke. Smirke was at his strongest when he subordinated motif to mass. Wilkins was quite the reverse. His talent was for detail rather than composition. And when his particular brand of detail went out of fashion in the first years of Victoria's reign, his reputation slumped dramatically. By 1847 W. H. Leeds felt free to deliver a crushing verdict: the architect of University College (1827–28) (Plate 186) had been so obsessed by precedent that he was incapable of creating the unprecedented. 'Far better', he suggested, that the architect of St. George's Hospital (1828–29) had 'never seen Athens or Magna Graecia'. 'Infinitely better' too, for the architect of the National Gallery (1834–38) (Plate 229), 'if instead of labouring to convince us that the Temple of Solomon was a building of the Grecian Doric order, he had applied himself to more diligent and real artistic study at his own drawing board'. Leeds, indeed, was a prime agent in the destruction of the Greek Revival as a fashionable norm. A belligerent, snuff-taking, stuttering recluse, he belaboured Greek Revivalists unmercifully throughout the 1830s and 1840s. But it was left to James Elmes to deliver the *coup de grace*. Wilkins's buildings, he wrote in 1847 in the *Civil Engineer and Architect's Journal*, were 'all of one family, one school, one style—pedantry. . . . So much Greek, so much gold was a saying of Samuel Johnson; so much Greek, so much *cold*, was the practice of William Wilkins—for no liberty would he give or take, no line or member would he use but for which he could not find a precedent in some ancient Greek building—and the older and more formal it was the better. He was a Greek puritan and an archaic methodist. . . . Had he been a sculptor he would have cut off the Hyacinthian locks of the god of Day; he would have deprived Jupiter of his ambrosial curls, as Delilah did Samson—and sent them both into Olympus like a couple of Roundheads. . . . Should the Emperor of Russia, in imitation of the Empress Catherine, erect another ice palace at Petersburgh, no man could have executed the freezing task so well as the cold and chaste architect of Downing College. . . . Yet . . . [he was] perhaps the best educated classic that has honoured the profession of architecture since Sir Christopher Wren. Had the talents of Mr. Wilkins been directed solely to literature, Grecian archaeology, the higher branches of mathematics, or to an accurate delineation of those antiquities which he so profoundly admired, he would have obtained a higher standing among the great men of his country, than he does among its architects; lacking, as he does, the architect's greatest qualities—invention and freedom from pedantry. His was the very mummy of the art—as cold, as lifeless, and as much bound up by the bands of precedent'.

At least Wilkins never had to read such diatribes himself: by the time Elmes penned that caustic epitaph its subject had been dead eight years. Smirke, however, lived on into the High Victorian period—so of course did Decimus Burton—and year after year he had to endure the slings and arrows of outraged critics. His fall from grace really began with the controversy over the rebuilding of the Houses of Parliament after the great fire of 1834. Both William IV and Sir Robert Peel tried hard to secure him the commission without the trouble of competition. Pugin guessed as much, and reported to E. J. Wilson: 'that execrable designer Smirke has already given his opinion which may be reasonably supposed to be a prelude to his selling his diabolical plans and detestable details . . . his career has gone on too long and this will be a capital opportunity to show up some of his infamous programmes'. Smirke failed to get the job. But his career went on. And, throughout the 1840s, as Barry's star soared to its meridian, he was subject to a tidal wave of abuse. In 1844 the 'classic genius' of the Regency was publicly referred to as 'an architectural Lazarus'.

The Greek Revival certainly had a bad press from the Victorians. Crabb Robinson had prophesied that Nash's metropolitan improvements would 'give a sort of glory to the Regent's government, which will be more felt by remote posterity than the victories of Trafalgar and Waterloo'. And perhaps he was right. But by the 1840s such enthusiasm had completely evaporated. Pugin's generation condemned Smirke's London Bridge Approaches, Nash's Regent Street and the bulk of Bloomsbury and Belgravia as monotonous, insipid and specious. William White was not alone in thinking the cube 'an excruciating proportion'. Ruskin dismissed the 'proportion of masses' as 'mere doggerel'. There is admittedly a mechanical sameness about much Greek Revival work. In the 1830s English Architecture—as Wilberforce remarked of the Church of England—nearly died of dignity, and of monotony too. Smirke, commented the *Library of the Fine Arts* in 1831, 'seems to have got all his architecture "by heart", or rather by rote . . .'. And Wilkins openly admitted the same disability. When he was asked at Cambridge how he managed to design so much, he replied: 'it was possible to do a great deal by method'. By 1832 even George Wightwick, himself something of a hack, was complaining that 'every carpenter who builds a row of ordinary houses on speculation, gives them porticoes and Greek scrolls, honeysuckle ornaments, and sarcophagi . . . the display without the meaning —the semblance without the substance'. No wonder, his critics starkly muttered, Smirke was ambidextrous: anyone could draw those repetitious mouldings with either hand.

In his Edinburgh Lectures of 1853, John Ruskin heaped coals of fire upon the heads of the last exponents of pure Greek Revivalism—the architects of the Athens of the North. Edinburgh New Town he dismissed as no more than 'a wilderness of square-cut stone'. In his *Stones of Venice* (1851–53) he had already roundly condemned the classic style as 'utterly devoid of all life, virtue, honourableness or power of doing good. It is base, unnatural, unfruitful, unenjoyable, and impious. Pagan in its origin, proud and unholy in its revival, paralysed in its old age . . . an architecture invented . . . to make plagiarists of its architects, slaves of its workmen, and Sybarites of its inhabitants; an architecture in which intellect is idle, invention impossible, but in which all luxury is gratified and all insolence fortified'.

In 1884 comes the first hint of change. That veteran controversialist, J. T. Emmett, told his readers in *The Quarterly Review* that the recent surfeit of Gothic and Italian was enough 'to reconcile us with renewed thankfulness to the pure Greek work which we still possess from the hands of Smirke and Soane, Wilkins and—best of all—Cockerell'. But then Emmett always disliked being in a majority. Augustus Hare was much more typical. By the end of the Victorian period he considered the Regency quite beyond the pale. 'Regent's Park', he wrote, and 'the ugly terraces which surround it . . . exhibit all the worst follies of the Grecian architectural mania which disgraced the beginning of this century'. As for the Inwoods' St. Pancras Church (Plates 26, 28): 'The slight portico is quite crushed by a ludicrous tower, which presents two copies of the Temple of the Winds at Athens, the smaller on top of the larger. The interior is taken from the Erechtheion. The side porticoes are adorned with Canephorae from the Pandroseion. The utter failure of this church as a work of art, and its cost—£76,679—did much towards the great reaction in favour of the gothic style'. Such misplaced severity took a long time to simmer down. After the First World War Sir Reginald Blomfield —admittedly in a French context—was still talking of architects who lost their way 'in the catacombs of the Classic Revival'. It was not until 1914 that Sir Albert Richardson published his *Monumental Classic Architecture*. And it was not until the 1920s that Sir John Betjeman 'first found Cheltenham sublime'. Even today Sir John Summerson, having christened St. Pancras 'the queen of early nineteenth-century churches', still feels obliged to ask: 'what did the reproduction of Greek Doric ever do for English architecture except produce an affectation of modernity by being archaic and an affectation of refinement by being pedantic?'. The pendulum swings slowly.

*   *   *

One Victorian critic in particular has cast a shadow over our understanding of the whole subject of the Greek Revival. And his criticisms cannot simply be ignored. That critic was James Fergusson, one of the earliest and most articulate prophets of functionalism. His *History of the Modern Styles of Architecture* first appeared in 1862. As a popular textbook—supplementing his two volume *Handbook of Architecture* (1855)—it held its place against all competitors until the arrival of Banister Fletcher's *History of Architecture on the Comparative Method* (1896). Unlike Banister Fletcher, Fergusson made few concessions to objectivity. His very title characterized the whole of architectural history since the Renaissance as a procession of *styles*, an elaborate fancy-dress ball. His preface set out the basic reason. Architecture had ceased to be 'a quasi-natural art . . . carried out in every part of the globe on the same well-understood and universally acknowledged principles'. Its logical purity had been corrupted by 'individual tastes and caprices'. The virus of historicism had polluted the very springs of architectural design. The evolution of 'true styles' had been replaced by 'imitative styles', the production of counterfeit replicas. Architecture had lost its innocence and become a self-conscious parody of itself, constantly looking over its shoulder at the achievements of its own past. Fergusson's whole volume was, therefore—on his own admission—no more than 'a critical essay on the history of the aberrations of the art during the last four centuries'.

Such criticisms, of course, were not peculiarly applicable to the Greek Revival. The Gothic Revival, too, was formally anathematized: 'no perfectly truthful building has been erected in Europe since the Reformation'; since the Renaissance 'all architects have been composing in a dead language'; 'where Art is a true art, it is as naturally practised, and as easily understood, as a vernacular literature . . . and so it was in Greece and Rome, and so, too, in the Middle Ages. But with us it is little more than a dead corpse, galvanised into spasmodic life by a few selected practitioners, for the amusement and delight of a small section of the specially educated classes . . . [Such an art can never be] a living and real form of artistic utterance'.

Now, the traditional defence of architectural revivalism is based on the linguistic analogy: architectural forms—between the sixteenth and the nineteenth centuries—constituted an inherited language through which the architect operated, in the same way as a poet or novelist. Fergusson took this argument and tried to turn it into a stick to belabour the very revivalists who used it:

> What the Iliad and the Aenied were to Milton, the Pantheon and the Temple of Peace were to Wren. It was necessary he should try to conceal the Christian church in the guise of a Roman temple. . . . The sonorous prose of Johnson finds its exact counterpart in the ponderous productions of Vanbrugh, and the elegant Addison finds his reflex in the correct tameness of Chambers. The Adams tried to reproduce what they thought was purely Classical Art, with the earnest faith with which Thomson believed he was reproducing Virgil's Georgics when he wrote the 'Seasons'. But here our parallel ends. The poets had exhausted every form of imitation, and longed for 'fresher fields and pastures new', and in the beginning of this century wholly freed themselves from the chains their predecessors had prided themselves in wearing; but, just as the architects might have done the same, Stuart practically discovered and revealed to his countrymen the beauties of Greek Art. Homer and Sophocles had long been familiar to us; —the Parthenon and the Temple on the Ilissus were new. The poets had had the distemper; the architects had still to pass through it; and for fifty long years the pillars of the Parthenon or the Ilissus Temple adorned churches and gaols, museums and magazines, shop fronts and city gates— everything and everywhere. At last a reaction set in against this absurdity; not, alas, towards freedom, but towards a bondage as deep, if not so degrading—[the Gothic].

Well, Fergusson pressed his case too hard. Neither the ablest Greek Revivalists, nor the ablest Gothic Revivalists, can be dismissed as mere pedantic copyists. And Fergusson almost admitted as much in his rather more sympathetic treatment of the Renaissance. He attempted to distinguish between the classic revival of the Renaissance and the Classical Revival of the eighteenth and nineteenth centuries on the grounds that, in the latter case alone, revivalism equalled reproduction:

> St. Peter's and St. Paul's though using Classical details, and these only, are still essentially Christian churches; the Escurial and Versailles are the resi-

dences of kings of the age in which they were built, and do not pretend to be anything else. No one could ever mistake St. Peter's for a Roman Temple; and Versailles is as unlike the Palace of the Caesars as any two buildings could well be. . . . But the Walhalla pretends to be an absolute and literal reproduction of the Parthenon; so does the Madeleine of a Roman Temple; and the architect has failed in his endeavours if you are able to detect in St. George's Hall, Liverpool, any feature which would lead you to suppose the building might not belong to the age of Augustus. . . . The architects of the Renaissance had a distinct principle before them, which was, how to adapt Classical details so as to make them subservient to modern purposes. . . . If the Revival architects have a principle, it is that modern purposes should be made subservient to foregone architectural styles.

That, of course, is an exaggeration. Fergusson emphasized only one half of the Neo-Classical equation—archaeology—and neglected the other—rationalist theory. Had he ever heard of Laugier? And how would he have countered Laugier's triple argument based on stylistic evolution, apparent utility and expressive ornament? Still, Fergusson was quite right in believing that at some point during the Neo-Classical phase the precarious balance between imitation and invention had been upset by the popularity of associative values.

Once the fashion was introduced it became a mania. Thirty or forty years ago no building was complete without a Doric portico, hexastyle or octastyle, prostylar or distyle in antis; and no educated man dared to confess ignorance of a great many very hard words which then became fashionable. Churches were most afflicted in this way; next to these came Gaols and County Halls,—but even Railway Stations and Panoramas found their best advertisements in these sacred adjuncts; and terraces and shop fronts thought they had attained the acme of elegance when either a wooden or plaster caricature of a Grecian order suggested the classical taste of the builder. In some instances the founders were willing to forego the commonplace requirements of light and air, in order to carry out their classical aspirations; but in nine cases out of ten a slight glance round the corner satisfies the spectator that the building is not erected to contain a statue of Jupiter or Minerva, and suffices to dispel any dread that it might be devoted to the revival of the impure worship of Heathen deities.

In brief, the symbolic had become more important than the tectonic. 'Geometrical mania' gave way to a new spasm of style-mongering. Kaufmann describes this process as 'the disguising of novel geometric forms with pseudo-classical apparel'. Smirke would have thought it architectural transvestism. Instead of following the logic of Neo-Classicism towards the goal of modernity, architects fell back on the comforting thought that attempts to discover a wholly new style were no more likely to be successful than the search for a fourth primary colour. In a way this was the inevitable result of a basic flaw in Neo-Classical theory. Laugier's doctrine of 'apparent utility', as adapted by Neo-Classical architects, was rationalist rather than functionalist. It made for a system of design aptly described by Sir John Summerson as 'subjunctive': architecture 'as if'. As the nineteenth century progressed the disparity between fact and fiction, structure and decoration, became more and more pronounced. Smirke's designs may have been borne up by Gallic logic, but they also depended on cast iron and concrete. Lodoli's thought had in fact anticipated this situation: if the material changes, so also must the system of expressive ornament. And Cockerell was aware of such implications. He recorded a conversation with his friend Sanford in 1822 as follows: 'Sanford's conversation on architecture, the common cant, why should we follow eternally the same round of architecture, why repeat the same thing, why should not genius invent a new order—why, because the materials, necessities and uses, principles of strength and stability must be ever invariable'. Now, even in 1822, that was not quite true. And Cockerell's irritation indicates an inner measure of doubt: Nash and Smirke were already experimenting with cast iron beams. In a conversation with Brönstedt in 1826 he 'instanced the impropriety of making a Grecian column in iron because its proportion is adapted to marble or stone in which the mind finds a correct adjustment of the strength of material to the weight to be carried—but if the strength of the material as in iron is quadrupled (or even in larger proportion) there is a manifest waste of strength and superfluous application of means to end'.

But neither Nash, Smirke nor Cockerell could bring themselves to abandon an architectural vocabulary geared first to wooden and then to masonry construction—nor, for that matter, could any other Neo-Classicist. Nash, of course, didn't care. Smirke buried his doubts beneath the burden of his own success. And Cockerell allowed the romantic elements in his own nature to override the classical. So the gap between form and function began to widen. And it was a division accelerated by the popularity of revivalist decor. Popularity eventually killed the Greek Revival by making motif more important than mass. The archaeological element in the equation became more important than the experimental. J. C. Loudon rushed in where even Nash had feared to tread. And third-rate architects like Edwin J. Dangerfield made their fortune with classical conglomerates like the Clock Tower at Herne Bay (1837) (Plate 213).

But when Fergusson came to the point, and stopped belabouring both Gothic and Classic, and tried to suggest an alternative, a style suitable to the second half of the nineteenth century, he himself could only fall back on the Renaissance. Even in America he found no clue to the great conundrum. Even in the New World he found the same historicist obsessions writ large: 'whatever faults we have committed in this respect, the Americans have exaggerated them'. Despairing equally of both combatants in the Battle of the Styles, he turned to 'a "tertium quid", a style which, for want of a better name, is sometimes called the Italian, but should be called the common-sense style'. And this 'compromise between classicality and commonsense' was peculiarly suitable precisely because of its imperfections. 'Never having attained the completeness which debars all further progress, as was the case in the purely Classical or in the perfected Gothic styles, it not only admits of, but insists on, progress. . . . It can use either pillars or pinnacles as may be required. It admits of towers, and spires, or domes. It can either indulge in plain walls, or pierce them with innumerable windows. It knows no guide but common sense, it owns no master but true taste . . . and more than this, it requires thought, where copying has hitherto sufficed'.

And so, when it came to the acid test, when the great panjandrum himself had to design a building—the tiny Marianne North Gallery (1882) in Kew Gardens, for example—he adopted an emasculated Renaissance style, free of symbolic absurdities, and largely free of architectural merit. In other words, Fergusson was as much the victim of circumstances as the revivalists he attacked: he succeeded in impaling himself on his own barbed phrases. Historicism was *the* Victorian style; and Fergusson, whether he liked it or not, was a Victorian through and through—his own encyclopaedic volumes were a triumph of that historical process of thinking which he affected to despise.

As for Fergusson's general accusation of classical copyism, the answer to that easy gibe had already been suggested by Piranesi and Robert Adam. Piranesi urged that in borrowing from ancient art one ought to show oneself 'of an inventive, and I had almost said, of a creating genius'. 'Rules often cramp the genius', wrote Adam; genius must have liberty 'to transform the beautiful spirit of antiquity with novelty and variety'. But Fergusson did not live long enough to receive a real answer from Sir Edwin Lutyens, the last great exponent of the British classical tradition. In two letters of 1903 to Sir Herbert Baker, he reminds us of the crucial difference between copying and re-creating:

> That time-worn doric order—a lovely thing—I have the cheek to adopt. You can't copy it. To be right you have to take it and design it. . . . You cannot copy: you find if you do you are caught, a mess remains.
>
> It means hard labour, hard thinking, over every line in all three dimensions and in every joint; and no stone can be allowed to slide. If you tackle it in this way, the Order belongs to you, and every stroke, being mentally handled, must become endowed with such poetry and artistry as God has given you. You alter one feature (which you have to, always), then every other feature has to sympathise and undergo some care and invention. Therefore it is no mean game, nor is it a game you can play lightheartedly . . . You cannot play originality with the Orders. They have to be so well digested that there is nothing but essence left. When they are right they are curiously lovely—unalterable as plant forms . . . The perfection of the Order is far nearer nature than anything produced on impulse or accident-wise.

That was the true voice of Neo-Classicism, belated but true none the less. Laugier and Cockerell could themselves have said no more. The Greeks had a word for it: *mimesis*, creative imitation. And it is within the context of the mimetic process that the architecture of the Greek Revival must be judged. As a movement it lacks a logical epilogue. The 'first revolution' at the end of the eighteenth century remained unfinished. The 'second revolution' at the end of the nineteenth century was still a long way off. Kaufmann's 'revolutionary patterns' were 'engulphed' in a 'deluge of forms'. The romantic strand in the creative process had temporarily overwhelmed the classic. The Modern Movement had to wait. But to dismiss the bulk of the nineteenth century as a revivalist interlude —and therefore, necessarily, an age of decline—is to pervert the whole process of historical judgment. To condemn C. R. Cockerell—even by implication—for not building like Mies Van Der Rohe is as foolish as condemning George III for not ruling like George VI.

Fergusson's final shot—a would-be trump card he inherited from Ruskin—was the claim that classicism was a mandarin style, the prerogative of an educated elite, without appeal to the man in the street. That criticism has turned out to be a double-edged weapon. A hundred years later, when Fergusson's functionalist dream has become the air-conditioned nightmare, that same man in the street longs only to escape into the kinder world of yesterday's styles. As we move into a Neo-Romantic phase, Fergusson's rationalism seems rather less appealing than the romantic symbolism against which he fought. The Romantics look like having the last word—even if the language they use is no longer Neo-Classical.

Nevertheless, it is undeniable that the Greek Revival has had few public supporters in England since its eclipse in the 1830s. Perhaps after all it was too much of an alien style, imperfectly assimilated and inadequately understood. All stylistic revivals suffer similar disabilities. Kaufmann summed up the problem as follows: 'Forms and system . . . become antagonistic when forms of an earlier system recur in a later one because of some new scholarly interest in them, or for some other extra-artistic reason. This is why we have the feeling of something unsound in every revival, or even of something insane. Forms recur; systems don't. Through the centuries Greek forms were applied again and again, but never in later times were homes arranged in the Greek manner, just as mankind may eventually copy institutions like the archonate, the consulate, or the senate, but never again live under Athenian or Roman law'. True enough. But the Greek Revival also suffered from disabilities which were peculiar to itself. As Payne Knight pointed out, there was always something rather incongruous about

> . . . poor Baalbec dwindled to the eye
> And Paestum's fanes with columns six feet high.

Unlike the Gothic Revival, the Greek Revival lacked indigenous roots. Unlike the Palladianism of the eighteenth century, it lacked the accumulated riches of a continuously evolving system. Unlike the Oriental and Egyptian Revivals, it lacked even the alibi of escapism. Imported into England, its transplantation was a risky operation, and its flowering brief and dramatic—as befitted an exotic from the Aegean. But there the simile must end. For the Greek Revival flourished longest and most fruitfully not in fashionable southern England—where it was quickly eclipsed by the Italianate—but among the smoke and mist of Scotland. And it was in fact in Scotland—even while Fergusson was hailing the collapse of the movement—that the Greek Revival produced its eponymous hero: 'Greek' Thomson.

Alexander Thomson was not a copy-book Greek. Yet he was sufficiently Grecian to justify his title. He held steadfast to the laws of Grecian building, but he ignored the rules of mere revivalism. Even more than Cockerell he was an eclectic. The ancient world was his quarry—Greece, Egypt, Syria, India—but copying played no part in his process of design. Fergusson he must have known by heart—both Fergussons: the historian and the aesthetic philosopher. He played Fergusson at his own game—absorbing old styles in pursuit of new—and he won. He too dared to ask: 'How is it that there is no modern style of architecture?'. But unlike Fergusson, he set about supplying a tangible answer. When William Burges urged his pupils to 'devote some time to the drawings of Mr. Thomson of Glasgow', he added: 'they represent buildings in Greek architecture, but certainly the best modern Greek architecture it has ever been my lot to see'. His ambition was the same as Schinkel's: 'to build not as the Greeks built, but as they would have built had they lived now'.

Thomson was a self-taught Grecian. He had no formal academic training, and never visited Greece. His inspiration came not from Greece but from the Greek Revival itself, its publications and its monuments. For him Hamilton's High School (Plates 233, 239) and Elmes's St. George's Hall (Plates 225–28) were the acme of architectural design. But his range of experience scarcely extended even to Edinburgh and Liverpool. He spent all his life in Glasgow. He was steeped in its Grecian traditions; and all around him, he found antique echoes in the streets of his native town: the Agora and the Thrasyllus Monument in John Taylor's Custom House (1840); the Ilissus Temple in old Wellington Street Church; the Tower of the Winds in the corner houses at St.

George's Cross; the Lysicrates Monument in the Merchant's House in Hutcheson Street; the Erechtheion in Archibald Elliott Jnr.'s Royal Bank of Scotland (1827) (Plate 246); and the Parthenon in William Stark's dour Court House (1807–14) (Plate 182). From the larger world of High Victorian architecture Thomson stood aloof. Hibbert's extraordinary Harris Library and Museum at Preston (1822–93) (Plate 190) has no connection with him: it belongs to neither the English nor the Scottish tradition. That was why Goodhart-Rendel included Thomson in his gallery of 'Rogue Architects'. 'His knowledge', wrote Lionel Budden, 'was for the most part empyric and gained with infinite difficulty. He stood alone both in philosophy and practice'. His gods were Hamilton, Playfair, Schinkel and Klenze. His masters, if any, were local men like John Baird and Charles Wilson. His genius was his own.

Thomson will of course always be remembered for three Glasgow buildings: the United Presbyterian churches at Caledonia Road (1856–57), St. Vincent Street (1857–59), and Queen's Park (1867–69). Three comments will have to suffice.

First, Queen's Park Church (Plate 46), now demolished:

> The forms are modelled with a sole regard to their aesthetic impact on the imagination. . . . The long line of the ground storey, with its simple pilasters, cut by the mighty entrance, with the three deep shadows above the entablature; the plain wall surface of the frontispiece, with that most remarkable motive of the four truncated columns; the flat band with rosettes surrounding them, instead of the ordinary architraves—all these are means designed with rare subtlety to create in the imagination the impression of massive strength and the sense of mystery that seemed to Thomson inherent in the idea of a temple. . . . His enthusiasm was for the abstract possibilities of his art. . . . The barbaric colonnettes, the dwarf antae, and the strange door heads are themselves grotesquely disharmonic. Yet the greatness of Thomson's intention prevails. . . . His grimly intellectual insistence on the power of dead-weight construction to achieve the most titanic results was too vital a thing in its realisation to be obscured by adventitious excrescences. His work is effective out of all proportion to its size, though the scale is never forced. Thomson naturally thought in the Grand Manner, and the quality of his genius asserts itself in the large facility of his massing. [Sir Reginald Blomfield.]

Second, St. Vincent Street Church (Plate 43), now the home of the Spiritualist National Church:

The site of St. Vincent Street, which Thomson handled with spectacular drama, is the first ingredient of his success there. Since the land falls steeply both to the west and more particularly to the south, a large substructure had to be built up. This was turned into a gigantic plinth which juts out from the side of the hill in imitation, surely of the substructure of the Parthenon, or at least the temple of Nike Apteros. This 'plinth' contains in fact the ground floor of the church . . . but it appears as an unusually large foundation for the temple which stands above. This temple has columns only at its ends; for along the sides, below a row of square clerestory windows, are 'aisles' with nearly continuous glazing divided only by pairs of coupled square columns. Near each end of the outer aisle walls is added one of Thomson's strangest and most arresting devices, a tall, nearly rectangular pylon imposed on the outside of the coupled colonnade and rising well clear of the cornice; the slight batter of the uprights of these pylons gives a distinctly Egyptian effect. . . . The appearance of great strength in the substructure is reinforced by the treatment of the lower windows. A band of stonework five courses deep is recessed all round the church: into this is set a continuous projecting band of stone in the form of a square zig-zag, rather like a very elementary key-pattern. The square spaces between the uprights of the pattern are filled alternately with windows and blank panels: the uprights act as window jambs, the horizontals as lintels to the windows (which have no projecting sills) and sills to the panels (which have no projecting lintels). Since the windows are set very deep, there is heavy cast shadow between the uprights: the effect is unusually massive. Above all is the nearly indescribable steeple. This begins on a plain tower, square in section, near the top of which is, on each side, a large T-shaped opening, in the horizontal part of which are inset two Egyptianesque caryatids in the form of sideways-facing busts which support the lintel. Above this the tower has four small, slightly bulging corner turrets which end in pinnacles. Between the pinnacles is a cylindrical drum flattened on four sides with a recurrence of the pylon motif used at the ends of the aisles . . . The drum is topped with a cylindrical peristyle which has columns in the shape of fat cornshocks or shaving brushes. Finally, the dome is like a long-drawn-out policeman's helmet with a kind of sugar castor on top, for which the inspiration appears to be Hindu. It is all—intentionally of course—very odd, Thomson's most extravagant and capricious display of the heterogeneous motifs which continued to fascinate him all his life. [Andor Gomme and David Walker.]

And thirdly, Caledonia Road Church (Plates 42, 44, 45):

A compelling overall logic pulls it together. What strength comes from the placing of the doorways and the alternating broad and narrow bands of stone! What a perfect sense of balance one has, as one looks at the church from its main viewpoint, the south-east! How sure is Thomson's eye in relating the height of his asymmetrically placed tower to the horizontal lines of the street front to the right! How convincingly the mass of the 'temple' helps in the linking of the vertical and horizontal accents which, without it, would be far too starkly juxtaposed! And how much Thomson has made of so unpromising a site! It is one of Glasgow's greatest buildings—indeed one of the greatest nineteenth century buildings anywhere. [Andor Gomme and David Walker.]

A new world is already visible in Thomson's work. In Kaufmann's Darwinian conspectus—from Ledoux to Corbusier—'Greek' Thomson is surely the 'missing link'. His Picturesque villas—notably 25, Mansion House Drive, Langside (1856) (Plate 162) and Holmwood, Netherlee Road, Cathcart (1856–58) (Plate 160)—seem to anticipate the young Frank Lloyd Wright. His domestic terraces—notably Moray Place (1859) (Plate 158) and Great Western Terrace (1869)—solve the conundrum that puzzled Nash by combining logical planning with Grecian details and modernistic, geometrical forms. His commercial designs—notably Grosvenor Building (1859), Buck's Head Building (*c.* 1863) and Egyptian Halls (1871–73) (Plate 249)—incorporate vertical metal stanchions and horizontal glazing bands in a way that seems almost to prophesy the early Chicago School. And in all his work his bizarre detail, his free handling of form, his penchant for the interpenetration of spatial elements—all these anticipate some of the qualities of *art nouveau*. In 1890, fifteen years after his death, the Alexander Thomson Travelling Studentship was appropriately won by C. R. Mackintosh. Thomson's work looked forwards and backwards: he anticipates some of the ideas of the Modern Movement, and he justifies the ideals of the Greek Revival. He seized upon the trabeated unit of the Grecian style as a formula capable of indefinite extension in an age of cast-iron and glass. By spurning all use of the arch, he chose to fight his architectural battles with one hand tied behind his back. He even believed that Stonehenge was 'more scientifically constructed than York Minster'. But within the limits of his chosen medium 'Greek' Thomson was unbeatable.

Sir Reginald Blomfield's judgement of 1904 is still worth quoting:

Thomson . . . was possibly the most original thinker in architecture of the nineteenth century . . . born with a deep and tenacious instinct for form . . . he turned his back on the architectural excesses of his youth and deliberately settled down to abstract . . . composition. While most of his contemporaries were scratching about in the rubbish-heaps of medieval detail, Thomson was soaring aloft in the spacious solitudes of pure architecture . . . he possessed an extraordinary power of handling large architectural forms; that is, he thought out his ideas in blocks and masses of building, not piecemeal in detail. . . . Occasionally his fancy ran riot in barbarisms . . . his . . . details [are often] . . . surprisingly bad. Nor, again, does he seem to have had the instinct of the great constructor . . . the arch he abhorred. . . . His methods are of primitive simplicity—those of the Greek builders in fact, and only practicable with the splendid stone at his disposal. But where Thomson was strong, with a strength sometimes amounting to genius, was in his mastery of abstract form. . . . Thomson was a prophet, and too far ahead of his time. At a period when the Gothic infatuation was at its height, when the revivalist architect was raging up and down the length of the land, and the rising generation was busily occupied with the skilful reproduction of its own sketch-books, this solitary Scotchman made his stand for the art of architecture single-handed. . . . He made no secret of his convictions . . . that architecture is something more profound than archaeological scene-painting, and . . . that the ideal of the upholsterer's shop is not the ideal of architecture.

Just how cut off from the rest of his profession Thomson became is demonstrated by two designs which he prepared towards the close of his career. In the first, his unsubmitted scheme for the Albert Memorial (1861), he produced a Graeco–Egyptian fantasy which comes closer to the sublimity of John Martin than to the quieter world of Gilbert Scott— the architecture of *Pandemonium*, in fact, miraculously implanted in Hyde Park. In the second, his defeated proposal for the Natural History Museum at Kensington (*c.* 1863), he produced a gigantic echo of Hamilton's High School, Klenze's Valhalla and Schinkel's Schauspielhaus. What Edinburgh, Munich and Berlin had thought nearly two generations before, Glasgow was still thinking in the 1870s—though Thomson's design characteristically included many of his own inimitable touches, elephant caryatids, for instance. Not surprisingly, the Kensington commission went to a man whose finger pressed more closely on the High Victorian pulse, Alfred Waterhouse. Still, the sheer drama of Thomson's scheme— what he called its 'interpenetrating masses'—makes us regret that he never fulfilled one major architectural ambition on his home ground:

the design for a new university high up on Gilmore Hill. Glasgow was destined never to boast a Thomsonian Clydeside Acropolis.

With 'Greek' Thomson, the Greek Revival in British architecture comes to an end. The *Beaux Arts* classicism of J. J. Burnet and his successors—Graeco–Roman Re-Revival in Blomfield's Regent Street— belongs to a different tradition, French in ancestry and largely Renaissance in inspiration. The splendours of Edwardian Baroque were much more than a tailpiece to the Greek Revival, and as such they deserve separate treatment elsewhere. As Professor Robert Kerr put it in 1874, 'Thomson . . . carried the Hellenic motive back to meet the Egyptian, and modernized both with much painstaking of detail. He hoped to be the founder of a new school, but that was impossible'. Thomson was *sui generis*. He had several imitators, but no disciples. His Schinkelesque mannerisms were continued by James Sellars at Kelvinside Academy (1877) and St. Andrew's Halls (1873–77; gutted 1962) (Plate 247). Indeed, the latter was one of the most grandiloquent performances in the whole Greek Revival movement. But, if we exclude 'Greek' Thomson, there are no significant developments within the Glaswegian Grecian tradition, between Elgin Place Congregational Church (John Burnet Snr., 1856) and St. George's in the Fields (Hugh Barclay, 1886). Even in Glasgow, tenaciously adhering to unfashionable traditions, the Greek Revival had been exhausted by the early 1870s. Gomme and Walker conclude: 'none of Thomson's direct successors really knew how to benefit from his example or to understand what he had done to the remnants of the classical tradition. Like all great artists who have inherited a tradition formed into a different context of civilization, Thomson not only absorbed it into himself but adapted it and reformed it into something which could once again be a living and expressive medium. . . . When Thomson turned a classical colonnade into a nearly continuous window band divided by stone mullions, he was indeed changing the possibilities of expression for a new generation. But by then the artistic consciousness of the time had become too fragmented to respond'.

At least one modern critic—A. Trystan Edwards—considers Thomson essentially a Romantic. Queen's Park Church (Plate 46), for example, is condemned for its accidental 'conglomeration of features'; and these superficially random conjunctions are held to make it 'Romantic, and

Romantic in the worst sense of the word'. Now Thomson's addiction to Picturesque composition is certainly a Romantic trait. But in that respect he shares his Romanticism with every major British Neo-Classicist. No. In Thomson's work classic and romantic—cool restraint and wild indulgence—are subtly and brilliantly combined, and the effect is all the greater for their combination. In this way he embodies both major components in the British Greek Revival.

For the Greek Revival has several faces. It was never as Greek as it set out to be. It was always a synthetic style, a compound of Palladian tradition, Neo-Classical abstraction and Romantic Hellenism: precise archaeology diluted by Renaissance conventions, ordered by rationalist theory, idealized in pursuit of the Arcadian dream, and belatedly realized among the back streets of sooty Glasgow. At the peak of its popularity, B. R. Haydon pinpointed its appeal to the latent Puritanism of English aesthetics: 'its simplicity, I take it, is suitable to English decision'. Later on, beneath this Anglo–Saxon reticence, Bulwer Lytton sensed its imperial connotations: 'the handwriting of our race, in this practical nineteenth century, on its square plain masonry and Doric shafts'. But it was not until the end of the Edwardian age that Geoffrey Scott explained the permanent aesthetic appeal of classic forms, and Sir Albert Richardson demonstrated in words and photographs the 'amazing tractability of Hellenistic art'.

'All good art', suggested F. L. Lucas, 'is first Romantic, then becomes Classical'. The Greek Revival reversed this process: romantic and classic elements run right through the movement, but in the end its romantic energies came to dominate its classical components. Was it, therefore, not 'good art'? Of course there was a good deal of associationalism about the movement, and it was that which finally destroyed its potential. Instead of remaining a vehicle geared to compositional experiment, it became no more than an alternative system of decoration. The objective values of pure form were submerged in the subjectivity of the Picturesque and the Sublime. Wotton's Vitruvian goals—'commoditie, firmnesse and delighte'—were superseded by the atectonic criteria of Romantic historicism. But at the last moment the movement was rescued by its greatest exponent. If any man could walk the romantic–classic tightrope, that man was 'Greek' Thomson.

'The historian', writes M. L. Clarke, 'whose business it is to observe rather than to criticize, will not look behind the columns or beneath the pediments to spy out weaknesses of design and poverty of invention. He will be content to accept these buildings as signs of the hellenizing taste of the period . . . and will see in these efforts to reproduce the forms of ancient Greece one of the many instances of the way in which modern Europe returns to the source from which so much of her art and thought and literature derives'. He will accept the Arcadian vision on its own terms: dappled sunlight on stone or stucco; the chiselled profile and the massy column; nobility, serenity,

> An awful Stillness, and sublime Repose.

The Greek Revival was in some respects a failure. But at least its failures were appropriately heroic. And the attitudes from which it sprang were not entirely meaningless.

PART THREE

Greek Revival Architecture in Britain: a Photographic Survey

LIST OF PLATES

155

CHURCHES

14-15. Nicholas Revett: New St Lawrence Church, Ayot St Lawrence, Hertfordshire (1778-9). N.M.R.: Nicholas Cooper.

16. The Temple of Apollo, Delos (J. Stuart and N. Revett, *Antiquities of Athens* iii, 1794, ch. x, pl. 1). R.I.B.A.

17. James 'Athenian' Stuart and William Newton: Hospital Chapel, Greenwich (1779-99), ceiling under organ loft. Warburg Institute.

18-19. Joseph Bonomi and the 4th Earl of Aylesford: St. James, Great Packington, Warwickshire (1789-90). *Country Life*.

20-2. James Wyatt: St. Mary, Dodington, Gloucestershire (*c.* 1799-1808). A. F. Kersting; N.M.R.: Reece Winstone.

23. George Steuart: St. Chad, Shrewsbury (1790-2). N.M.R.

24. Wesleyan Methodist Chapel, Bridport, Dorset (*c.* 1825). N.M.R.

25. John Slater: St. Patrick (R.C.), Toxteth, Liverpool (1821-7). N.M.R.

26. H. W. and W. Inwood: St. Pancras Church, London (1819-22). N.M.R.

27. H. W. and W. Inwood: All Saints, Camden Town, London (1822). N.M.R.

28. H. W. and W. Inwood: St. Pancras Church, London (1819-22). Caryatid Porch. N.M.R.

29. H. W. and W. Inwood: St. Peter's Chapel, Regent Square, London (1824-6). Demolished. N.M.R.

30. Charles Hollis: All Saints, Poplar, London (1821-3). N.M.R.

31. Francis Bedford: St. George, Camberwell, London (1822-4). N.M.R.

32. John Nash: Specimen Design for the Church Commissioners (1818). R.I.B.A.

33. Sir John Soane: Schemes for Commissioners' Churches (*c.* 1818), drawn by J. M. Gandy. Sir John Soane's Museum.

34. Sir John Soane: Schemes for Commissioners' Churches (*c.* 1818), drawn by J. M. Gandy. Sir John Soane's Museum.

35. John Nash: Specimen Design for the Church Commissioners (1818). R.I.B.A,

36. Sir Robert Smirke: All Saints, Markham Clinton, Nottinghamshire (1831-2). N.M.R.

37. Archibald Elliot: Forbes Mausoleum, Callendar House, Stirlingshire (1816). S.N.M.R.

38. John Foster: Huskisson Monument, St. James's Cemetery, Liverpool (1836). N.M.R.

39. Thomas Cundy Snr. and Jnr.: Tower, St. Matthew, Normanton, Rutland (1826-9). N.M.R.

40. John Foulston: St. Catherine, Plymouth, Devon (1823). Demolished. N.M.R.

41. Sir John Soane: Soane Tomb, St. Pancras Gardens, London (1816), drawn by J. Wightman. V. and A.

42. Alexander 'Greek' Thomson: United Presbyterian Church, Caledonia Road, Glasgow (1856–7). S.N.M.R.

43. Alexander 'Greek' Thomson: United Presbyterian Church, St. Vincent Street, Glasgow (1859). T. and R. Annan.

44–5. Alexander 'Greek' Thomson: details, Caledonia Road Church. S.N.M.R.

46. Alexander 'Greek' Thomson: United Presbyterian Church, Queen's Park, Glasgow (1867). Demolished. S.N.M.R.

HOUSES

47. James 'Athenian' Stuart: The Banqueting House, Mount Stewart, Co. Down (*c*. 1780). Patrick Rossmore.

48. James 'Athenian' Stuart: Doric Temple, Hagley Park, Worcestershire (1758–9). *Country Life.*

49. Thomas Wright and James 'Athenian' Stuart: Shepherd's Monument, Shugborough, Staffordshire (*c*. 1756 and *c*. 1764). N.M.R.

50. James 'Athenian' Stuart: Tower of the Winds, Shugborough, Staffordshire (1764). N.M.R.

51. James 'Athenian' Stuart: Tower of the Winds, Shugborough, ceiling. N.M.R.

52. James 'Athenian' Stuart: Doric Temple, Shugborough, Staffordshire (*c*. 1764). N.M.R.

53. Thomas Wright: Landscape and Ruins, Shugborough, Staffordshire, painted by C. Dahl (*c*. 1769). *Country Life.*

54. The Choragic Monument of Lysicrates (J. Stuart and N. Revett, *Antiquities of Athens* i, 1762, ch. iv, pl. 3). R.I.B.A.

55. James 'Athenian' Stuart: 'Demosthenes Lanthorn', Shugborough, Staffordshire (1770). N.M.R.

56. The Arch of Hadrian (J. Stuart and N. Revett, *Antiquities of Athens* iii, 1794, ch. iii, pl. 4). R.I.B.A.

57. James 'Athenian' Stuart: 'The Triumphal Arch', Shugborough, Staffordshire (1764). N.M.R.

58. John Vardy and James 'Athenian' Stuart: Great Room, Spencer House, London (*c*. 1760–5). *Country Life.*

59. Robert Adam: Ante Room, Syon House, Middlesex (*c*. 1761–5). N.M.R.

60. Robert Adam: Portico, Osterley Park, Middlesex (1762–80). N.M.R.

61. Robert Adam: South Front, Kedleston Hall, Derbyshire (completed 1765). N.M.R.

62. Robert Adam: Sculpture Gallery, Newby Hall, Yorkshire (*c.* 1767–80). *Country Life.*

63. James Wyatt: Drawing Room, Castle Coole, Co. Fermanagh (1790–7). *Country Life.*

64. Robert Adam: Library Ante Room, Syon House, Middlesex (*c.* 1761–5). N.M.R.

65. James Wyatt: Lantern, Dodington Park, Gloucestershire (1796–1813). N.M.R.

66. James Wyatt: Entrance Hall, Heveningham Hall, Suffolk (c. 1784). *Country Life.*

67. Francis Johnston and James Wyatt: Castle Coole, Co. Fermanagh (1790–7). *Country Life.*

68. James Wyatt: Dodington Park, Gloucestershire (1796–1813). *Country Life.*

69. James Wyatt: Portico, Goodwood House, Sussex (*c.* 1800). *Country Life.*

70. Henry Holland: Porte Cochère, Woburn Abbey, Bedfordshire (1787–96). Demolished 1950. N.M.R.

71. Henry Holland: Sculpture Gallery, Woburn Abbey, Bedfordshire (1787–89 and 1801–03). Since altered. N.M.R.

72. Nicholas Revett: Portico, Standlynch [Trafalgar House], Wiltshire (1766). *Country Life.*

73. Thomas Lee: Arlington Court, Devon (1820–3). Reece Winstone.

74. George Steuart: Portico, Attingham Hall, Shropshire (1783–5). N.M.R.

75. Details, Paestum (T. Major, *The Ruins of Paestum*, 1768).
   inset Benjamin Latrobe: Portico capital, Hammerwood House, Sussex (*c.* 1793). Dora Wiebenson.

76. Sir John Soane: Dairy, Hammels Park [Crofton Grange], Hertfordshire (1783). Demolished. Sketch by G. Richardson. V. and A.

77. Nicholas Revett: Island Temple, West Wycombe Park, Buckinghamshire (1778–80), painted by Thomas Daniell (1781). *Country Life.*

78. Jeffry Wyatt: Nant-y-Bellan Tower, Wynnstay Park, Denbighshire (*c.* 1800). N.M.R.

79. Jeffry Wyatt: Ruins [Temple of Augustus], Virginia Water, Windsor Great Park, Berkshire (1826). N.M.R.

80. J. B. Rebecca: Greek and Gothic; Castle Goring, Sussex (1791–1825). A. J. Rowan.

81. Sir Thomas Robinson: Porch, Rokeby, Yorkshire (*c.* 1731). *Country Life.*

82–3. Francis Sandys: Ickworth, Suffolk (1796–1830). A. F. Kersting. N.M.R.

84–6. James Playfair: Cairness House, Aberdeenshire (designed 1789; built 1791–7). S.N.M.R.

87. Sir John Soane: Entrance Lodges, Tyringham Hall, Buckinghamshire (1792–7). N.M.R.

88. Sir John Soane: Entrance Hall, Bentley Priory, Stanmore, Middlesex (1789–99). N.M.R.

89. Staircase, Northwick Park, Blockley, Gloucestershire (?1828). N.M.R.

90. George Dance Jnr.: Portico, Stratton Park, Hampshire (1803–6). House rebuilt. N.M.R.

91. George Dance Jnr.: Staircase, Stratton Park, Hampshire (1803–6). Demolished. N.M.R.

92. Grange Park, Hampshire. Sketch by W. A. Nesfield. D. Linstrum.

93. William Wilkins: E. Portico, Grange Park, Hampshire (1804–9). N.M.R.

94. The Theseion (J. Stuart and N. Revett, *Antiquities of Athens* iii, 1794, ch. i, pl. 3). R.I.B.A.

95. The Choragic Monument of Thrasyllus (J. Stuart and N. Revett, *Antiquities of Athens* ii, 1787, ch. iv, pl. 3). R.I.B.A.

96. William Wilkins: E. Portico, Grange Park, Hampshire (1804–9). N.M.R.

97. William Wilkins, C. R. Cockerell *et al.* Grange Park, Hampshire (1804–9; 1823–6 etc.). N.M.R.

98. Edward Haycock Snr.: Millichope, Shropshire (1840). *Country Life.*

99. John Nash: Stonelands, Dawlish, Devon (*c.* 1825). N.M.R.

100. C. R. Cockerell: Derry Ormonde, Cardiganshire (1824). N.M.R.

101. Aberglasney, Carmarthenshire (*c.* 1825 ?). N.M.R.

102. James Knowles: Silverton Park, Devon (1839–45). Demolished. N.M.R.

103. William Burn: Camperdown, nr. Dundee, Angus (1824–6). S.N.M.R.

104. Decimus Burton: Greenough's Villa [later Grove House; now Nuffield Lodge], Regent's Park, London (1822–4). Since altered. V. and A.

105. Decimus Burton: Holwood House, Keston, Kent (1823–6). V. and A.

106. James Milne: 3–23, St. Bernard's Crescent, Edinburgh (1825). S.N.M.R.

107. Doorway, Morton Manor, nr. Carlisle, Cumberland (*c.* 1820). N.M.R.

108. Decimus Burton: Holwood House, Keston, Kent (1823–6). N.M.R.

109. C. A. Busby: Sussex Square, Brighton, Sussex (*c.* 1830). Reece Winstone.

110. Columbia Terrace, Cheltenham, Gloucestershire (1820–5). Eagle Photos, Cheltenham.

111. John Dobson: Balcony, Eldon Square, Newcastle-upon-Tyne (1824–6). N.M.R.

112. Decimus Burton: The Colosseum, Regent's Park, London (1823–7). Demolished 1875. N.M.R.

113. John Nash: Cumberland Terrace, Regent's Park, London (1826). N.M.R.

114. James 'Athenian' Stuart: Lichfield House, 15 St. James's Square, London (1764–6). Alterations by James Wyatt *c.* 1791. Eric de Maré.

115. John Nash: Carlton House Terrace, London (1827–9). N.M.R.

116. A. H. Wilds: Entrance, Park Crescent, Worthing, Sussex (1829). T. S. R. Boase.

117. J. M. Gandy: Doric House, Sion Hill, Bath (*c.* 1810). Sandra Blutman.

118. Benjamin Latrobe: Capitals, Ashdown House, Sussex (*c.* 1794). Sandra Blutman.

119. William Hardy: Letheringsett Hall, Norfolk (1808–9). *Country Life.*

120. Thomas Harrison: Obelisk House, Allerton, Lancashire (1815). Dismantled. Sandra Blutman.

121. Archibald Elliot: Loggia, The Haining, Selkirk (*c.* 1819). S.N.M.R.

122. Edward Haycock Snr. ?: Capitals, Entrance Lodge, Brogyntyn, Shropshire (*c.* 1811). N.M.R.

123. George Dance Jnr.: Staircase, Ashburnham Place, Sussex (1813–17). Demolished. *Country Life.*

124–5. Thomas Hopper: Leigh Court, Abbotsleigh, Somerset (1814). A. F. Kersting.

126. C. R. Cockerell: Staircase, Oakley Park, Shropshire (*c.* 1820). *Country Life.*

127–8. John Nash, Caledon, co. Tyrone (*c.* 1812). *Country Life.*

129. John Nash? and Richard Payne Knight: Dining Room, Downton Castle, Herefordshire (1782). *Country Life.*

130. John Nash: Library, Caledon, co. Tyrone (*c.* 1812). *Country Life.*

131. Peter Nicholson: Corby Castle, Cumberland (1812–17). *Country Life.*

132. C. R. Cockerell: Oakley Park, Shropshire (*c.* 1820). *Country Life.*

133. Bayfordbury, Hertfordshire (1759–62, 1809–12). *Country Life.*

134. Decimus Burton: Grimston Park, Yorkshire (1840–50). *Country Life.*

135. Edward Haycock Snr.: Portico, Clytha House, Monmouthshire (*c.* 1830). N.M.R.

136. Detail: Clytha House, Monmouthshire. N.M.R.

137. Detail: Torwood Cottage, Laurencekirk, Kincardineshire (*c.* 1830). S.N.M.R.

138. Francis Johnston: Townley Hall, Co. Louth (1794). *Country Life.*

139. John Kent and C. H. Tatham: Colonnade, Paultons, nr. Romsey, Hampshire (1805 and *c.* 1828). Demolished. *Country Life.*

140. John Kent and C. H. Tatham: Hall, Paultons, nr. Romsey, Hampshire (1805 and *c.* 1828). Demolished. *Country Life.*

141. W. J. Donthorn: Elmham Hall, Norfolk (*c.* 1825–30). Demolished. N.M.R.

142. Sir Robert Smirke: Normanby Park, Lincolnshire (1821). *Country Life.*

143. H. E. Goodridge: Lansdown Tower, Bath (1825–6). N.M.R.

144–5. Sir Charles Monck, Sir William Gell and John Dobson: Belsay Hall, Northumberland (1810–17). *Country Life.*

146–7. Sir Charles Monck, Sir William Gell and John Dobson: Belsay Hall, Northumberland (1810–17). *Country Life.*

148. John Dobson: Meldon Park, Northumberland (1832). *Country Life.*

149. John Dobson: Nunneykirk Hall, Northumberland (1825). *Country Life.*

150. Henry Bassett: Burton Park, Sussex (1831). *Country Life.*

151. H. E. Goodridge: Bathwich Grange [now Montebello], Bath (1828–30). N.M.R.

152. John Dobson: Nunneykirk Hall, Northumberland (1825). *Country Life.*

153–4. John Dobson: Longhurst, Northumberland (1828). *Country Life.*

155–6. Archibald Simpson: Strathcathro House, Angus (1827). S.N.M.R.

157. H. E. Goodridge: Bathwick Hill House, Bath (1828). N.M.R.

158. Alexander 'Greek' Thomson: Moray Place, Strathburgo, Glasgow (1859). S.N.M.R.

159. Alexander 'Greek' Thomson: Arran View, Airdrie, Lanarkshire (1867). S.N.M.R.

160. Alexander 'Greek' Thomson: Holmwood House, Netherlee Road, Glasgow (1856–8). A. McLaren Young.

161. Alexander 'Greek' Thomson: 200 Nithsdale Road, Glasgow. S.N.M.R.

162. Alexander 'Greek' Thomson: Double Villa, 25–25a, Mansion House Drive, Langside, Glasgow (1856). S.N.M.R.

PUBLIC BUILDINGS

163. James Wyatt: Radcliffe Observatory, Oxford (1773–94). Batsford.

164. Thomas Johnson: County Gaol, Warwick (1779–82). N.M.R.

165. Sir John Soane: Unexecuted scheme for Brasenose College, Oxford (1807). V. and A.

166. Sir John Soane: Princes Street Vestibule, Bank of England, London (1804–5). Bank of England. N.M.R.

167. Sir John Soane: Lantern, Old Dividend Office, Bank of England, London (1818). Since rebuilt. Bank of England.

168. Sir John Soane: Council Chamber, Freemasons' Hall, London (1828). V. and A.

169. Sir John Soane: Threadneedle Street Facade, Bank of England, London (1823–6). Since rebuilt. Bank of England.

170. Sir John Soane: 13, Lincoln's Inn Fields [now Sir John Soane's Museum], London (1812 onwards). Eric de Maré.

171–2. Thomas Harrison: Chester Castle (1788–1822), Portico and Shire Hall (1791–1801). *Country Life.*

173–4. Thomas Harrison: Visionary schemes for a National Valhalla (*c.* 1814–5).

175. Thomas Harrison: Propylaeum, Chester Castle (1810–22). *Country Life.*

176. Thomas Harrison: Grosvenor Bridge, Chester (1827–31). *Country Life.*

177. Sir John Soane: Scheme for a Palace in Hyde Park, London (1779). V. and A.

178. Decimus Burton: Screen, Hyde Park Corner, London (1825). N.M.R.

179. Decimus Burton: Constitution Arch, Hyde Park Corner, London (1846; moved 1883). N.M.R.

180–1. Sir Robert Smirke: Covent Garden Theatre (1808–9). Burnt and rebuilt 1856–8. R.I.B.A.

182. William Stark: Court House, Glasgow, (*c.* 1807–14; altered 1913). S.N.M.R.

183. George Dymond and Charles Fowler: The Higher Market, Exeter (1835–8). A. F. Kersting.

184. William Wilkins: Downing College, Cambridge (designed 1804: built 1807–20). N.M.R.

185. C. R. Cockerell: Competition design for University Library, Cambridge (1830). V. and A.

186. William Wilkins and J. P. Gandy-Deering: University College, London (1827–8). N.M.R.

187–8. C. R. Cockerell: Competition designs for University Library, Cambridge (1830 and 1836). V. and A.

189. Sir Robert Smirke: The British Museum, London (1823–47). A. F. Kersting.

190. James Hibbert: Harris Library and Museum, Preston, Lancashire (1882–93). Bedford Lemere.

191. Cattle Market, Bodmin, Cornwall (1839). N.M.R.

192. Fragments on the Isle of Delos, (J. Stuart, N. Revett and J. Woods *Antiquities of Athens* iv, 1816, ch. vi, pl. 2.) R.I.B.A.

193. Sir Robert Smirke: Old Council House, Bristol (1822–7). N.M.R.: N. Cooper.

194. Sir Robert Smirke: County Buildings, Perth (1816–19). N.M.R.: N. Cooper.

195. James Thomson?: Observatory (originally a windmill), Dumfries (1834–8). S.N.M.R.

196. J. C. Mead: Observatory, Cambridge (1822–3). N.M.R.

197. James Matthews: Music Hall, Union Street, Aberdeen (1858). S.N.M.R.

198. John Forbes: Pittville Pump Room, Cheltenham (1825–30). Eagle Photos.

199. John Forbes: Pittville Pump Room, Cheltenham (1825–30). Eagle Photos.

200. Tunnel Baths, Ilfracombe, Devon (1836). N.M.R.

201. Custom House, Falmouth, Cornwall (*c.* 1830). N.M.R.

202. W. H. Seth-Smith: The Pantechnicon, Motcomb Street, London (1830). N.M.R.

203. George and James Pain: Portico, Male Prison, Cork (1818). Maurice Craig.

204. R. Tattershall.: Cumberland Infirmary, Carlisle (1830–32; extended 1870–3). N.M.R.

205. William Wilkins: Portico, Archaeological Museum, York (1827–30). N.M.R.

206. Robert Chaplin: Railway Station, Ashby-de-la-Zouch, Leicestershire (1849). N.M.R.

207. John Dobson: Central Exchange, Grey Street and Market Street, Newcastle-upon-Tyne (1825). N.M.R.

208. D. J. Humphris: General Hospital, Cheltenham (1848–9; extended 1929). N.M.R.

209. Shop Front, 8 Argyll Street, Bath (*c.* 1825). N.M.R.

210. Philip Hardwick: Propylaeum, Euston Station, London (1836–9). Demolished, 1961. Bedford Lemere.

211. Decimus Burton: Athenaeum Club (1827–30; altered 1899). Bedford Lemere.

212. John Nash, Edward Blore and James Pennethorne: Buckingham Palace, London (1826 onwards); bomb damage 1941. Central Press.

213. Edwin J. Dangerfield: Clock Tower, Herne Bay, Kent (1837). N.M.R.

214. John Foulston: Buildings in Ker Street, Devonport, Plymouth, Devon (1823–4). R.I.B.A.

215. John Foulston: The Athenaeum, Plymouth, Devon (1818). Destroyed in the Second World War. R.I.B.A.

216. E. Park and J. Bowden: Court House, Dundalk, Co. Louth (1813–18). Maurice Craig.

217. John Bowen: Market Hall, Bridgwater, Somerset (1834). Reece Winstone.

218–9. Henry Roberts: Fishmongers' Hall, London (1831–4). *Country Life*.

220–1. John Wood, James Wyatt and John Foster: Town Hall, Liverpool (1749–54; 1789–92; 1796– *c.* 1820). A. F. Kersting. *Country Life*.

222. J. A. Hansom, F. Welch and C. Edge: Town Hall, Birmingham (1832–61), N.M.R.

223. C. R. Cockerell: Ashmolean Museum, Oxford (1841–5).

224. Sir Robert Smirke: Royal College of Physicians [now part of Canada House], Trafalgar Square, London (1822–4). N.M.R.

225–8. Harvey Lonsdale Elmes, C. R. Cockerell and Robert Rawlinson: St. George's Hall, Liverpool (1842–54). A. F. Kersting; *Country Life*; N.M.R.; *Country Life*.

229. William Wilkins: National Gallery, Trafalgar Square, London (1834–8), *background* James Gibbs: St. Martin-in-the-Fields (1722–6). N.M.R.

230. C. R. Cockerell: Bank of England, Liverpool (1845). N.M.R.

231. Thomas Telford: St. Katherine's Docks, Stepney, London (1825–8). *Architectural Review*.

232. R. S. Pope: *right* Old Council House extension, Bristol (1828); W. B. Gingell and T. R. Lysaght: *centre* Lloyds Bank, Bristol (1854–8). Nicholas Cooper.

233. Thomas Hamilton: Design for the Royal High School, Edinburgh (*c.* 1825). S.N.M.R.

234. C. R. Cockerell and W. H. Playfair: National Monument, Calton Hill, Edinburgh (1822–9). S.N.M.R.

235. W. H. Playfair: Design for the Scottish National Gallery, Edinburgh (*c.* 1845). National Galleries of Scotland.

236. W. H. Playfair: *right* Royal Scottish Academy (1822–6; 1832–5) and *centre* Scottish National Gallery (1850–7), Edinburgh. S.N.M.R.

237. W. H. Playfair: *left* National Gallery (1850–7); and *background* New College (1846), Edinburgh. Edwin Smith, Edinburgh University Press.

238. W. H. Playfair: Dugald Stewart Monument, Calton Hill, Edinburgh (1831–2). S.N.M.R.

239. Thomas Hamilton: Royal High School, Edinburgh (1825–9). S.N.M.R.

240. Thomas Hamilton: Royal College of Physicians, Edinburgh (1844–6). S.N.M.R.

241. Thomas Hamilton: National Gallery of Scotland, Unexecuted design. S.N.M.R.

242. Thomas Hamilton: Royal High School, Edinburgh (1825–9). S.N.M.R.

243. G. M. Kemp: Visionary view of Calton Hill, Edinburgh (1843). S.N.M.R.

244. Thomas Hamilton: Royal High School, Edinburgh (1825–9). S.N.M.R.

245. W. H. Playfair: Surgeons Hall, Edinburgh (1829–32). S.N.M.R.

246. Archibald Elliot Jnr.: Royal Bank of Scotland, Glasgow (*c.* 1827). S.N.M.R.

247. James Sellars: St. Andrew's Halls, Glasgow (1873–7; gutted 1962).

248. W. Clarke and G. Bell Snr.: County Buildings and Courthouses, Glasgow (1844). S.N.M.R.

249. Alexander 'Greek' Thomson: Egyptian Halls, Union Street, Glasgow (1871–3). S.N.M.R.

250. Alexander 'Greek' Thomson: Grecian Building, Sauchiehall Street, Glasgow (*c.* 1865). S.N.M.R.

N.M.R.: National Monuments Record, London.
S.N.M.R.: National Monuments Record of Scotland, Edinburgh.

CHURCHES

The Greek Revival was well suited to the design of private chapels, sepulchral monuments and mausolea. 'Athenian' Stuart, Ignatius Bonomi, James Wyatt and Sir Robert Smirke were all involved in memorable projects of this sort. The style was, however, less easily adapted to the requirements of the conventional parish church: the ubiquitous Commissioners' Churches erected in the years after Waterloo were by no means uniformly successful. Nevertheless, even in that field, the achievements of John Nash, Sir John Soane and the Inwood family were considerable. And, right at the end of the movement, 'Greek' Thomson's Glasgow churches proved just how flexible the Grecian style could be.

14. Nicholas Revett: New St. Lawrence Church, Ayot St. Lawrence.

15. Nicholas Revett: New St. Lawrence Church, Ayot St. Lawrence, Hertfordshire (1778–9), from the south-east.

16. The Temple of Apollo, Delos (J. Stuart and N. Revett, *Antiquities of Athens* iii, 1794, ch. x, pl. 1).

17. James 'Athenian' Stuart and William Newton: Hospital Chapel, Greenwich (1779–99), ceiling under organ loft.

18 and 19. Joseph Bonomi and the 4th Earl of Aylesford: St. James, Great Packington,
Warwickshire (1789–90).

20. James Wyatt: St. Mary, Dodington, Gloucestershire (*c.* 1779–1808).

21 and 22. James Wyatt: St. Mary, Dodington, Gloucestershire (c. 1799–1808).
Central window of dome. Exterior.

23. George Steuart: St. Chad, Shrewsbury (1790–2).

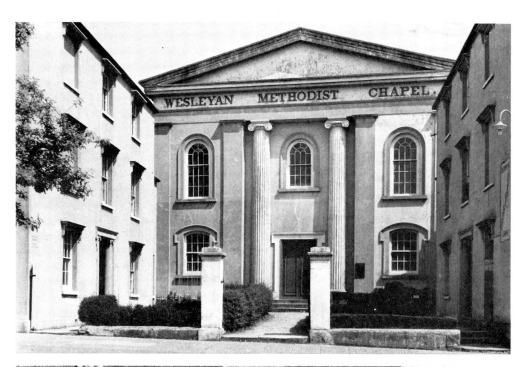

24. Wesleyan Methodist Chapel, Bridport, Dorset (*c.* 1825).

25. John Slater: St. Patrick (R.C.), Toxteth, Liverpool (1821–7). S.W. entrance colonnade.

26. H. W. and W. Inwood: St. Pancras Church, London (1819–22).

27. H. W. and W. Inwood: All Saints, Camden Town, London (1822).

28. H. W. and W. Inwood: St. Pancras Church, London (1819–22). Caryatid porch.

29. H. W. and W. Inwood: St. Peter's Chapel, Regent Square, London (1824–6).
Capitals, west front.

30. Charles Hollis: All Saints, Poplar, London (1821–3).

31. Francis Bedford: St. George, Camberwell, London (1822–4).

32. John Nash: Specimen Design for the Church Commissioners (1818).

33. Sir John Soane: Schemes for Commissioners' Churches (*c.* 1818), drawn by J. M. Gandy.

34. Sir John Soane: Schemes for Commissioners' Churches (*c.* 1818), drawn by J. M. Gandy.

35. John Nash: Specimen Design for the Church Commissioners (1818).

36. Sir Robert Smirke: All Saints, Markham Clinton, Nottinghamshire (1831–2).

37. Archibald Elliot: Forbes Mausoleum, Callendar House, Stirlingshire (1816).

39. Thomas Cundy Snr. and Jnr.: St. Matthew, Normanton, Rutland

38. John Foster: Huskisson Monument, St. James's Cemetery,

41. Sir John Soane: Soane Tomb, St. Pancras Gardens, London (1816), drawn by J. Wightman.

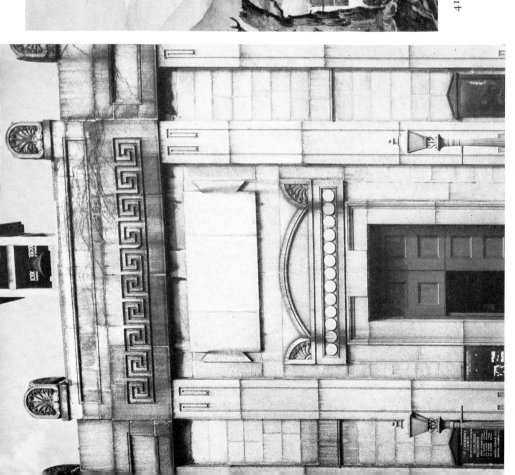

40. John Foulston: St. Catherine, Plymouth, Devon (1823). Demolished.

43. Alexander 'Greek' Thomson: United Presbyterian Church, St. Vincent Street, Glasgow (1859).

42. Alexander 'Greek' Thomson: United Presbyterian Church, Caledonia Road, Glasgow (1856–7).

44 and 45. Alexander 'Greek' Thomson: details, Caledonia Road Church.

46. Alexander 'Greek' Thomson: United Presbyterian Church, Queen's Park, Glasgow (1867). Demolished.

HOUSES

The Greek Revival originated in a Neo-Classical vision of Arcadia. Appropriately, some of its most characteristic monuments consisted of temple-fronted houses in a Romantic landscape setting. 'Athenian' Stuart, Nicholas Revett, George Dance, William Wilkins, C. R. Cockerell, H. E. Goodridge, John Dobson and William Burn were only a few of the many architects involved in this combination of Neo-Classicism and the Picturesque. Town houses lent themselves less readily to such a formula, except in the Nash terraces of Regent's Park. And even in the sphere of country-house design the Greek Revival was often only skin-deep: the Palladian villa-plan persisted long after the eclipse of Palladianism. In fact the history of the Grecian style in British domestic architecture is less a tale of dogmatic revivalism than a story of progressive synthesis and adaptation—from Robert Adam to 'Greek' Thomson.

47. James 'Athenian' Stuart: The Banqueting House, Mount Stewart, Co. Down (*c.* 1780).

48. James 'Athenian' Stuart: Doric Temple, Hagley Park, Worcestershire (1758–9).

49. Thomas Wright and James 'Athenian' Stuart: Shepherd's Monument, Shugborough, Staffordshire (c. 1756 and c. 1764).

50. James 'Athenian' Stuart: Tower of the Winds, Shugborough, Staffordshire (1764).

51. James 'Athenian' Stuart: Tower of the Winds, Shugborough, ceiling.

52. James 'Athenian' Stuart: Doric Temple, Shugborough, Staffordshire (*c.* 1764).

53. Thomas Wright: Landscape and Ruins, Shugborough, Staffordshire, painted by C. Dahl (*c.* 1769).

55. James 'Athenian' Stuart: 'Demosthenes Lanthorn',
Shugborough, Staffordshire (1764-70)

54. The Choragic Monument of Lysicrates (J. Stuart and
N. Revett, *Antiquities of Athens* i 1762 ch iv pl 4)

57. James 'Athenian' Stuart: 'The Triumphal Arch', Shugborough, Staffordshire (1764).

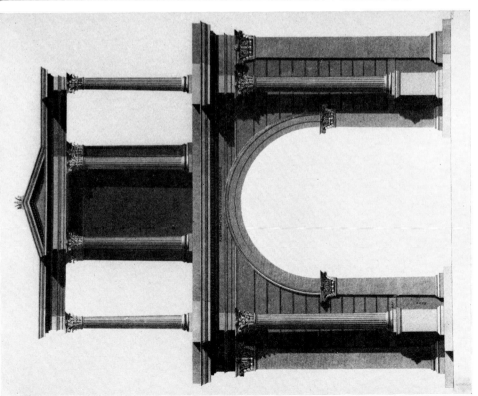

56. The Arch of Hadrian (J. Stuart and N. Revett, *Antiquities of Athens* iii, 1794, ch. iii, pl. 4).

58. John Vardy and James 'Athenian' Stuart: Great Room, Spencer House, London (*c.* 1760–5).

59. Robert Adam: Ante Room, Syon House, Middlesex (*c.* 1761–5).

60. Robert Adam: Portico, Osterley Park, Middlesex (1762–80).

61. Robert Adam: South Front, Kedleston Hall, Derbyshire (completed 1765).

62. Robert Adam: Sculpture Gallery, Newby Hall, Yorkshire (*c.* 1767–80).

63. James Wyatt: Drawing Room, Castle Coole, Co. Fermanagh (1790–7).

64. Robert Adam: Library Ante Room, Syon House, Middlesex (c. 1761–5).

65. James Wyatt: Lantern, Dodington Park, Gloucestershire (1796–1813).

66. James Wyatt: Entrance Hall, Heveningham Hall, Suffolk (*c.* 1784).

67. Francis Johnston and James Wyatt: Castle Coole, Co. Fermanagh (1790–7).

68. James Wyatt: Dodington Park, Gloucestershire (1796–1813).

69. James Wyatt: Portico, Goodwood House, Sussex (*c.* 1800).

70. Henry Holland: Porte Cochère, Woburn Abbey, Bedfordshire (1787–96). Demolished 1950.

71. Henry Holland: Sculpture Gallery, Woburn Abbey, Bedfordshire (1787–89 and 1801–3). Since altered.

72. Nicholas Revett: Portico, Standlynch [Trafalgar House], Wiltshire (1766).

73. Thomas Lee: Arlington Court, Devon (1820–3).

74. George Steuart: Portico, Attingham Hall, Shropshire (1783–5).

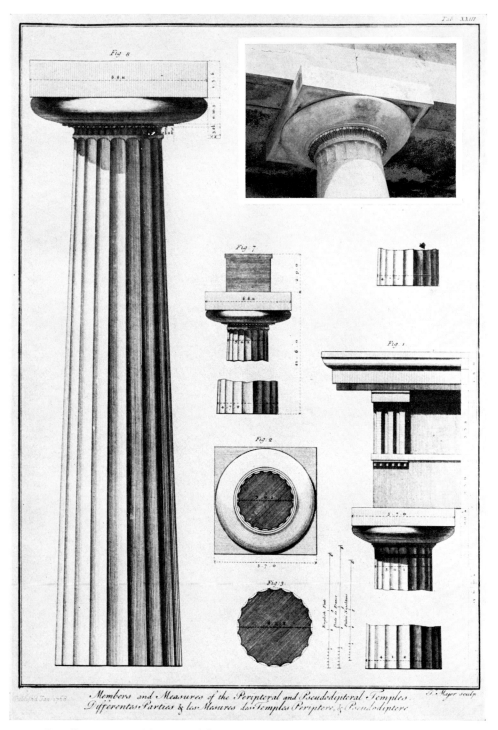

Members and Measures of the Peripteral and Pseudodipteral Temples
Differentes Parties & les Mesures des Temples Periptere, & Pseudodiptere

75. Details, Paestum (T. Major, *The Ruins of Paestum* 1768).
Inset Benjamin Latrobe: Portico capital, Hammerwood House, Sussex (*c.* 1793).

76. Sir John Soane: Dairy, Hammels Park [Crofton Grange], Hertfordshire (1783). Demolished. Sketch by G. Richardson.

77. Nicholas Revett: Island Temple, West Wycombe Park, Buckinghamshire (1778–80), painted by Thomas Daniell (1781).

78. Jeffry Wyatt: Nant-y-Bellan Tower, Wynnstay Park, Denbighshire (*c.* 1800).

79. Jeffry Wyatt: Ruins [Temple of Augustus], Virginia Water, Windsor Great Park Berkshire (1826).

80. J. B. Rebecca: Greek and Gothic, Castle Goring, Sussex (1791–1825).

81. Sir Thomas Robinson: Porch, Rokeby, Yorkshire (*c.* 1731).

82 and 83. Francis Sandys: Ickworth, Suffolk (1796–1830).

84 and 85. James Playfair: Cairness House, Aberdeenshire (designed 1789; built 1791–7).

86. James Playfair: Cairness House, Aberdeenshire (designed 1789; built 1791–7).

87. Sir John Soane: Entrance Lodges, Tyringham Hall, Buckinghamshire (1792–7).

88. Sir John Soane: Entrance Hall, Bentley Priory, Stanmore, Middlesex (1789–99).

89. Staircase, Northwick Park, Blockley, Gloucestershire (? 1828).

91. George Dance Jnr.: Staircase, Stratton Park, Hampshire (1803–6).
Demolished.

90. George Dance Jnr.: Portico, Stratton Park, Hampshire (1803–6).
House rebuilt.

92. Grange Park, Hampshire. Sketch by W. A. Nesfield.

93. William Wilkins: E. Portico, Grange Park, Hampshire (1804–9).

94. The Theseion (J. Stuart and N. Revett, *Antiquities of Athens* iii, 1794, ch. i, pl. 3).

95. The Choragic Monument of Thrasyllus (J. Stuart and N. Revett, *Antiquities of Athens* ii, 1787, ch. iv, pl. 3).

96. William Wilkins: E. Portico, Grange Park, Hampshire (1804–9).

97. William Wilkins, C. R. Cockerell *et al*. Grange Park, Hampshire (1804–9; 1823–6 etc).

98. Edward Haycock, Snr.: Millichope, Shropshire (1840).

99. John Nash: Stonelands, Dawlish, Devon (*c.* 1825).

100. C. R. Cockerell: Derry Ormonde, Cardiganshire (1824).

101. Aberglasney, Carmarthenshire (c. 1825?).

102. James Knowles: Silverton Park, Devon (1839–45). Demolished.

103. William Burn: Camperdown, nr. Dundee, Angus (1824–6).

104. Decimus Burton: Greenough's Villa [later Grove House; now Nuffield Lodge], Regent's Park, London (1822–4). Since altered.

105. Decimus Burton: Holwood House, Keston, Kent (1823–6).

107. Doorway, Morton Manor, nr. Carlisle, Cumberland (c. 1820).

106. James Milne: 3–23, St. Bernard's Crescent, Edinburgh (1825).

109. C. A. Busby: Sussex Square, Brighton, Sussex (*c.* 1830).

108. Decimus Burton: Holwood House, Keston, Kent (1823–6).

110. Columbia Terrace, Cheltenham, Gloucestershire (1820–5).

111. John Dobson: Balcony, Eldon Square, Newcastle-upon-Tyne (1824–6).

112. Decimus Burton: The Colosseum, Regent's Park, London (1823–7). Demolished 1875.

113. John Nash: Cumberland Terrace, Regent's Park, London (1826).

114. James 'Athenian' Stuart: Lichfield House, St. James's Square, London (1764–6). Alterations by James Wyatt *c*. 1791.

115. John Nash: Carlton House Terrace, London (1827–9).

116. A. H. Wilds: Entrance, Park Crescent, Worthing, Sussex (1829).

117. J. M. Gandy: Doric House, Sion Hill, Bath (*c.* 1810).

118. Benjamin Latrobe: Capitals, Ashdown House, Sussex (*c.* 1794).

120. Thomas Harrison: Obelisk House, Allerton, Lancashire (1815).

119. William Hardy: Letheringsett Hall, Norfolk (1808–9).

122. Edward Haycock Snr.?: Capitals, Entrance Lodge, Brogyntyn, Shropshire (c. 1811).

121. Archibald Elliot: Loggia, The Haining, Selkirk (c. 1819).

123. George Dance Jnr.: Staircase, Ashburnham Place, Sussex (1813–17). Demolished.

124 and 125. Thomas Hopper: Leigh Court, Abbotsleigh, Somerset (1814).

126. C. R. Cockerell: Staircase, Oakley Park, Shropshire (*c.* 1820).

127 and 128. John Nash: Caledon, Co. Tyrone (*c.* 1812).

129. John Nash? and Richard Payne Knight: Dining Room, Downton Castle, Herefordshire (1782).

130. John Nash: Library, Caledon, Co. Tyrone (*c.* 1812).

131. Peter Nicholson: Corby Castle, Cumberland (1812–17).

132. C. R. Cockerell: Oakley Park, Shropshire (*c.* 1820).

133. Bayfordbury, Hertfordshire (1759–62, 1809–12).

134. Decimus Burton: Grimston Park, Yorkshire (1840–50).

135. Edward Haycock Snr.: Portico, Clytha House, Monmouthshire (c. 1830).

136. Detail: Clytha House, Monmouthshire.

137. Detail: Torwood Cottage, Laurencekirk, Kincardineshire (*c.* 1830).

138. Francis Johnston: Townley Hall, Co. Louth (1794).

139. John Kent and C. H. Tatham: Colonnade, Paultons, nr. Romsey, Hampshire (1805 and *c.* 1828). Demolished.

140. John Kent and C. H. Tatham: Hall, Paultons, nr. Romsey, Hampshire (1805 and *c*. 1828). Demolished.

141. W. J. Donthorn: Elmham Hall, Norfolk (c. 1825–30). Demolished.

142. Sir Robert Smirke: Normanby Park, Lincolnshire (1821).

143. H. E. Goodridge: Lansdown Tower, Bath (1825–6).

144. Sir Charles Monck, Sir William Gell and John Dobson: Belsay Hall, Northumberland (1810–17).

145. Sir Charles Monck, Sir William Gell and John Dobson: Belsay Hall,
Northumberland (1810–17).

146 and 147. Sir Charles Monck, Sir William Gell and John Dobson: Belsay Hall, Northumberland (1810–17).

148. John Dobson: Meldon Park, Northumberland (1832).

149. John Dobson: Nunneykirk Hall, Northumberland (1825).

150. Henry Bassett: Burton Park, Sussex (1831).

151. H. E. Goodridge: Bathwich Grange [now Montebello], Bath (1828–30).

152. John Dobson: Nunneykirk Hall, Northumberland (1825).

153 and 154. John Dobson: Longhurst, Northumberland (1828).

155 and 156. Archibald Simpson: Strathcathro House, Angus (1827).

157. H. E. Goodridge: Bathwick Hill House, Bath (1828).

158. Alexander 'Greek' Thomson: Moray Place, Strathburgo, Glasgow (1859).

159. Alexander 'Greek' Thomson: Arran View, Airdrie, Lanarkshire (1867).

160. Alexander 'Greek' Thomson: Holmwood House, Netherlee Road, Glasgow (1856–8).

162. Alexander 'Greek' Thomson: Double Villa, Mansion House

Drive, Langside, Glasgow. 1856.

161. Alexander 'Greek' Thomson: 200 Nithsdale Road, Glasgow.

PUBLIC BUILDINGS

The Greek Revival was pre-eminently a style fitted for public buildings. Banks, court-houses, prisons, museums, art galleries, libraries, observatories, colleges, clubs, hospitals, asylums, schools, shops, markets, theatres—the early nineteenth century was in many ways a golden age for urban improvements in Britain, and the Greek Revival supplied a format which was appropriately monumental. The examples selected here have been chosen to show a wide range of building-types and to illustrate the different ways in which the style was handled by a number of leading architects, notably James Wyatt, Sir John Soane, Thomas Harrison, Sir Robert Smirke, William Wilkins, C. R. Cockerell, Harvey Lonsdale Elmes, Thomas Hamilton, W. H. Playfair and 'Greek' Thomson.

163. James Wyatt: Radcliffe Observatory, Oxford (1773–94).

164. Thomas Johnson: County Gaol, Warwick (1779–82).

165. Sir John Soane: Unexecuted scheme for Brasenose College, Oxford (1807).

166. Sir John Soane: Princes Street Vestibule, Bank of England, London (1804–5).

167. Sir John Soane: Lantern, Old Dividend Office, Bank of England, London (1818). Since rebuilt.

168. Sir John Soane: Council Chamber, Freemasons' Hall, London (1828).

169. Sir John Soane: Threadneedle Street Facade, Bank of England, London (1823–6). Since rebuilt.

170. Sir John Soane: 13, Lincoln's Inn Fields [now Sir John Soane's Museum], London (1812 onwards).

171 and 172. Thomas Harrison: Chester Castle (1788–1822), Portico and Shire Hall (1791–1801).

173 and 174. Thomas Harrison: Visionary schemes for a National Valhalla (*c.* 1814–15).

175. Thomas Harrison: Propylaeum, Chester Castle (1810–22).

176. Thomas Harrison: Grosvenor Bridge, Chester (1827–31).

177. Sir John Soane: Scheme for a Palace in Hyde Park, London (1779).

178. Decimus Burton: Screen, Hyde Park Corner, London (1825).

179. Decimus Burton: Constitution Arch, Hyde Park Corner, London (1846; moved 1883).

180 and 181. Sir Robert Smirke: Covent Garden Theatre (1808–9). Burnt and
rebuilt 1856–8.

182. William Stark: Court House, Glasgow (*c.* 1807–14; altered 1913).

183. George Dymond and Charles Fowler: The Higher Market, Exeter (1835–8).

184. William Wilkins: Downing College, Cambridge (designed 1804: built 1807–20).

185. C. R. Cockerell: Competition design for University Library, Cambridge (1830).

186. William Wilkins and J. P. Gandy-Deering: University College, London (1827–8).

187 and 188. C. R. Cockerell: Competition designs for University Library, Cambridge (1830 and 1836).

189. Sir Robert Smirke: The British Museum, London (1823–47).

190. James Hibbert: Harris Library and Museum, Preston, Lancashire (1882–93).

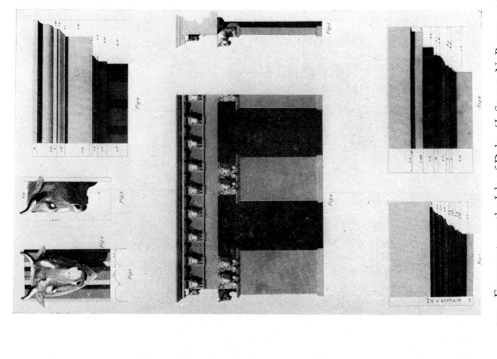

192. Fragments on the Isle of Delos (J. Stuart, N. Revett and J. Woods *Antiquities of Athens* iv, 1816, ch. vi, pl. 2).

191. Cattle Market, Bodmin, Cornwall (1839).

194. Sir Robert Smirke: County Buildings, Perth (1816–19).

193. Sir Robert Smirke: Old Council House, Bristol (1822–7).

196. J. C. Mead: Observatory, Cambridge (1822–3).

195. James Thomson?: Observatory (originally a windmill), Dumfries (1824–8).

198. John Forbes: Pittville Pump Room, Cheltenham (1825–30).

197. James Matthews: Music Hall, Union Street, Aberdeen (1858).

199. John Forbes: Pittville Pump Room, Cheltenham (1825–30).

200. Tunnel Baths, Ilfracombe, Devon (1836).

201. Custom House, Falmouth, Cornwall (*c.* 1830).

202. W. H. Seth-Smith: The Pantechnicon, Motcomb Street, London (1830).

204. R. Tattershall: Cumberland Infirmary, Carlisle (1830–32).

203. George and James Pain: Portico, Male Prison, Cork (1818).

206. Robert Chaplin: Railway Station, Ashby-de-la-Zouch, Leicester-shire (1849).

205. William Wilkins: Portico, Archaeological Museum, York, (1827–30).

207. John Dobson: Central Exchange, Grey Street and Market Street, Newcastle-upon-Tyne (1825).

208. D. J. Humphris: General Hospital, Cheltenham (1848–9).

209. Shop Front, Argyll Street, Bath (*c.* 1825).

210. Philip Hardwick: Propylaeum, Euston Station, London (1836–9). Demolished, 1961.

211. Decimus Burton: Athenaeum Club (1827–30; altered 1899).

212. John Nash, Edward Blore and James Pennethorne: Buckingham Palace, London (1826 onwards); bomb damage 1941.

213. Edwin J. Dangerfield: Clock Tower, Herne Bay, Kent (1837).

214. John Foulston: Buildings in Ker Street, Devonport, Plymouth, Devon (1823–3).

215. John Foulston: The Athenaeum, Plymouth, Devon (1818). Destroyed in the Second World War.

216. E. Park and J. Bowden: Court House, Dundalk, Co. Louth (1813–18).

217. John Bowen: Market Hall, Bridgwater, Somerset (1834).

218 and 219. Henry Roberts: Fishmongers' Hall, London (1831–4).

220 and 221. John Wood, James Wyatt and John Foster: Town Hall, Liverpool (1749–54; 1789–92; 1796–c. 1820).

222. J. A. Hansom, F. Welch and C. Edge: Town Hall, Birmingham (1832–61).

223. C. R. Cockerell: Ashmolean Museum, Oxford (1841–5).

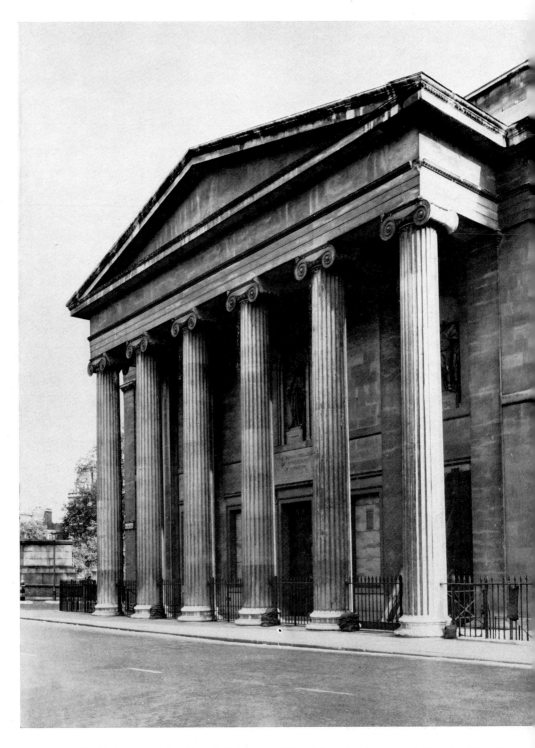

224. Sir Robert Smirke: Royal College of Physicians [now part of Canada House] Trafalgar Square, London (1822–4).

225 and 226. Harvey Lonsdale Elmes, C. R. Cockerell and Robert Rawlinson:
St. George's Hall, Liverpool (1842–54).

227. Harvey Lonsdale Elmes, C. R. Cockerell and Robert Rawlinson: St. George's Hall, Liverpool (1842–54).

228. Harvey Lonsdale Elmes, C. R. Cockerell and Robert Rawlinson: St. George's Hall, Liverpool (1842–54).

230. C. R. Cockerell: Bank of England, Liverpool (1845).

229. William Wilkins: National Gallery, Trafalgar Square, London (1834–8); *background* James Gibbs: St. Martin-in-the-Fields

231. Thomas Telford: St. Katherine's Docks, Stepney, London (1825–8).

232. R. S. Pope: *right* Old Council House extension, Bristol (1828); W. B. Gingell and T. R. Lysaght: *centre* Lloyds Bank, Bristol (1854–8).

233. Thomas Hamilton: Design for the Royal High School, Edinburgh (*c.* 1825).

234. C. R. Cockerell and W. H. Playfair: National Monument, Calton Hill, Edinburgh (1822–9).

235. W. H. Playfair: Design for the Scottish National Gallery, Edinburgh (*c.* 1845).

236. W. H. Playfair: *right* Royal Scottish Academy (1822–6; 1832–5) and *centre* Scottish National Gallery (1850–7), Edinburgh.

238. W. H. Playfair: Dugald Stewart Monument, Calton Hill, Edinburgh (1831–2).

237. W. H. Playfair: *left* National Gallery (1850–7); and *background* New College (1846), Edinburgh.

240. Thomas Hamilton: Royal College of Physicians, Edinburgh (1844–6).

239. Thomas Hamilton: Royal High School, Edinburgh (1825–9).

241. Thomas Hamilton: National Gallery of Scotland, Unexecuted design.

242. Thomas Hamilton: Royal High School, Edinburgh (1825–9).

243. G. M. Kemp: Visionary view of Calton Hill, Edinburgh (1843).

244. Thomas Hamilton: Royal High School, Edinburgh (1825–9).

245. W. H. Playfair: Surgeons Hall, Edinburgh (1829–32).

246. Archibald Elliot Jnr.: Royal Bank of Scotland, Glasgow (c. 1827).

247. James Sellars: St. Andrew's Halls, Glasgow (1873–7; gutted 1962).

248. W. Clarke and G. Bell Snr.: County Buildings and Courthouses Glasgow (1844).

249. Alexander 'Greek' Thomson: Egyptian Halls, Union Street, Glasgow (1871–3).

250. Alexander 'Greek' Thomson: Grecian Building, Sauchiehall Street, Glasgow (c.1865).

Bibliography

(Place of publication: London unless otherwise stated)

I PRIMARY

PERIODICALS

Annals of the Fine Arts (1817–20).
Architectural Magazine, ed. J. C. Loudon (1834–8).
Arnold's Magazine of the Fine Arts (1831–4).
The Art-Union (1839–48); continued as *The Art Journal* (1849–   ).
Athenaeum (1828–1921).
La Belle Assemblée (1806–32).
Builder (1843–1966); continued as *Building* (1966–   ).
British Almanac and Companion (1827–1913).
Civil Engineer and Architect's Journal (1837–67).
Edinburgh Review (1802–1929).
European Magazine (1782–1826).
Gentleman's Magazine (1731–1868).
Library of the Fine Arts (1831–3).
Monthly Magazine (1796–1843).
Quarterly Review (1809–1967).
Repository of Arts, published by R. Ackermann (1809–29).
R.I.B.A. Transactions/Papers/Journal (1842–   ).
Scots Magazine (1739–1826).
Surveyor, Engineer and Architect (1840–2); continued as *Architect, Engineer and Surveyor* (1843).

SEPARATE WORKS

Aberdeen, G. (Earl of), *An inquiry into the principles of beauty in Grecian architecture* (1822).
Adam, R., *Ruins of the Palace of the Emperor Diocletian, at Spalatro, in Dalmatia* (1764).
Adam, R. & J., *Works in Architecture*, 3 vols. (1778–1822).
Adam, W., *Vitruvius Scoticus*, 2 vols. (Edinburgh, 1720–40).
Aikin, E., *Designs for Villas* (1808).

Bibliography

Aikin, E., *An Essay on the Doric Order of Architecture* (1810).

Alison, Rev. A., *Essays on the Nature and Principles of Taste* (Edinburgh, 1790; 1811).

Allason, T., *Picturesque Views of the Antiquities of Pola, in Istria* (1819).

Angell, S., and Evans, T., *Sculptured Metopes discovered among the ruins of the temples of . . . Selinus in Sicily . . . 1823* (1826).

Babin, J. P. [and Spon, J.], *Relation de l'état présent de la ville d'Athènes* (Lyon, 1674).

Barry, J., *A letter to the Dilettanti Society, respecting . . . the improvement of public taste* (1798).

Barthélemy, J., *Travels of Anacharsis the Younger in Greece*, 5 vols. (Paris, 1788); trans. W. Beaumont, (1794).

— *Travels in Italy . . . in a series of Letters Written to . . . Count Caylus* (trans., 1802).

Bayardi, O. A., *Catalogo degli antichi monumenti disotterati dalla discoperta città di Ercolano* (Naples, 1755).

Bellicard, J. C., *Observations upon the Antiquities of the town of Herculaneum* (1753).

Bent, J. T. (ed.), *Early Voyages and Travels in the Levant . . . Thomas Dallam [and] . . . John Covel* (Hakluyt Society, 1893).

Berkenhout, J., *The ruins of Paestum or Posidonia* (1767).

Biddulph, W., *The Travels of certaine Englishmen into Africa, Asia, Troy* (1609).

Billington, J., *The Architectural Director* (1834).

Blondel, J. F., *De la distribution des maisons de plaisance, et de la décoraticion des Edifices en général* (Paris, 1737).

— *Discours sur la nécessité de l'étude de l'architecture* (Paris, 1754).

— *Architecture francaise, ou recueil des plans, élévations, coupes et profils des églises, maisons royales, palais . . .* (Paris, 1752–6).

— *Cours d'architecture, ou traité de la décoration, distribution et construction des bâtiments* (Paris, 1771–7).

Blouet, A., *Expédition de Morée* (Paris, 1831).

Blount, Sir H., *A Voyage into the Levant* (1636).

Borioni, A., and Venuti, R., *Collectanea Antiquitatum Romanorum* (1736).

Bos, L., *Antiquities of Greece* (1772).

Breval, J. D., *Remarks on several Parts of Europe* (1726).

Britton, J., *et al.*, *Beauties of England and Wales*, 18 vols. (1801–15).

— *The Union of Architecture, Sculpture and Painting* (1827).

— *Bath and Bristol* (1829).

— *Modern Athens . . . or Edinburgh in the 19th Century* (1829).

— and Brayley, E. W., *Devonshire and Cornwall Illustrated* (1832).

— and Pugin, A., *Illustrations of the Public Buildings of London*, 2 vols. (1823–8), with supplement ed. W. H. Leeds (1838).

Brøndsted, P. H., *Voyages dans la Grèce, accompagnés de récherches archéologiques . . .*, 2 vols. (Paris, 1826, 1830).

— *The Bronzes of Siris . . . in the British Museum* (1836).

Brydone, P., *A Tour through Sicily and Malta* (1773).

Bibliography

Burke, E., *A Philosophical Enquiry into the Origin of our Ideas on the Sublime and the Beautiful* (1757); ed. J. T. Boulton (1958).

Burrow, E. J., *The Elgin Marbles* (1817).

B[urton], J[ames], *Views at St. Leonards, near Hastings* [1828].

Busby, C. A., *Designs for Villas and Country Houses* (1808).

Cameron, C., *The Baths of the Romans explained and illustrated* (1772).

Campbell, C., *Vitruvius Britannicus*, 3 vols. (1717–25); continued by J. Wolfe and J. Gandon, 2 vols. (1725 etc.).

Camus, Le, *Le génie de l'architecture* (Paris, 1780).

Canova, A., and Visconti, E. Q., *A letter to the Earl of Elgin, and two memoirs . . . on . . . the collection of the Earl of Elgin* (1816).

Cassas, L. F., *Grandes Vues Pittoresques, Grèce* (Paris, 1813).

Caylus, Comte de, *Recueil d'Antiquités Egyptiennes, Étrusques, Grecques, Romaines*, 7 vols. (Paris, 1752–67).

— *Voyage d'Italie, 1714–1715* (Paris, 1914).

Chambers, W., *A treatise on Civil Architecture* (1759; ed. J. Gwilt, 1825).

Chandler, R., Revett N., and Pars, W., etc., *Ionian Antiquities*, 4 vols. (1769–1881).

— — *Travels in Asia Minor* (Oxford, 1775; ed. Edith Clay, 1972).

— — *Travels in Greece* (Oxford, 1776).

Chishull, E., *Travels in Turkey and back to England* (1747).

Choiseul-Gouffier, M. G. H. F., Count de, *Voyage pittoresque de la Grèce*, 2 vols. (Paris, 1782, 1809).

Ciriaco, P. (d'Ancona), *Epigramata reperta per Illyricum . . .* (C. Morini?, Rome, 1664?).

— *La Roma antica di Ciriaco d'Ancona*, ed. C. Huelsen (Rome, 1907).

— *Ciriaco d'Ancona e la sua descrizione autografa del Peloponneso . . . in Fontes Ambrosiana* ii, ed. R. Sabbadini (Florence, 1913).

Clarke, E. D., *Travels in Various Countries of Europe, Asia and Africa*, 6 vols. (1810–23).

Cleghorn, G., *Remarks on the intended restoration of the Parthenon of Athens as the National Monument of Scotland* (Edinburgh, 1824).

Cochin, C. N., and Bellicard, J. C., *Observations sur les antiquités d'Herculanum* (Paris, 1754).

Cockerell, C. R., *Travels in Southern Europe and the Levant 1810–1817*, ed. S. P. Cockerell (1903).

Cordemoy, J. L. de, *Nouveau traité de toute l'architecture, ou l'Art de bastir* (Paris, 1706).

Coryate, T., [Purchas, S.], *Master Thomas Coryates travels to, and Observations in Constantinople . . . and his journey thence to Aleppo, Damasco, and Jerusalem* (1625).

Cottingham, L. N., *The Smith and Founder's Director* (1824).

Craven, Elizabeth, Lady, *A Journey through the Crimea to Constantinople* (1789).

Dallaway, J., *Constantinople Ancient and Modern, with excursions to the shores and islands of the Archipelago, and to the Troad*, 2 vols. (1797).

Dalton, R., *Antiquities and Views in Greece and Egypt* (1752).

167

Bibliography

Desgodetz, A., *The Ancient Buildings of Rome* (1771); trans. G. Marshall 2 vols. (1771, 1795).

Digby, Sir K., *Journal of a Voyage into the Mediterranean . . . A.D. 1628*, ed. J. Bruce (1868).

Dodwell, E., *Views in Greece* (1821).

— *A classical and topographical Tour through Greece, during the years 1801, 1805, and 1806*, 2 vols. (1819).

— *Views and descriptions of Cyclopian, or, Pelasgic Remains in Greece and Italy* (1834).

Donaldson, T. L., and Cockburn, J. P., *Pompeii* (1827).

— — *A Collection of . . . Doorways* (1833).

— — *A Review of the Professional Life of Sir John Soane* (1837).

Douglas, Hon. F. S. N., *Memorandum on the Subject of the Earl of Elgin's Pursuits in Greece* (1810, 1811, 1815).

— *An Essay on certain points of resemblance between the ancient and modern Greeks* (1813 ed.).

Drummond, A., *Travels through different cities of Germany, Italy, Greece and several parts of Asia* (1754).

Dubut, L. A., *Architecture civile, maisons de ville et de campagne* (Paris, 1803).

Dumont, G. M., *Les Ruines de Paestum* (1769).

Dupré, L., *Voyage à Athènes et à Constantinople* (Paris, 1825).

Durand, J. N. L., *Recueil et parallèle des édifices de tout genre, anciens et modernes* (Paris, 1801).

— *Essai sur l'histoire générale de l'Architecture* (1809).

— *Précis des Leçons d'Architecture données à l'École Polytechnique* (Paris, 1802–9).

Elmes, J., *Lectures on Architecture* (1823).

— *Metropolitan Improvements* (1829).

English, E. F., and Maddox, W., *Views of Lansdown Tower, Bath* (1844).

Fergusson, J., *Observations on the British Museum, National Gallery and National Record Office* (1849).

— *An historical inquiry into the true principles of Beauty in Art, more especially with reference to Architecture* (1849).

— *History of the Modern Styles of Architecture*, ed. R. Kerr (1872).

Fischer von Erlach, J. B., *A plan of civil and historical architecture* (1737 ed.).

Flaxman, J., *Lectures on Sculpture* (1829).

Forbin, Comte de, *Travels in Greece, Turkey, and the Holy Land* (trans. 1820).

— *Recollections of Sicily* (1823).

Foulston J., *Public Buildings erected in the West of England* (1838).

Frémin, —, *Memoires critiques d'Architecture* (Paris, 1702).

Fuller, J., *Narrative of a tour through some parts of the Turkish Empire* (1829).

Galland, A., *Journal . . . pendant son séjour à Constantinople, 1672–1673*, ed. C. Schofer, 2 vols. (Paris, 1881).

Galt, J., *Voyages and travels in the years 1809, 1810, and 1811* (1812).

— *A Tour of Asia* (1820?).

Gandy, J., *Designs for Cottages, . . . and other Rural Buildings* (1805).

Gandy, J. P., and Gell, Sir W., *Pompeiana: the topography, edifices, and ornaments of Pompeii* (1817–19).

Gell, Sir W., *The Topography of Troy and its vicinity* (1804).

— *The Geography and Antiquities of Ithaca* (1807).

— *Argolis: The Itinerary of Greece* (1810).

— *Itinerary of the Morea* (1817).

— *Narrative of a journey in the Morea* (1823).

— *The Topography of Rome and its Vicinity*, 2 vols. (1834).

— *Pompeiana . . . the result of excavations since 1819*, 2 vols. (1832).

Gilpin, W., *Three Essays: on Picturesque Beauty* (1792).

Goethe, W., *Italian Tour*, trans. A. J. W. Morrison and C. Nisbet (1892); trans. W. H. Auden and E. Mayer (1962).

— [trans.], *Tagebuch einer Reise nach Sicilien von Henry Knight* [R. Payne Knight] in *Philipp Hackert. Biographische Skizze* (Tübingen, 1811).

Goldicutt, J., *Antiquities of Sicily* (1819).

— *Specimens of Ancient Decorations from Pompeii* (1825).

Goodwin, F., *Rural Architecture* (1835).

Gori, A. F., *Monumentum sive columbarium* (Florence, 1727).

— *Museum Florentinum*, 6 vols. (Florence, 1731–66).

— *Museum Etruscum* (Florence, 1737–43).

— *Antiquitates Etruscae* (Nuremberg, 1770).

Gourbillon, M., *Travels in Sicily* (1820).

Graevius, J. G., *Thesaurus Antiquitatum Romanorum* (1694–9).

Granville, A. B., *The Spas of England*, 2 vols. (1841).

Guys, P. A., *A Sentimental Journey through Greece*, 3 vols. (trans. 1772).

Hamilton, Sir W., *Account of the discoveries at Pompeii communicated to the Society of Antiquaries of London* (1777).

Hamilton, W. R., *Memorandum on the subject of the Earl of Elgin's pursuits in Greece* (1811).

— *Memorandum on the present state of the negotiation respecting the purchase of the Elgin marbles* (1816).

— — *Letters . . . to the Earl of Elgin, on the new Houses of Parliament* (1836, 1837).

— *Observations on a letter from W. R. H. . . . to the Earl of Elgin on the new Houses of Parliament* (1837).

— *Historical Notices of the Society of Dilettanti* (privately printed 1855).

Harding, S. [publisher], *Persepolis Illustrata* (1739).

Hardwick, T., *A Memoir of the Life of Sir William Chambers* (1825).

Hay, D. R., *The orthographic beauty of the Partheon referred to a law of nature* (Edinburgh/London, 1853).

Haydon, B. R., *The judgement of connoisseurs upon works of art compared with that of professional men* (1816).

— *Correspondence and Table Talk* (1875, 1876).

Haydon, B. R., *Autobiography and Memoirs*, ed. A. Huxley (1926).

— *The Diary of Benjamin Robert Haydon*, ed. W. B. Pope (Cambridge, Mass., 1960–3).

Haygarth, W., *Greece, a poem* (1814).

Hittorff, J. I., *Restitution du Temple d'Empédocle à Séluiante, ou l'Architecture polychrôme chez les Grecs* (Paris, 1851).

Hoare, Sir R. Colt, *Recollections abroad, during the year 1790. Sicily and Malta* (Bath, 1817).

Hobhouse, J. C., *A Journey through Albania and other provinces of Turkey in Europe and Asia, to Constantinople, during the years 1809 and 1810.* (1813).

Holland, Sir Henry, *Travels in the Ionian Isles, Albania, Thessaly, Macedonia . . . during the years 1812 and 1813* (1815).

Hope, T., *Household Furniture and Interior Decoration* (1807); ed. C. Musgrave (1970).

— *Costume of the Ancients*, 2 vols. (1812 ed.).

— *Anastasius: or, memoir of a Greek* 3 vols. (1819).

— *An historical essay on architecture* (1835).

Hosking, W., and Jenkins, J., *A Selection of Architectural and other ornament, Greek, Roman and Italian* (1827).

— — *Treatise on Architecture*, ed. A. Ashpital (1867).

Hugues, P. F. [D'Hancarville], *Collection of Etruscan, Greek, and Roman Antiquities, from the Cabinet of the Hon. W. Hamilton*, 4 vols. (Naples, 1766–7).

— *Monumens de la vie privée des douze Césars* (Nancy, 1780).

— *Monumens du culte secret des dames romains* (Nancy, 1784).

— *Veneres uti observantur in gemmis antiquis* (*c.* 1785).

— *Récherches sur l'Orgine, l'Esprit, et les Progrès des arts de la Grèce*, 3 vols. (1785).

Hughes, T. S., *Travels in Sicily, Greece, and Albania* (1820).

Hunt, P., *The literary remains of the late J. Twedell* (1816).

Inwood, H. W., *The Erechtheion at Athens* (1827).

— *Of the Resources of Design in the Architecture of Greece, Egypt, and other countries* (1834).

Ittar, S., *Raccolta degli antichi edifici di Catania* (Catania, 1812).

Justi, C., *Winckelmann*, 2 vols. (1866–72).

Kelsall, C., *A Letter from Athens* (1812).

— *Classical Excursion from Rome to Arpino* (Geneva, 1820).

Kinnard, W., *Antiquities at Athens and Delos* (1830).

Knight, H. Gally, *Phrosyne: a Grecian tale; Alashtar: an Arabian tale* (1817).

— *Relation d'une Excursion monumentale en Sicile et en Calabre* (Caen, 1839).

Knight, R. Payne, *An Account of the remains of the worship of Priapus* (1786).

— *The Landscape, A Didactic Poem . . . addressed to Uvedale Price Esq.* (1794).

— *An Analytical Enquiry into the Principles of Taste* (1805).

— *An inquiry into the symbolical language of ancient art and mythology* (1818).

Kruse, F. C. H., *Hellas*, 2 vols. (Leipzig, 1825–7).

Laborde, A. L. J. de, Count, *Collection des Vases Grecs de Mr le Comte de Lamberg* (Paris, 1813).

Laborde, L. E. S. J. Marquis de (ed.), *Athènes aux xv*ᵉ, *xvi*ᵉ, *et xvii*ᵉ *siècles*, 2 vols. (Paris, 1854).

Laing, D., *Buildings Public and Private* (1818).

Laugier, M. A., *Essai sur l'Architecture* (1753; revised ed. Paris, 1755).

— *Observations sur l'Architecture* (The Hague, 1765).

Laurent, P. E., *Recollections of a Classical Tour through various parts of Greece, Turkey, and Italy, in 1818 and 1819* (1821).

Leake, W. M., *Researches in Greece* i (1814).

— *The Topography of Athens* (1821).

— *Journal of a Tour in Asia Minor* (1824).

— *Travels in the Morea*, 3 vols. (1830).

— *Travels in Northern Greece*, 4 vols. (1835).

— *Peloponesiaca* (1846).

Lear, E., *Views in the Seven Ionian Islands* (1863).

Ledoux, C.-N., *L'architecture considérée sous le rapport de l'art, des moeurs et de la législation* (Paris, 1804).

Leeds, W. H., *The Travellers Club House . . . and the Revival of the Italian Style* (1839).

Legh, P., *The Music of the Eye, or essays on the Vitruvian analysis of architecture* (1831).

Le Roy, J. D., *Les Ruines des plus beaux monuments de la Grèce* (Paris, 1758).

— *Observations sur les Édifices des anciens peuples* (Amsterdam, 1767).

Lewis, S., *A Topographical Dictionary of England*, 4 vols. (1849); *Wales*, 2 vols. (1849).

Lithgow, W., *A most delectable, and true discourse, of an admired and painful peregrination from Scotland to the most famous Kingdomes in Europe, Asia, and Affrieke* (1614; Glasgow, 1906).

Lodoli, C., [Memmo, A.], *Elementi d'architettura Lodoliana, ossia l'arte del fabbricare con solidità e con eleganza non capricciosa* (1833).

London Interiors (1841).

Loudon, J. C., *Encyclopaedia of Cottage, Farm and Villa Architecture* (1833); revised by Mrs. Loudon (1846; 1867).

Lucas, P., *Voyage . . . fait en 1714 . . . dans la Turquie, l'Asie Sourie, Palestine, Haute et Basse Egypte*, 3 vols. ed. A. Barrier (Rouen, 1719).

— *Voyage du Sieur P. Lucas au Levant*, ed. C. C. Baudelot de Dairval (The Hague, 1705).

Magni, C., *Quanto di più curioso, e vago per la Turchia* (Parma, 1679).

— *Relazione della Citta d'Athene colle Provincie dell'Attica* (Parma, 1688).

— *Il più curioso e vago della Turchia* (Parma, 1704).

Major, T., *The Ruins of Paestum* (1768).

Marot, J., *Plan géométral du Temple de Balbec, situé en Grèce* (Paris?, 1680?).

Maundrell, H., *A Journey from Aleppo to Jerusalem at Easter, A.D. 1697* (1703).

Mayer, L., *Views in Egypt, Palestine and other parts of the Ottoman Empire* (1804).

Mazois, F., *Considerations sur la fame et la distribution des Théâtres antiques* (1820).

— and Gau M., *Les Ruines de Pompéi* (Paris, 1824–38).

Mengs, A. R., *Works*, trans. J. N. d'Azara (1796).

Bibliography

Middleton, C., *The Architect and Builder's Miscellany* (1799).

Milizia, F., *Dell' arte di vedere nelle belle arti del disegno secondo i principii di Sulzer* (1781).

— *Principi di Architettura Civile* (1785).

— *The Lives of celebrated Architects ancient and modern* (1768); trans. Mrs. E. Cresy (1826).

Mitford, W., *The History of Greece*, 5 vols. (1784–1818).

Montagu, J. (Earl of Sandwich), *A Voyage . . . round the Mediterranean in . . . 1738 and 1739*; ed. J. Cooke (1799).

Montagu, Lady Mary Wortley, *The Travel Letters of Lady Mary Wortley Montagu*, ed. A. W. Lawrence (1930).

— *Letters . . . during the embassy to Constantinople 1716–1718* (1819, ed.).

Montfaucon, B. de, *Antiquity explained, and represented in sculptures*, trans. D. Humphreys, 7 vols. (1721–5).

Morritt, J. B. S., *Letters descriptive of a Journey in Europe and Asia Minor in the years 1794–1796*, ed. G. Mandarin (1914).

Moryson, F., *An Itinerary* (1617); ed. C. Hughes (1903).

Moses, H., *A collection of antique vases* (1814).

— *Select Greek and Roman Antiquities* (1817).

— *Vases from the Collection of Sir Henry Englefield Bt.* [1819].

— *Designs of modern costume* (1823).

Neale, J. P., *Views of Seats* 1st. series, 6 vols. (1818–23); 2nd series, 5 vols. (1824–9).

— *New Statistical Account of Scotland*, 15 vols. (Edinburgh, 1845).

Newton, W., *The Architecture of M. Vitruvius Pollio*, trans. (1771).

Nicholson, P., *The Student's Instructor* (1823).

— *An Architectural Dictionary*, 2 vols. (1819).

Normand, C. P. J., *Nouveau parallèle des ordres d'Architecture des Grecs, des Romains et des auteurs modernes* (Paris, 1825); trans. A. Pugin (1829); ed. R. A. Cordingley (1951).

Nointel, C. M. F. Olier, Marquis de, *Les Voyages . . ., 1670–1680*, ed. A. Vandal (1900).

Otter, W., *Life and Remains of the Rev. Edward Daniel Clarke* (1824).

Pancrazi, G. M., *Antichità Siciliane spiegate colle notizie generali di questo regno*, 2 vols. (Naples, 1751).

Paoli, P. A., *Paesti, quod Posidoniam etiam dixere, rudera* (Rome, 1784).

Papworth, J. B., *Rural Residences* (1818).

— *Hints on Ornamental Gardening* (1823).

— *An Essay on the principles of Design in Architecture* (1826).

Pausanias, *Guide to Greece*, ed. P. Levi, 2 vols. (1971).

Pennethorne, J., *The Elements and Mathematical Principles of the Greek Architects and Artists* (1844).

— *The Geometry and Optics of Ancient Architecture* (1878).

Penrose, F. Cranmer, *Two Letters from Athens* (1847).

— *An investigation of the principles of Athenian architecture* (1888, ed.).

Pergolesi, M. A., *Designs for Ornaments* (1777–91; ed. J. A. Heaton 1892).

Bibliography

Perry, C., *A View of the Levant* (1743).

Petty, W. [Marquis of Lansdowne], *A Catalogue of the Lansdowne Marbles* (1807).

Piranesi, G. B., *Antichità romane de' tempi della Republica, e de' primi imperatori*, 2 vols. (Rome, 1748).

— *Prima parte di architettura* (Rome, 1750).

— *Carceri* (Rome, 1760 ed.).

— *Della magnificenza ed architettura de' Romani* (Rome, 1761).

— *Osservazioni . . . sopra la lettre de M. Mariette . . . e Parere su l'architettura* (Rome, 1765).

— *Diverse maniere d' adornare i cammini* etc. (Rome, 1769).

— and F., *Différentes vues de . . . Pesto* (Rome, 1778).

— — *Antiquités de la Grande Grèce* 2 vols. (Paris, 1837 ed.).

— *Vasi, candelabri, cippi, sarcofagi, tripodi, lucerne ed ornamenti antichi* 2 vols. (Rome, 1778).

Piranesi, F., and P., *Antiquités d'Herculanum* 6 vols. (Paris, 1804–6).

Pococke, R., *A Description of the East and some other countries* 2 vols. (1743–5).

Ponce, M., *Tableaux et Arabesques antiques* (Paris, 1838 ed.).

Ponsonby, W., (Earl of Bessborough), *Catalogue des pierres gravées* (London, 1761).

Potter, J., *Archeologica Graecae: or the Antiquities of Greece.* (Oxford, 1697–9).

Price, Sir U., *An Account of the statues . . . in Greece, trans. from Pausanias* (1780).

— *An Essay on the Picturesque as Compared with the Sublime and the Beautiful* 2 vols. (1794–8).

— *A Letter . . . on the application of the practice as well as the principles of landscape painting to landscape gardening* (1795).

— *A Dialogue on the distinct Characters of the Picturesque and the Beautiful* (Hereford, 1801).

Pullan, R. P., and C. T. Newton, *A History of the Discoveries of Halicarnassus, Cnidus, and Branchidae* (1862).

Quatremere de Quincy, A.-C., *Architecture*, 3 vols. (Paris; Liege, 1788–1825).

— *De l'Architecture Egyptienne . . . comparée sous les mêmes rapports à l'Architecture Grecque* (Paris, 1803).

— *Le Jupiter Olympien, ou l'art de la sculpture antique considérée* (Paris, 1815).

— *Lettres . . . sur les marbres d'Elgin* (Rome, 1818).

— *The Destination of Works of Art, trans.* (1821).

— *Restitution des deux Frontons du Temple de Minerve à Athènes* (Paris, 1825).

— *Monuments et Ouvrages d'art antiques* (Paris, 1829).

— *Dictionnaire historique d'Architecture* (Paris, 1832).

Randolph, B., *The present state of the Morea* (1686).

— *The Present State of the Islands in the Archipelago* (Oxford, 1687).

Rehberg, F., *Drawings faithfully copied from nature at Naples* [Lady Hamilton's attitudes] (1794).

'Report from the Select Committee of the House of Commons on the Earl of Elgin's Collection of Sculptured Marbles', *Parliamentary Papers* 1816, iii, 49–225.

Bibliography

Repton, H., *Sketches and Hints on Landscape Gardening* (1795).

— *Observations on the Theory and Practice of Landscape Gardening* (1803).

— *Fragments on the Theory and Practice of Landscape Gardening* (1816).

Richardson, G., *Iconology*, 2 vols. (1778, 1779).

— *A Treatise on the Five Orders of Architecture* (1787).

— *Thirty Capitals . . . from the Antique* (*c.* 1795).

— *New Vitruvius Britannicus*, 2 vols. (1802–8).

Riedesel, J. H., *Travels through Sicily and that part of Italy formerly called Magna Graecia. And a tour through Egypt* (1773).

Riou, S., *The Grecian Orders of Architecture* (1768).

Roche, P. de la, *An Essay on the Orders of Architecture . . . and the introduction of a new great order, called the Britannic Order* (1769).

Roe, Sir T., *Negotiations . . . in his embassy to the Ottoman Porte, from the year 1621 to 1628* (1740).

St. Non, J. C. R. de., *Voyage Pittoresque ou Description des Royaumes de Naples et de Sicile* 5 vols. (Paris, 1781–6).

Sandys, G., *A Relation of a Journey begun An. Dom. 1610* (1615).

Santi Bartoli, P., *Gli Antichi Sepolchri ovvero Mausolei Romani* (Rome, 1697; new ed. 1768).

Santi Bartoli, P., and Bartoli, F., *Picturae antiquae cryptorum romanorum* (Rome, 1738).

— — *Receuil de Peintures antiques* (Paris, 1757).

Sayer, R., *Ruins of Athens and Other Valuable Antiquities in Greece* (1759).

Semper, G., *On the study of Polychromy and its revival* (1851).

— *On the Origin of Polychromy in Architecture. An Apology for the colouring of the Greek Court in the Crystal Palace* (1854).

Soane, Sir John, *Plans, Elevations and Sections of Buildings* (1788).

— *Designs in Architecture* (1790).

— *Sketches in Architecture* (1793).

— *Designs for Public and Private Buildings* (1828).

— *Civil Architecture. Designs for completing some of the public buildings in Westminster* (1829).

— *Descriptions of the House and Museum . . . of Sir John Soane* (1832).

— *Description of three Designs for the two Houses of Parliament . . . 1779, 1794 and 1796* (1835).

— *Library Catalogue* (privately printed, 1878).

— *Lectures on Architecture . . . 1809–1836*; ed. A. T. Bolton (1929).

Spon, J., *Repouse à la Critique publiée par M. Guillet sur le Voyage de Grèce* (Lyon, 1679).

— *Recherches curieuses d'antiquité* (Lyon, 1683).

— and Wheeler, Sir G., *Voyage d'Italie, de Dalmatie, de Grèce et du Levant . . . 1675 and 1676* (Lyon, 1678–80).

Stackelberg, O. M. von., *Der Apollotempel zu Bassae in Arcadien* (Rome, 1826).

— *La Grèce. Vues pittoresques et topographiques* (Paris, 1834).

Stanhope, Lady Hester, *Travels*, 3 vols., ed. C. L. Meryon (1846).

Bibliography

Steven, W., *The History of the High School at Edinburgh* (Edinburgh, 1849).

Stuart, J., and Revett, N., *The Antiquities of Athens* 4 vols. (1762–1816).

Swan, C., *Journal of a Voyage up the Mediterranean* 2 vols. (1826).

Tatham, C. H., *Ancient Ornamental Architecture . . . in Rome and other parts of Italy* (1799).

Ternite, W., *Wandgemälde von Pompeji und Herculanum* (1839).

Texier, C., *Asie Mineure, description geographique, historique et archéologique* (1835).

Thomson, A., 'Art and Architecture', *The British Architect* i (1874), 274–8, 354–7; ii (1874), 50–52, 82–84, 272–4, 317–18. (Reprinted Manchester, 1874).

— 'Glasgow University' *Glasgow Architectural Soc. Proceedings* (1865–7).

Thuermer, J., *Ansichten von Athen und seinen Deukmahlen* (1825 ?).

Tischbein, W., *Collection of engravings from ancient vases . . . the collection of Sir William Hamilton* (Naples, 1791–5).

Tooke, A. [and Moses, H.], *The Pantheon* (1824 ed.).

Tournefort, J. Pitton de, *A Voyage into the Levant* (trans. 1741).

Twedell, Rev. R. (ed.), *The Remains of the late John Twedell* (1815).

Valadier, G., *Progetti architettonici* (Rome, 1807).

— *Raccolta delle più insigni Fabbriche di Roma antica* (Rome, 1810–26).

Vaudoyer, A. L. T., *et al., Grands Prix d'Architecture* (Paris, 1779–83, 1791, 1806).

Walpole, Rev. Robert, *Memoirs relating to European and Asiatic Turkey . . . and various countries of the East* 2 vols. (1817–20).

Walsh, R., *A residence at Constantinople, during . . . the commencement, progress, and termination of the Greek and Turkish Revolutions* 2 vols. (1836).

Watkins, T., *Travels through Swisserland, Italy, Sicily, the Greek Islands to Constantinople . . . in the years 1787, 1788, 1789* 2 vols. (1792).

Whaley, T., *Memoirs, including his journey to Jerusalem* (1797); ed. Sir E. Sullivan (1906).

Whateley, T., *Observations on Modern Gardening* (1771).

Wheeler, Sir G., *A journey into Greece* (1682).

Wightwick, G., *The Palace of Architecture* (1840).

Wilkins, W., *The Antiquities of Magna Graecia* (Cambridge, 1807).

— (ed.) [and Aberdeen, G. Earl of], *The civil architecture of Vitruvius* (1812).

— *Atheniensia, or remarks on the topography and buildings of Athens* (1816).

— *Prolusiones Architectonicae: or Essays on subjects connected with Greek and Roman Architecture* (1837).

Williams, H. W., *Travels in Italy, Greece, and the Ionian Islands* 2 vols. (Edinburgh, 1820).

Winckelmann, J. J., *Anmerkungen über die Baukunst der Alten* (Dresden, 1762).

— *Reflections on the Painting and Sculpture of the Greeks* (1755), trans. H. Fuseli (1765).

— *The History of Ancient Art* (1764), trans. G. H. Lodge, 2 vols. (1881).

— *Opere*, Italian trans., 12 vols. (Prato, 1830–4).

— *Writings on Art*, ed. D. Irwin (1972).

Wood, R., *The Ruins of Palmyra* (1753).

— *The ruins of Balbec* (1757).

Bibliography

Wordsworth, C., *Athens and Attica* (1836).

Worsley, Sir R., *Museum Worsleyanum* 2 vols. (1794–1803).

Zahn, W., *Les plus beaux monuments . . . de Pompeii, d'Herculaneum, et de Stabiae* (Berlin, 1828).

II SECONDARY

UNPUBLISHED THESES

Bohan, P. J., 'James and Decimus Burton' (Ph.D., Yale, 1961).

Crook, J. Mordaunt, 'The Career of Sir Robert Smirke, R.A.' (D.Phil., Oxon, 1961).

Dodd, Patricia, 'Belsay, Northumberland: House and Gardens' (B. A. Leeds, 1966).

I. Fisher, 'Thomas Hamilton of Edinburgh, Architect and Town Planner' (B. A. Oxon, 1965).

Hall, I. G., 'Methods of Decoration and Arrangement of English Greek Revival Buildings, 1750–1850' (M.A., Manchester, 1959).

— 'Classical Architecture in Manchester, 1700–1850' (Ph.D., Manchester, 1963).

Law, G., 'Greek Thomson' (B.A. Cantab., 1950).

Lewis, C. D., 'Greece and the Greek Revival, 1759–1809' (B.A. Cantab., 1962).

Liscombe, R., 'William Wilkins' (Ph.D., London, 1972).

Proudfoot, C., 'C. H. Tatham' (B.A. Cantab., 1970).

Roberts, H., 'Joseph Bonomi' (B.A. Cantab., 1970).

Rosenblum, R., 'The International Style of 1800: a Study in Linear Abstraction' (Ph.D., New York University, 1956).

Stillman, D., 'The Genesis of the Adam Style' (Ph.D., Columbia, 1960).

Sweetman, J. E., 'Shaftesbury and Art Theory in 18th c. England' (Ph. D., London University, 1955).

Walkley, G., 'William Wilkins' (R.I.B.A. Medal Essay, 1947).

Whiffen, M., 'The Architecture of Sir Charles Barry in Manchester' (Manchester, 1950).

MONOGRAPHS, BIOGRAPHIES ETC.

Allen, B. Sprague, *Tides in English Taste, 1619–1800*, 2 vols. (Cambridge, Mass., 1937).

[Arts Council], *The Romantic Movement: Council of Europe Exhibition Catalogue* (1959).

— *Charles Cameron* (1968).

— *The Age of Neo-Classicism: Council of Europe Exhibition Catalogue* (1972).

Ayrton, E., *The Doric Temple* (1961).

Balfour, Lady Frances, *George, 4th Earl of Aberdeen*, 2 vols. (1923).

Barbier, C. P., *William Gilpin: his drawings, teaching and theory of the Picturesque* (1963).

Barry, A., *Life and Works of Sir Charles Barry* (1870).

Bate, W. J., *From Classic to Romantic, Premises of Taste in 18th c. England* (Cambridge, Mass., 1946).

Bibliography

Baumgarten, S., *Le Crépuscule Neo-Classique: Thomas Hope* (Paris, 1958).

Bellot, H. Hale, *University College, London, 1826–1926* (1929).

Bertrand, L., *La Fin du Classicisme et le retour à l'antique dans la seconde metié du xviiie siècle et les premières annés du xixe en France* (Paris, 1897).

Birnstingle, H. J., *Sir John Soane* (1925).

Boase, T. S. R., *English Art, 1800–70* (Oxford, 1959).

Boe, A., *From Gothic Revival to Functional Form* (Oxford, 1957).

Bolton, A. T., *The Architecture of Robert and James Adam, 1758–94*, 2 vols. (1922).

— *Pitzhanger Manor, Ealing* (1927).

— *The Portrait of Sir John Soane* (1927).

Bowie, J. and Thimme, D. (eds.), *The Carrey Drawings of the Parthenon Sculptures* (Indiana, 1972).

Bradbury, R., *The Romantic Theories of Architecture of the Nineteenth Century in Germany, England and France* (New York, 1934).

Butler, Eliza, M., *The Tyranny of Greece over Germany* (Cambridge, 1935).

Carpenter, R., *The Esthetic Basis of Greek Art* (1921).

Carritt, E. F., *A Calendar of British Taste from 1669 to 1800* (1949).

Casson, S., *Greece and Britain* (1943).

Chambers, F. P., *History of Taste* (New York, 1932).

Chandler, G., *William Roscoe of Liverpool* (1953).

Childe-Pemberton, W. A., *The Earl Bishop: Frederick Hervey, Bishop of Derry, Earl of Bristol*, 2 vols. (1925).

Clark, H. F., *The English Landscape Garden* (1948).

Clarke, M. L., *Greek Studies in England, 1700–1830* (Cambridge, 1945).

Clifford, D., *A History of Garden Design* (1962).

Collins, P., *Changing Ideals in Modern Architecture, 1750–1950* (1965).

Colvin, H. M., *A Biographical Dictionary of English Architects, 1660–1840* (1954).

Crook, J. Mordaunt, *Haileybury and the Greek Revival: the architecture of William Wilkins* (Hoddesdon, 1964).

— *The Greek Revival* (R.I.B.A. Drawings Series, 1968).

— *The British Museum* (1972).

— and Port, M. H., *The History of the King's Works*, vol. VI, 1782–1851, ed. H. M. Colvin (1972).

Cust, L., and Colvin, S., *History of the Society of Dilettanti* (1898).

Dale, A., *James Wyatt, Architect, 1746–1813* (1936; revised 1956).

Davis, T., *The Architecture of John Nash* (1960).

— *John Nash* (1966).

De Zurco, E. R., *Origins of Functionalist Theory* (New York, 1957).

Dobson, Margaret, *Memoir of John Dobson* (1885).

Draper, J. W., *18th Century English Aesthetics, a bibliography* (Heidelberg, 1931).

Eitner, L. E. A., *Neoclassicism and Romanticism, 1750–1850*, 2 vols (Englewood, 1970).

Fairchild, H. N., *The Noble Savage: A Study in Romantic Naturalism* (New York, 1928).

Bibliography

Ferriman, Z. D., *Some English Philhellenes* (1917).

Fleming, J., *Robert Adam and his Circle in Rome* (1962).

Focillon, H., *G. B. Piranesi* (Paris, 1918).

Fothergill, B., *Sir William Hamilton* (1969).

Frantz, R. W., *The English Traveller and the Movement of Ideas, 1660–1732* (Lincoln, Neb., 1934).

Furst, Lilian, *Romanticism* (1969).

Giedion, S., *Space, Time and Architecture* (Cambridge, Mass., 1941).

Gloag, J. and Bridgewater, D., *Cast Iron in Architecture* (1948).

Goodhart-Rendel, H. S., *English Architecture Since the Regency* (1953).

Grigson, G., *The Romantics: an Anthology* (1942).

Grousset, R., *L'Empire du Levant* (Paris, 1946).

Halsband, R. (ed.), *The Life of Lady Mary Wortley Montagu* (Oxford, 1956).

— *Letters of Lady Mary Wortley Montagu,* 3 vols. (1965–7).

Halsted, J. B., *Romanticism: selected documents* (1969).

Hamlin, T., *Greek Revival Architecture in America* (1944).

Harris, Eileen, *The Furniture of Robert Adam* (1963).

Harris, J., *Regency Furniture Design* (1961).

— *Sir William Chambers* (1970). Contributions by Eileen Harris and J. Mordaunt Crook.

Hatfield, H. C., *Winckelmann and his German Critics, 1755–81* (New York, 1943).

Hautecoeur, L., *Rome et la Renaissance de l'Antiquité à la fin du xviiie siècle* (Paris, 1912).

Hawley, H., *Neo Classicism, Style and Motif* (Cleveland, 1964).

Herrmann, W., *Laugier and Eighteenth-Century French Theory* (1962).

Hipple, W. J., *The Beautiful, The Sublime, and The Picturesque in 18th c. British Aesthetic Theory* (Carbondale, 1957).

Hitchcock, H.-R., *Early Victorian Architecture in Britain,* 2 vols. (New Haven, 1954).

— *Architecture: 19th and 20th Centuries* (1958; 1963).

Hobhouse, Hermione, *Thomas Cubitt* (1971).

Hofmann, W., *The Earthly Paradise: Art in the Nineteenth Century* (New York, 1961).

Houghton, W. E., ed. *The Wellesley Index to Victorian Periodicals 1824–1900* i (1966).

Hussey, C., *The Picturesque, Studies in a Point of View* (1927; 1967).

— *English Country Houses: Early, Mid and Late Georgian,* 3 vols. (1954–8).

— *English Gardens and Landscapes, 1700–50* (1967).

Irwin, D., *English Neoclassical Art* (1966).

Ison, W., *The Georgian Buildings of Bath* (1948).

— *The Georgian Buildings of Bristol* (1952).

Jones, Barbara, *Follies and Grottoes* (1953).

Kaufmann, E., *Von Ledoux bis Le Corbusier* (Vienna, 1933).

— *Architecture in the Age of Reason* (Cambridge, Mass., 1955).

Kliger, S., *The Goths in England* (Cambridge, Mass., 1952).

Klopper, P., *Von Palladio bis Schinkel* (Eszlingen, 1911).

Krauss, F., *Paestum: Die Griechischen Tempel* (Berlin, 1941).

Bibliography

Larrabee, S. A., *English Bards and Grecian Marbles* (New York, 1943).

— *Hellas Observed* (1957).

Lawrence, A. W., *Greek Architecture* (1957).

Lees-Milne, J., *The Age of Adam* (1947).

Leppmann, W., *Winckelmann* (1971).

Levin, H., *The Broken Column: an essay in Romantic Hellenism* (Cambridge, Mass., 1931).

Lewis, Lesley, *Connoisseurs and Secret Agents in 18th c. Rome* (1961).

Linstrum, D., *Sir Jeffry Wyatville* (Oxford, 1972).

Lovejoy, A. O., *Essays in the History of Ideas* (1948).

Lucas, F. L., *The Decline and Fall of the Romantic Ideal* (New York, 1936).

Macleod, R., *Style and Society: architectural ideology in Britain, 1835–1914* (1971).

Malakis, E., *French Travellers in Greece, 1770–1820* (Philadelphia, 1925).

Malins, E., *English Landscape and Literature* (1966).

Manwaring, Elizabeth, *Italian Landscape in 18th c. England* (New York, 1925).

Marsden, J. H., *Memoir of the Life and Writings of W. M. Leake* (1864).

Marshall, R., *Italy in English Literature, 1755–1815* (New York, 1934).

Mortiennsen, R. D., *The Idea of Space in Greek Architecture* (Johannesburg, 1964).

Michaelis, A., *Ancient Marbles in Great Britain*; trans. C. A. M. Fennell (1882).

— *A Century of Archaeological Discoveries*; trans. B. Kahnweiler (1908).

Miller, W., *The English in Athens before 1821* (1926).

Monk, S. H., *The Sublime, a study of critical theories in 18th c. England* (New York, 1935).

Newton, E., *The Romantic Rebellion* (1962).

Omont, H. A., *Documents sur l'imprimeme à Constantinople au xviiie siecle* (Paris, 1895).

— (ed.), *Athènes au xviie siecle* (Paris, 1898).

— (ed.), *Missions archéologiques françaises en Orient au xviie et xviiie siècles* (1902).

— (ed.), *Voyages à Athènes, Constantinople et Jerusalem de François Arnaud* (1909).

— *Minoide Mynas et ses missions en Orient, 1840–1855* (Paris, 1916).

Oncken, A., *Friedrich Gilly* (Berlin, 1935).

Panofsky, E., *Idea: A Concept in Art Theory* (Columbia, S. Carolina, 1968).

Papworth, W., *J. B. Papworth* (1879).

— (ed.), *Dictionary of Architecture* (Architectural Publication Society), 8 vols. (1852–92).

Parks, R. O. (ed.), *Piranesi Exhibition Catalogue* (Northampton, Mass., 1962).

Pater, W., *Works,* 10 vols. (1910 ed.).

Pevsner, Sir Nikolaus, *The Buildings of England*, 46 vols. (Harmondsworth, 1951—).

— *Studies in Art, Architecture and Design*, 2 vols. (1968).

Pilcher, D., *The Regency Style* (1947).

Pinguad, L., *Choiseul-Gouffier, la France en Orient sous Louis xvi* (1887).

Praz, M., *On Neo-Classicism,* 1940; trans. A. Davidson (1969).

Quennell, P., *Romantic England: Writing and Painting, 1717–1851* (1970).

Reilly, P., *An Introduction to Regency Architecture* (1948).

Richardson, Sir Albert, *Monumental Classic Architecture in Great Britain and Ireland during the 18th and 19th centuries* (1914).

Richardson, Sir Albert, and Gill, C. Lovett, *Architecture in the West of England* (1924).

— *Robert Mylne, Architect and Engineer 1733–1811* (1955).

Roberts, J. F. A., *William Gilpin and Picturesque Beauty* (Cambridge, 1944).

Robertson, D. S., *A Handbook of Greek and Roman Architecture* (1929).

Rocheblave, S., *Essai sur le Comte de Caylus: l'homme, l'artiste, l'antiquaire* (Paris, 1892).

Rodd, Sir R., *The Englishman in Greece* (1910).

Rosenau, Helen, *The Ideal City* (1959).

— *Social Purpose in Architecture: Paris and London compared, 1760–1800* (1971).

St. Clair, W., *Lord Elgin and the Marbles* (1967).

— *That Greece Might Still Be Free* (1972).

Saunders, Ann, *Regent's Park* (Newton Abbot, 1969).

Saxl, F., and Wittkower, R., *British Art and the Mediterranean* (1948).

Scott, G., *The Architecture of Humanism* (1914).

Searight, Sarah, *The British in the Middle East* (1969).

Sicilianos, D., *Old and New Athens*; trans. Robert Liddell (1960).

Simpson, W. D., *Archibald Simpson* (Aberdeen, 1947).

Smith, C. Harcourt, *The Society of Dilettanti* (1932).

Smith, L. Pearsall, *Four Words, Romantic, Originality, Creative, Genius* (Oxford, 1924).

Spencer, T., *Fair Greece, Sad Relic* (1954).

Steegman, J. E., *The Rule of Taste from George I to George IV* (1936).

— *Consort of Taste, 1830–70* (1950).

Stern, B. H., *The Rise of Romantic Hellenism in English Literature, 1732–86* (Menasha, Wisconsin, 1940).

Stevens, G. P. et al., *The Erechtheum* (1927).

Stewart, C., *Stones of Manchester* (1956).

Stillman, D., *The Decorative Work of Robert Adam* (1966).

Stokoe, F. W., *German Influence in the English Romantic Period, 1788–1815* (Cambridge, 1926).

Stroud, Dorothy, *Capability Brown* (1950).

— *Henry Holland* (1950).

— *The Architecture of Sir John Soane* (1961).

— *Humphry Repton* (1962).

— *Henry Holland* (1966).

— *George Dance, Architect, 1741–1825* (1971).

Summerson, Sir John, *John Nash, Architect to George IV* (1935).

— *Heavenly Mansions and other essays on architecture* (1949; New York, 1963).

— *Sir John Soane* (1952).

— *The Classical Language of Architecture* (1964).

— *Architecture in Britain, 1530–1830* (Harmondsworth, 1953; 1970).

— *Victorian Architecture: Four Studies in Evaluation* (New York, 1970).

Survey of London, 28 vols. to date (1896—).

Swarbrick, J., *Robert Adam and his Brothers* (1915).

Bibliography

Taylor, F. H., *The Taste of Angels. A History of Art Collecting from Rameses to Napoleon* (1948).

Tipping, H. Avray, *English Homes*, Period VI, 1760–1820 (1926).

Turnor, R., *James Wyatt* (1950).

Ward, H., *History of the Athenaeum* (1926).

Watkin, D., *Thomas Hope and the Neo-Classical Idea* (1968).

Weber, S. H., *Voyages and Travels in Greece, the Near East and Adjacent Regions previous to . . . 1801* (Catalogue of the Gennadius Library, American School of Classical Studies, Athens, 1953).

Whiffen, M., *Stuart and Georgian Churches: the architecture of the Church of England outside London, 1603–1837* (1947–8).

Whitney, L., *Primitivism and the Idea of Progress in English Popular Literature of the 18th c.*, intro. A. O. Lovejoy (Baltimore, 1934).

Wiebenson, Dora, *Sources of Greek Revival Architecture* (1969).

Wilkes, L., and Dodds, G., *Tyneside Classical* (1964).

Wood, C. A., *A History of the Levant Company* (1935).

Woodbridge, K., *Landscape and Antiquity, Aspects of English Culture at Stourhead, 1718–1838* (Oxford, 1971).

Woodhouse, C. M., *The Philhellenes* (1969).

Young, E. and W., *Old London Churches* (1956).

Youngson, A. J., *The Making of Classical Edinburgh* (1966).

ARTICLES

Barclay, D. and Blomfield, R., 'Alexander Thomson', *Architectural Rev.* xv (1904), 181–95.

Barman, C., 'Fishmongers' Hall', *Country Life*, lxv (1929), 82–90.

Bence-Jones, M., 'Cork', *Country Life*, cxlii (1967), 250–3, 306–9.

Binney, M., 'Great Packington, Warwicks.', *Country Life*, cxlviii (1970), 102–6, 162–6, 226–9; cl (1971), 110–15.

— 'Charles Barry', *Country Life*, cxlvi (1969), 494–8, 550–2, 622–4.

Block, G. D. M., et al., 'Euston Station', *Country Life*, cxxvii (1960), 554–6; *Architectural Rev.* lxxiv (1933), 104.

Blutman, Sandra, 'Beaumont Lodge, Berkshire, and the British Order', in *The Country Seat: Studies . . . presented to Sir John Summerson*, ed. H. M. Colvin and J. Harris (1970), 181–4.

— 'Castle Goring, Sussex', in *The Country Seat: Studies . . . presented to Sir John Summerson,* ed. H. M. Colvin and J. Harris (1970), 205–8.

Bolton, A. T., 'West Wycombe, Bucks.', *Country Life*, xxxix (1916), 16–24, 48–54.

— 'Heaton Park, Manchester', *Country Life*, xxxvi (1914), 710–17.

— 'Tyringham, Newport Pagnell, Bucks.', *Country Life*, xlii (1917), 628–34; *Architectural Rev.*, lxv (1929), 56–64, 142–3.

Bibliography

Bolton, A. T., 'Hagley Park, Worcs.', *Country Life*, xxxviii (1915), 520–8.

Brackett, O., 'Langley Park, Norfolk', *Country Life*, lxii (1927), 16–23, 567–70; lxiii (1928), 467–570.

Budden, L., 'Alexander Thomson', *Builder*, xcix (1910), 215–19.

Butchart, R., 'Lost Opportunities: an account of some of Edinburgh's Unrealised Projects', *The Book of the Old Edinburgh Club*, xxx (1959), 36–59.

Buttle, D., 'James Wyatt and the Early Greek Revival', *Studies in Architectural History*, ed. W. A. Singleton (1956), 70–88.

Clark, H. F., '18th century Elysiums', *Warburg Institute Jnl.*, vi (1943), 165–89.

— 'The Sense of Beauty in the 18th, 19th and 20th centuries: aesthetic values in English landscape appreciation', *Landscape Architecture*, xlvii (1957), 465–9.

Cockerell, R. P., 'The Life and Works of C. R. Cockerell', *Architectural Rev.*, xii (1902), 43–7, 129–46.

Codrington, G., 'Dodington Park, Glos., *Architectural Rev.*, lxxi (1932), 95–100.

Cornforth, J., 'The United Service Club, London', *Country Life*, cxxxi (1962), 832–5.

— et al., 'Normanby Park, Lincs.', *Country Life*, xxx (1911), 170–6; cxxx (1961), 346–9.

— 'Trentham, Staffs.', *Country Life*, cxliii (1968), 176–80, 228–31, 282–5.

— 'Bowood, Wilts.', *Country Life*, cli (1972), 1448–51, 1546–50, 1610–13.

Crook, J. Mordaunt, 'Sir Robert Smirke: a pioneer of concrete construction', *Trans. of the Newcomen Society*, xxxviii (1965–6), 5–22.

— 'Architect of the Rectangular, a reassessment of Sir Robert Smirke', *Country Life*, cxli (1967), 846–8.

— 'Sir Robert Smirke: a centenary florilegium', *Architectural Rev.*, cxlii (1967), 208–10.

— 'Sir Robert Smirke: a Regency Architect in London', *Jnl. of the London Society* (1968), No. 381/2–11.

— 'The Villas in Regent's Park', *Country Life*, cxliv (1968), 22–5, 84–7.

— 'Broomhall, Fife', *Country Life*, cxlvii (1970), 242–6.

— 'The Pre-Victorian Architect: Professionalism and Patronage', *Architectural History*, viii (1969), 62–78.

— 'A Vanished Theatrical Masterpiece: Smirke's Covent Garden Theatre', *Country Life Annual* (1970), 102–5.

— 'Grange Park Transformed', in *The Country Seat: Studies . . . presented to Sir John Summerson*, ed. H. M. Colvin and J. Harris (1970), 220–8.

— 'The Architecture of Thomas Harrison', *Country Life*, cxlix (1971), 876–9, 944–7, 1088–91, 1539.

— 'Regency Architecture in the West Country: the Greek Revival', *Jnl. of the Royal Society of Arts*, cxix (1971), 438–51.

— 'The Fate of Neo-Classical Houses', *Country Life*, cli (1972), 1382–5.

— 'Neo-Classical Architecture at the Royal Academy', *Connoisseur*, clxxxi (1972), 14–17.

Dent, A. R., 'Barry and the Greek Revival', *Architecture*, 5th series, iii (1924–5), 225–36.

Dodd, E., 'C. R. Cockerell', in *Victorian Architecture*, ed. P. Ferriday (1963), 105–21.

Edwards, A. Trystan, 'Alexander Thomson', *Architect's Jnl.*, ix (1914), 334–6, 350–2.

Bibliography

Eliot, C., 'Athens in the Time of Lord Byron', *Hesperia*, xxxvii (1968), 134–58.

Fitzgerald, D., 'The Temple of the Winds: an Irish banqueting house', *Connoisseur*, clxvii (1968), 206–9.

Fleming, J., 'A Robert Adam Miscellany', *Architectural Rev.*, cxxiii (1958), 102–7.

French, C., Ebberley House, Devon, *Country Life*, cxxiii (1958), 827

Girouard, M., 'Sir Charles Barry', *Country Life*, cxxxiii (1960), 796–7.

— 'Longhirst, Meldon and Nunnykirk', *Country Life*, cxxxix (1966), 352–6, 406–9.

— and Paul, J., 'Neo-Classicism', *Architectural Rev.*, clii (1972), 168–70.

Goodhart-Rendel, H. S., 'The Work of Sir John Burnet', *Architect's Jnl.*, lvii (1923), 1066–1110.

— 'English Architecture, 1834–1934', in *The Growth and Work of the R.I.B.A.*, ed. J. A. Gotch (1934).

— 'Rogue Architects of the Victorian Era', *R.I.B.A. Jnl.*, lxi (1949), 251–9.

Grierson, H. J. C., 'Classical and Romantic', in *The Background to English Literature* (1934), 256–90.

Hamlin, J., 'The Greek Revival in America and some of its Critics', *Art Bulletin*, xxiv (1942), 244–58.

Harbron, D., 'The Modern Proteus: Sir Thomas Robinson Architect, 1700–1777', *Architectural Rev.*, lxxx (1936), 167–70.

Harris, Eileen, 'Burke and Chambers on the Sublime and the Beautiful', *Essays in the History of Architecture Presented to Rudolf Wittkower* (1967), 207–13.

Harris, J., 'Blondel at Stowe', *Connoisseur*, clv (1964), 173–6.

— 'C. R. Cockerell's, *Ichnographica Domestica*', *Architectural History*, xiv (1971), 5–29.

Havens, R. D., 'Simplicity, a Changing Concept', *Jnl. of the Hist. of Ideas*, xiv (1953).

Hobhouse, Hermione, 'The Building of Belgravia', *Country Life*, cxlv (1969), 1154–7, 1312–14.

Honour, H., 'Adaptations from Athens', *Country Life*, cxxiii (1958), 1120–1.

Hunt, J. D., 'Emblem and Expression in the Landscape Garden', *18th C. Studies*, iv (1971), 294–317.

Hussey, C., 'Dodington Park, Glos.', *Country Life*, lv (1924), 170–5; cxx (1956), 1176–9, 1230–3.

— 'Modern Garden Architecture at Tyringham, Bucks.', *Country Life*, lxv (1929), 740–6, 780–6.

— et al., 'Goodwood House, Sussex', *Country Life*, xviii (1905), 198–205; lxxii (1932), 38–44, 66–71.

— 'Burton Park, Sussex', *Country Life*, lxxx (1936), 38–43.

— 'Castlecoole, Co. Fermanagh', *Country Life*, lxxx (1936), 654–7, 682–7.

— 'Caledon, Co. Tyrone', *Country Life*, lxxxi (1937), 224–9, 250–5.

— 'Stourhead, Wilts.', *Country Life*, lxxxiii (1938), 608–14, 638–42.

— 'Belsay Castle, Northumberland', *Country Life*, lxxxviii (1940), 300–3, 324–8, 346–50.

— et al., 'Grimston Park, Yorks.', *Country Life*, x (1901), 464–70; lxxxvii (1940), 252–6, 276–80.

Bibliography

Hussey, C., 'Hall Place, West Meon, Hants.', *Country Life*, xcv (1944), 860–3, 904–7.

— 'The Bank of England', *Country Life*, xcvi (1944), 156–9.

— 'Trafalgar House, Wilts.', *Country Life*, xcviii (1945), 68–71, 112–15.

— et al., 'Linton Park, Kent', *Country Life*, v (1899), 176–80; xcix (1946), 578–81, 624–7.

— 'Stowe, Bucks.', *Country Life*, cii (1947), 526–9, 578–81, 626–9.

— 'Townley Hall, Co. Louth', *Country Life*, civ (1948), 178–81, 228–31.

— 'Ashburnham Place, Sussex', *Country Life*, cxiii (1953), 1158–60, 1246–50, 1334–8.

— 'Shugborough, Staffs.', *Country Life*, cxv (1954), 510–13, 590–3, 676–9.

— 'A Classical Landscape Park—Shugborough, Staffs.', *Country Life*, cxv (1954), 1126–9, 1220–3.

— 'Ickworth Park, Suffolk', *Country Life*, cxvii (1955), 678–81.

— 'The Opening of Woburn Abbey', *Country Life*, cxvii (1955), 854–8.

— 'Woburn Abbey, Beds.', *Country Life*, cxviii (1955), 434–7, 488–91.

— 'Rokeby, Yorks.', *Country Life*, cxvii (1955), 1302–5.

— 'Oakley Park, Shropshire', *Country Life*, cxix (1956), 380–3, 426–9.

— 'Prestwold Hall, Leics.', *Country Life*, cxxv (1959), 828–31, 890–3, 948–51.

— 'Alton Towers, Staffs.', *Country Life*, cxxvii (1960), 1246–9, 1304–7.

— 'Future of the Pantechnicon', *Country Life*, cxxxix (1966), 714–16.

— 'Calverly Park, Tunbridge Wells', *Country Life*, cxlv (1969), 1080–3, 1166–9.

Jenkins, F. I., 'John Foulston and the Public Buildings in Plymouth, Stonehouse and Devonport', *Jnl. Soc. Architectural Historians* (U.S.A.), xxvii (1968), 124–35.

Jones, R. P., 'The Life and Work of Harvey Lonsdale Elmes', *Architectural Rev.*, xv (1904), 231–45.

— 'The Life and Work of Decimus Burton', *Architectural Rev.*, xvii (1905), 154–64.

Kaufmann, E., 'Claude-Nicolas Ledoux, Inaugurator of a New Architectural System', *Jnl. Soc. Architectural Historians* (U.S.A.), iii (1943), 12–20.

— 'At an Eighteenth-Century Crossroads: Algarotti vs. Lodoli', *Jnl. Soc. Architectural Historians* (U.S.A.), iv (1944), 23–9.

— 'Three Revolutionary Architects—Boullée, Ledoux and Lequeu', *Trans. American Philosophical Soc.*, xl (1952).

Kerr, H. F., 'Edinburgh: The Modern Athens', *Country Life*, lviii (1925), 172–9.

Kimball, F., 'Romantic Classicism in Architecture', *Gazette des Beaux Arts* (1944), 95–112.

— 'Piranesi, Algarotti and Lodoli', *Essays in Honour of Hans Tietze* (New York, 1958), 309–16.

Lang, S., 'R. Payne Knight and the Idea of Modernity', in *Concerning Architecture: Essays . . . presented to Nikolaus Pevsner*, ed. Sir J. Summerson (1968), 85–97.

— 'The Early Publications of the Temples at Paestum', *Jnl. of the Warburg and Courtauld Institutes*, xiii (1950), 48–64.

Law, G., 'Greek Thomson', *Architectural Rev.*, cxv (1954), 307–16.

Lea, J., 'Ayot St. Lawrence Church', *Country Life*, xciii (1943), 360, 538.

Lees-Milne, J., 'Shugborough', *Connoisseur*, clxiv (1967), 211–5.

Bibliography

Legrand, Ph.–E., 'Contribution à l'Histoire des Marbres du Parthenon', *Revue Archeologique* 3rd Series, xxv (1894).
— 'Encore les Marbres du Parthenon', *Revue Archeologique* 3rd Series, xxvi (1895).
— 'Biographie de Louis François Sebastien Fauvel', *Revue Archeologique* 3rd series, xxx–xxxi (1897).
Lewis [Lawrence], Lesley, 'The Architects of the Chapel of Greenwich Hospital', *Art Bulletin*, xxiv (1927), 260–7.
— 'Stuart and Revett: their Literary and Architectural Careers', *Jnl. of the Warburg Institute,* ii (1938–9), 128–46.
Leyland, J., et al., 'Stoke Park, Bucks.', *Country Life*, i (1897), 724–6; xiv (1903), 168–74.
— 'Rokeby, Yorks.', *Country Life*, ii (1897), 405–7.
Liscombe, R., 'Economy, character and durability: specimen designs for the Church Commissioners, 1818', *Architectural History*, xiii (1970), 43–57.
Little, B., 'Cambridge and the Campus', *Virginia Mag. of History and Biography*, lxxiv (1971), 190–201.
Martin, G., 'The National Gallery', *Burlington Mag.*, cxiii (1971), 318–29.
McCarthy, M., 'Sir Roger Newdigate and Piranesi', *Burlington Mag.*, cxiv (1972), 466–72.
— 'Documents on the Greek Revival', *Burlington Mag.*, cxiv (1972).
McWilliam, C., 'James Playfair's Designs for Ardkinglas, Argyll', in *The Country Seat: studies . . . presented to Sir John Summerson*, ed. H. M. Colvin and J. Harris (1970), 193–8.
Meeks, C. V. L., 'Picturesque Eclecticism', *Art Bulletin*, xxxii (1950), 226–35.
— 'Creative Eclecticism', *Jnl. Soc. Architectural Historians* (U.S.A.), xii (1953), 15–18.
Metcalf, Priscilla, 'Silverton Park, Devon', in *The Country Seat: studies . . . presented to Sir John Summerson*, ed. H. M. Colvin and J. Harris (1970), 234–6.
Michaelis, A., 'Supplement on Marbles at Broomhall', *Journal of Hellenic Studies*, (1884).
Middleton, R. D., 'The Abbé de Cordemoy and the Graeco-Gothic Ideal: a Prelude to Romantic Classicism', *Jnl. Warburg and Courtauld Institutes*, xxv (1962), 278–320 and xxvi (1963), 90–123.
Nares, G., 'Corby Castle, Cumberland', *Country Life*, cxv (1954), 32–5, 92–5.
— 'Hardenhuish Church, Wilts.', *Country Life*, cvii (1950), 319–20.
— 'The Athenaeum', *Country Life*, cix (1951), 1018–22.
— 'Hagley Hall, Worcs.', *Country Life*, cxxii (1957), 546–9, 608–11.
— 'Cranbury Park, Hants.', *Country Life*, cxx (1956), 944–7, 1058–61, 1116–19.
Oswald, A., 'Birmingham Town Hall, 1834–1934', *Country Life*, lxxvi (1934), 372–3.
— 'Tatton Park, Cheshire', *Country Life*, cxxxvi (1964), 162–5, 232–6, 292–6.
— 'Some Recent Work at Fishmongers' Hall and Leathersellers' Hall', *Country Life*, cxii (1952), 1564–7.
— 'Carlton House Terrace: An Early Controversy', *Country Life*, cix (1951), 700–1.
— 'Paultons, Romsey, Hants.', *Country Life*, lxxxiv (1938), 276–81.
— 'West Wycombe Park, Bucks.', *Country Life*, lxxiii (1933), 466–71, 494–9.

Bibliography

Oswald, A., 'The London Institution', *Country Life*, lxxix (1936), 378–83.
— 'The Mansion House, London', *Country Life*, lxxii (1932), 514–20, 544–9.
O'Sullivan, H., 'The Court House, Dundalk', *Journal of the Co. Louth Archaeological Soc.*, xv (1962), 131–43.
Panofsky, E., 'Et in Arcadia Ego', in *Philosophy and History*, ed. R. Klibansky and H. J. Paten (1936), 223–54. Reprinted in *Meaning in the Visual Arts* (New York, 1955).
Pevsner, N., 'Richard Payne Knight', *Art Bulletin*, xxi (1949), 293–320.
— and Lang, S., 'Apollo or Baboon', *Architectural Rev.* civ (1948), 271–9.
Pite, A. Beresford, 'The Work of William Wilkins', *R.I.B.A. Jnl.*, xl (1933), 121–33.
Porcelli and Girouard, M., 'Mount Edgecumbe, Cornwall', *Country Life*, cxxviii (1960), 1550–3, 1598–1601.
Praz, M., 'Herculaneum and European Taste', *Magazine of Art*, xxxii (1939), 684–93, 727.
Reilley, C. H., 'St. George's Hall, Liverpool,' *Country Life*, lxii (1927), 127–31.
— 'The Town Hall, Liverpool', *Country Life*, lxii (1927), 120–7.
Rix, M., 'Attingham Hall, Shropshire', *Country Life*, cxvi (1954), 1350–3.
Rosenau, Helen, 'Dance the Younger', *R.I.B.A. Jnl.*, liv (1947), 502–7.
— 'The Engravings of the Grands Prix of the French Academy of Architecture', *Architectural History*, iii (1966).
Rowan, A., 'Georgian Edinburgh', *Country Life*, cxlii (1967), 956–9, 1052–5.
— 'Paxton House, Berwickshire', *Country Life*, cxlii (1967), 364–7, 422–5, 470–3.
— 'Poor William Pars', *Country Life Annual* (1970), 116–18.
Smith, A. H., 'Lord Elgin and his Collection', *Jnl. of Hellenic Studies*, xxxvi (1916), 163–372.
Spencer, Earl, 'Spencer House, London', *Country Life*, lx (1926), 660–7, 698–704.
Stanton, Phoebe, 'Pugin: Principles of Design versus Revivalism', *Jnl. Soc. Architectural Historians* (U.S.A.), xiii (1954), 20–5.
Stillman, D., 'Robert Adam and Piranesi', *Essays in the History of Architecture Presented to Rudolf Wittkower*, ed. D. Fraser, H. Hibbard and M. J. Lewine (1967), 197–206.
— 'The Gallery for Lansdowne House', *Art Bulletin*, lii (1970), 75–80.
Stroud, Dorothy, 'Hyde Park Corner', *Architectural Rev.*, cvi (1949), 397–9.
— 'Woburn Abbey, Beds.', *Country Life*, cxxxviii (1965), 98–102, 158–61.
Summerson, Sir John, 'Soane: the Case-History of a Personal Style', *R.I.B.A. Jnl.*, lviii (1951), 83–91.
— 'The Classical Country House in 18th-Cent. England' [Cantor Lectures], *Jnl. Royal Soc. Arts*, xvii (1959), 539–87.
— 'Country House Typology', *Architectural Rev.*, cxxvii (1960), 81–2.
— 'The Architectural Setting' in *The Eighteenth Century*, ed. A. Cobban (1970), 41–94.
[Sutton, D.] 'The Neo-Classic Ideal', *Apollo*, lxxviii (1963), 334–43.
Taylor, G. C., 'Nuneham Courteney, Oxon.', *Country Life*, xc (1941), 866–70, 910–13.
Taylor, J., 'Charles Fowler', *Architectural History*, xi (1968), 57–74.
Taylor, N., 'The Awful Sublimity of the Victorian City', in H. J. Dyos and M. Wolff (eds.), *The Victorian City: Images and Realities*, ii (1972).

Tipping, H. Avray, 'Clumber, Notts.', *Country Life*, xxiv (1908), 352–9, 384–90.

— 'Spetchley Park, Worcs.', *Country Life*, xl (1916), 42–8, 70–5.

— 'Downton Castle, Herefs.', *Country Life*, xlii (1917), 36–42.

— 'Rokeby, Yorks.', *Country Life*, xlii (1917), 276–82, 300–5.

— 'Hamilton Palace, Lanarkshire', *Country Life*, xiv (1919), 662–71, 716–23, 748–55.

— 'Bayfordbury, Herts.', *Country Life*, lvii (1925), 92–9, 124–33.

— 'Ickworth, Suffolk', *Country Life*, xviii (1905), 870–7; lviii (1925), 668–75, 698–705.

— 'Attingham, Shropshire', *Country Life*, xlix (1921), 158–66, 186–93.

— 'Heaton Park, Lancs.', *Country Life*, lviii (1925), 322–8, 354–60.

Tselos, Dimitri, 'Joseph Gandy, Prophet of Modern Architecture', *Magazine of Art*, xxxiv (1941), 251 et seq.

Turley, R., 'John Dobson', *Architectural Rev.*, xcix–c (1946), 141–6.

Vermeule, C. C. and Bothmer, D. von, 'Notes on a New Edition of Michaelis', *American Jnl. of Archaeology*, lix (1955), 129–50; lx (1956), 321–50; lxiii (1959), 139–66; 329–48.

Walker, D., and McNeill, P., 'Greek Thomson', *Glasgow Rev.* Summer, 1965.

— 'James Sellars', *Scottish Art Rev.*, xi (1967), i, 16–19 and ii, 21–6.

— and McWilliam, C., 'Cairness, Aberdeenshire', *Country Life*, cxlix (1971), 184–7, 248–51.

Walkley, G., 'William Wilkins', *Country Life*, lxxxvi (1939), 689.

Warren, T. H., 'Nuneham Courteney, Oxon.', *Country Life*, xxxiv (1913), 746–55.

Watkin, D., 'Charles Kelsall: the quintessence of Neo Classicism', *Architectural Rev.*, cxl (1966), 109–12.

— 'Buckland Filleigh, Devon', in *The Country Seat: Studies . . . presented to Sir John Summerson*, ed. H. M. Colvin and J. Harris (1970), 229–33.

— 'Letheringsett Hall, Norfolk', *Country Life*, cxli (1967), 18–21.

— and Proudfoot, C., 'C. H. Tatham', *Country Life*, cli (1972), 918–21.

Wellek, R., 'Romanticism re-examined', *Concepts of Criticism* (New Haven, 1963), 128–98; reprinted in *Romanticism Reconsidered*, ed. Northrop Frye (1963), 107–33.

Whiffen, M., 'An English Le Roy', *Architectural Rev.*, cxxvi (1959), 119–20.

Whistler, L., 'Stowe, Bucks.', *Country Life*, cviii (1950), 1002–6; cxxii (1957), 68–71, 390–3; cxxv (1959), 352–3.

Wiebenson, Dora, 'Greek, Gothic and Nature: 1750–1820', *Essays in Honor of Walter Friedlander*, ed. Marsyas (New York, 1965), 187–94.

Williamson, R. P. Ross, 'The Last Act at the Pantheon', *Architectural Rev.*, lxxxii (1937), i, 7–10.

Wilton-Ely, J., 'The Architectural Models of Sir John Soane', *Architectural History*, xii (1969), 5–38.

Wittkower, R., 'Piranesi's "Parere su l'Architettura"', *Jnl. of the Warburg Institute*, ii (1938–9), 147–58.

Index

(The bold figures refer to plate numbers)